Praise for *Reactive Systems in Java*

Convinced Reactive is right for your project? This is the book that will take your project from Reactive in theory to Reactive in production.

Make sure every member of your team reads this book.

—*K. Scott Morrison, CTO*

Clement and Ken wrote, by far, the most up-to-date book on reactive systems that is interwoven with theories and practical code examples. It is a must-read for anyone who wants to get a deep understanding of reactive systems, event-driven architecture, and asynchronous messaging in today's complex cloud native environments.

—*Mary Grygleski, Senior Developer Advocate, IBM*

As someone new to reactive programming and Quarkus, I found this book fascinating and extremely helpful. Its hands-on approach and illustrative examples were ideal for getting up to speed quickly.

—*Chris Mayfield, Associate Professor, James Madison University*

If you know where to look, reactive computer systems have been around for decades, but it's in recent times, with the advent of serverless and event-driven architectures, that we've really seen them elevated to the point where most application developers need to be aware of them. For Java developers, this book is the perfect way to find out what a reactive system is, how to reason about it, and how to build them in a reliable and scalable manner using the most popular Kubernetes-native framework out there, Quarkus. The added advantage is that the authors speak from years of real-world product experience.

—*Mark Little, VP Engineering, Red Hat*

Reactive Systems in Java

Resilient, Event-Driven
Architecture with Quarkus

Clement Escoffier and Ken Finnigan

Beijing · Boston · Farnham · Sebastopol · Tokyo

Reactive Systems in Java

by Clement Escoffier and Ken Finnigan

Published by O'Reilly Media, Inc., 1005 Gravenstein Highway North, Sebastopol, CA 95472.

O'Reilly books may be purchased for educational, business, or sales promotional use. Online editions are also available for most titles (*http://oreilly.com*). For more information, contact our corporate/institutional sales department: 800-998-9938 or *corporate@oreilly.com*.

Acquisitions Editor: Suzanne McQuade	**Indexer:** WordCo Indexing Services, Inc.
Development Editor: Jill Leonard	**Interior Designer:** David Futato
Production Editor: Caitlin Ghegan	**Cover Designer:** Karen Montgomery
Copyeditor: Sharon Wilkey	**Illustrator:** Kate Dullea
Proofreader: Kim Cofer	

November 2021:   First Edition

Revision History for the First Edition

2021-11-09:   First Release

See *http://oreilly.com/catalog/errata.csp?isbn=9781492091721* for release details.

978-1-492-09172-1

[LSI]

To Déborah, Flore, and Néo, who left us too early.
To Erin, Lorcán, and Daire.

Table of Contents

Preface... xiii

Part I.   Reactive and Quarkus Introduction

1. Reactive in a Nutshell... 3
   What Do We Mean by Reactive?   3
   Reactive Software Is Not New   4
   The Reactive Landscape   5
   Why Are Reactive Architectures So Well-Suited for Cloud Native
       Applications?   7
   Reactive Is Not a Silver Bullet   8

2. Introduction to Quarkus... 9
   Java on the Cloud   9
      Thorntail Example   13
      Quarkus Example   15
   The Quarkus Way   18
   Create Your First Quarkus Application   21
   Kubernetes with Quarkus in 10 Minutes   28
   Going Native   34
   Summary   38

Part II.   Reactive and Event-Driven Applications

3. The Dark Side of Distributed Systems............................... 43
   What's a Distributed System?   43

The New Kids on the Block: Cloud Native and Kubernetes Native
    Applications   46
The Dark Side of Distributed Systems   51
Fallacies of Distributed Computing in a Kubernetes World   52
A Question of Timing: The Synchronous Communication Drawback   54
Summary   60

4. Design Principles of Reactive Systems. **61**
Reactive Systems 101   61
Commands and Events   63
    Commands   63
    Events   64
    Messages   64
    Commands Versus Events: An Example   65
Destinations and Space Decoupling   68
Time Decoupling   70
The Role of Nonblocking Input/Output   71
    Blocking Network I/O, Threads, and Concurrency   71
    How Does Nonblocking I/O Work?   74
    Reactor Pattern and Event Loop   77
Anatomy of Reactive Applications   79
Summary   82

5. Reactive Programming: Taming the Asynchronicity. **83**
Asynchronous Code and Patterns   83
Using Futures   89
Project Loom: Virtual Threads and Carrier Threads   91
Reactive Programming   93
    Streams   94
    Operators   96
    Reactive Programming Libraries   100
Reactive Streams and the Need for Flow Control   100
    Buffering Items   101
    Dropping Items   102
    What Is Backpressure?   103
    Introducing Reactive Streams   103
    Be Warned: It's a Trap!   106
    Backpressure in Distributed Systems   106
Summary   107

Part III.   Building Reactive Applications and Systems with Quarkus

6. Quarkus: Reactive Engine. **111**
  The Imperative Model   112
  The Reactive Model   115
  Unification of Reactive and Imperative   116
  A Reactive Engine   120
  A Reactive Programming Model   120
  Event-Driven Architecture with Quarkus   121
  Summary   122

7. Mutiny: An Event-Driven Reactive Programming API. **123**
  Why Another Reactive Programming Library?   123
  What Makes Mutiny Unique?   124
  Mutiny Usage in Quarkus   125
  Uni and Multi   126
  Mutiny and Flow Control   128
  Observing Events   129
  Transforming Events   130
  Chaining Asynchronous Actions   131
  Recovering from Failure   133
  Combining and Joining Items   134
  Selecting Items   136
  Collecting Items   137
  Summary   138

8. HTTP with Reactive in Mind. **139**
  The Journey of an HTTP Request   140
  Say Hello to RESTEasy Reactive!   141
  What's the Benefit?   144
  Asynchronous Endpoints Returning Uni   146
  Dealing with Failure and Customizing the Response   148
  Streaming Data   151
    Raw Streaming   152
    Streaming JSON Array   153
    Using Server-Sent-Events   155
  Reactive Score   157
  Summary   158

9. Accessing Data Reactively. **159**
  The Problem with Data Access   159
  Nonblocking Interactions with Relational Databases   161

Using a Reactive ORM: Hibernate Reactive   162
What About NoSQL?   166
Interacting with Redis   166
Data-Related Events and Change Data Capture   170
Using Debezium to Capture Change   172
Summary   175

Part IV. Connecting the Dots

10. **Reactive Messaging: The Connective Tissue**. **179**
    From Reactive Applications to Reactive Systems   179
      Channels and Messages   180
      Producing Messages   181
      Consuming Messages   184
      Processing Messages   186
      Acknowledgments   187
      Connectors   189
    Building Message-Based Applications   189
      Message and Acknowledgment   191
      Failures and Negative Acknowledgment   193
      Stream Manipulation   193
      Blocking Processing   195
      Retrying Processing   195
    Putting Everything Together   196
    Summary   200

11. **The Event Bus: The Backbone**. **201**
    Kafka or AMQP: Picking the Right Tool   201
    Building Reactive Systems with Kafka   202
      Apache Kafka   202
      Point-to-Point Communication   208
      Publish/Subscribe   209
      Elasticity Patterns   209
      Dealing with Failures   210
      Backpressure and Performance Considerations   212
      Kafka on Kubernetes   213
    Building Reactive Systems with AMQP   216
      AMQP 1.0   217
      Point-to-Point Communication   217
      Publish/Subscribe   219
      Elasticity Patterns   220

    Acknowledgment and Redelivery   220
    Credit-Flow Backpressure Protocol   221
    AMQP on Kubernetes   221
  Summary   223

12. Reactive REST Client: Connecting with HTTP Endpoints. 225
  Interacting with an HTTP Endpoint   225
  The REST Client Reactive   228
    Mapping HTTP APIs to Java Interfaces   229
    Invoking the Service   231
  Blocking and Nonblocking   232
  Handling Failures   233
    Fallback   234
    Retries   236
    Time-out   236
    Bulkheads and Circuit Breaker   236
  Building API Gateways with the RESTEasy Reactive Client   238
  Using the REST Client in Messaging Applications   243
  Summary   248

13. Observing Reactive and Event-Driven Architectures. 249
  Why Is Observability Important?   249
  Health with Messaging   250
  Metrics with Messaging   256
  Distributed Tracing with Messaging   260
  Summary   264

Conclusion. 265

Index. 269

Preface

In the IT world, the limits of today are the gateways of tomorrow. In the last 50 years, the IT world has continuously evolved, tirelessly, always pushing the limits. These changes are due to not only technical progress, but also us, the consumers. As consumers, we continue to demand more and more from the software we interact with every day. In addition, our way of interacting with software has entirely changed. We can't live without mobile applications and devices and now accept receiving notifications all day long. The Internet of Things (IoT) is an emerging market promising many more innovations, increasing the number of events and data processed uninterruptedly. The cloud and Kubernetes have not only changed our usage but also radically transformed the way we design, develop, deploy, and maintain applications.

But don't be mistaken; all these revolutions come with a price. While they have enabled new uses and applications, they have also introduced massive complexity. Most software systems today are distributed systems. And distributed systems are hard to design, build, and operate, especially on the scale we need to implement these new modern applications. We need to handle failures, asynchronous communication, an ever-changing topology, the dynamic availability of resources, and so on. While the cloud promises unlimited resources, money is a limiting factor, and increasing the deployment density, meaning running more on fewer resources, becomes a stringent concern.

So, what about Reactive? It is not a library you use in your code or a magic framework. *Reactive* is a set of principles, tools, methodologies, and frameworks that lead to building *better* distributed systems. How *much* better? It depends on the system, but applications following the Reactive principles embrace distributed systems' challenges and focus on elasticity, resilience, and responsiveness, as explained in The Reactive Manifesto (*https://oreil.ly/fO6n0*).

In this book, we use the noun *Reactive*, with an uppercase *R*, to aggregate all the various facets of the reactive landscape, such as reactive programming, reactive systems, reactive streams, and so on. With this book, you'll learn how Reactive will help us face these new concerns and how it fits in cloud environments. After reading this book, you will be able to build reactive systems—resilient, adaptable, event-driven distributed systems.

Who Should Read This Book?

This book targets intermediate and advanced Java developers. It would be best if you were reasonably comfortable with Java; however, prior knowledge of reactive programming or even Reactive in general are not required. Many concepts in this book relate to distributed systems, but you do not need to be familiar with them either.

Reactive systems often rely on message brokers such as Apache Kafka or Advanced Message Queuing Protocol (AMQP). This book introduces the basic knowledge you need to understand how such brokers help in designing and implementing reactive systems.

Three distinct groups can benefit from this book:

- Developers who are building cloud native applications or distributed systems
- Architects seeking to understand the role of reactive and event-driven architectures
- Curious developers who have heard about Reactive and want a better understanding of it

With this book, you will start a journey toward understanding, designing, building, and implementing reactive architectures. You will not only learn how it helps to build *better* distributed systems and cloud applications, but also see how you can use reactive patterns to improve existing systems.

What About Quarkus?

Attentive readers would have noticed the mention of Quarkus in the subtitle of this book. But, so far, we haven't mentioned it. *Quarkus* is a Java stack tailored for the cloud. It uses build-time techniques to reduce the amount of memory used by the application and provide a fast startup time.

But Quarkus is also a reactive stack. At its core, a reactive engine enables the creation of concurrent and resilient applications. Quarkus also provides all the features you need to build distributed systems that can adapt to fluctuating loads and inevitable failures.

Throughout this book, we use Quarkus to demonstrate the benefits of the reactive approach and introduce various patterns and best practices. Don't panic if you don't have prior knowledge or experience with it. We will accompany you on the journey, guiding you at every step.

This book focuses on creating reactive applications and systems that leverage Quarkus capabilities and provides all the knowledge required to build such systems. We do not cover the complete Quarkus ecosystem, as this book concentrates on the Quarkus components that help in the construction of reactive systems.

Navigating This Book

If you are just discovering Reactive and want to know more about it, reading this book from cover to cover will leave you with an understanding of Reactive and how it can help you. If you are a seasoned reactive developer interested in Quarkus and its reactive features, you may want to skip the first part of this book and jump to the chapters that interest you the most.

Part I is a brief introduction, setting the context:

- Chapter 1 provides a brief overview of the reactive landscape, including its benefits and drawbacks.
- Chapter 2 presents Quarkus and its build-time approach to reducing startup time and memory usage.

Part II covers Reactive in general:

- Chapter 3 explains the complexities of distributed systems and the misconceptions; these are the reasons for being reactive.
- Chapter 4 presents the characteristics of reactive systems.
- Chapter 5 covers the various forms of asynchronous development models, with a focus on reactive programming.

Part III explains how to build reactive applications with Quarkus:

- Chapter 6 discusses the reactive engine and bridging imperative and reactive programming.
- Chapter 7 is a deep dive on SmallRye Mutiny, the reactive programming library used in Quarkus.
- Chapter 8 explains HTTP request characteristics and how we can be reactive with HTTP.
- Chapter 9 explains how you can use Quarkus to build highly concurrent and efficient applications interacting with a database.

The final part, Part IV, *connects the dots* and presents how you can build reactive systems with Quarkus:

- Chapter 10 dives into the integration of Quarkus applications with messaging technologies, an essential ingredient of reactive systems.

- Chapter 11 focuses on the integration with Apache Kafka and AMQP, and how to build reactive systems with them.

- Chapter 12 explores the various ways to consume HTTP endpoints from a Quarkus application and how to enforce resilience and responsiveness.

- Chapter 13 covers observability concerns in reactive systems, such as self-healing, tracing, and monitoring.

Getting You Ready

Throughout this book, you will see many examples of code. These examples illustrate the concepts covered in this book. Some are basic and run in an IDE, and others require a couple of prerequisites.

We cover these examples, one by one, throughout this book. Now, maybe you're not one for suspense. Or, more likely, maybe you're already tired of hearing us blather on at length and just want to see this working. If that's the case, simply point your browser to *https://github.com/cescoffier/reactive-systems-in-java* and feel free to kick the tires a bit. You can retrieve the code with Git using `git clone https://github.com/cescoffier/reactive-systems-in-java.git`. Alternatively, you can download a ZIP file (*https://oreil.ly/Ey74z*) and unzip it.

The code is organized by chapter. For example, the code related to Chapter 2 is available in the *chapter-2* directory (Table P-1). Depending on the chapter, the code may be split into multiple modules. For examples that are available in the code repository, the code snippet title in the book indicates the location of the file in the repository.

Table P-1. Code location per chapter

Chapter	Title	Path
Chapter 2	Introduction to Quarkus	*https://github.com/cescoffier/reactive-systems-in-java/tree/master/chapter-2*
Chapter 3	The Dark Side of Distributed Systems	*https://github.com/cescoffier/reactive-systems-in-java/tree/master/chapter-3*
Chapter 4	Design Principles of Reactive Systems	*https://github.com/cescoffier/reactive-systems-in-java/tree/master/chapter-4*
Chapter 5	Reactive Programming: Taming the Asynchronicity	*https://github.com/cescoffier/reactive-systems-in-java/tree/master/chapter-5*
Chapter 7	Mutiny: An Event-Driven Reactive Programming API	*https://github.com/cescoffier/reactive-systems-in-java/tree/master/chapter-7*

Chapter	Title	Path
Chapter 8	HTTP with Reactive in Mind	https://github.com/cescoffier/reactive-systems-in-java/tree/master/chapter-8
Chapter 9	Accessing Data Reactively	https://github.com/cescoffier/reactive-systems-in-java/tree/master/chapter-9
Chapter 10	Reactive Messaging: The Connective Tissue	https://github.com/cescoffier/reactive-systems-in-java/tree/master/chapter-10
Chapter 11	The Event Bus: The Backbone	https://github.com/cescoffier/reactive-systems-in-java/tree/master/chapter-11
Chapter 12	Reactive REST Client: Connecting with HTTP Endpoints	https://github.com/cescoffier/reactive-systems-in-java/tree/master/chapter-12
Chapter 13	Observing Reactive and Event-Driven Architectures	https://github.com/cescoffier/reactive-systems-in-java/tree/master/chapter-13

The examples from the code repository use Java 11, so be sure to have a suitable Java Development Kit (JDK) installed on your machine. They also use Apache Maven as the build tool. You don't have to install Maven, as the repository uses the Maven Wrapper (*https://oreil.ly/0oKc9*) (provisioning Maven automatically). However, if you prefer installing it, download it from the Apache Maven Project website (*https://oreil.ly/XgiCr*), and follow the instructions on the Installing Apache Maven page (*https://oreil.ly/nwJV9*).

To build the code, run mvn verify from the root of the project. Maven is going to download a set of artifacts, so be sure to have an internet connection.

This book covers Quarkus, a Kubernetes-native Java stack. You don't need to install anything to use Quarkus, as long as you have Java and Maven. It will download everything else automatically.

You will need Docker. Docker is used to create containers for our applications. Install Docker by following the instructions at the Get Docker page (*https://oreil.ly/DjBnj*).

Finally, several chapters illustrate the deployment of our reactive applications in Kubernetes. To deploy to Kubernetes, you first need kubectl, a command-line tool to interact with Kubernetes. Install it by following the instructions from the Kubernetes Install Tools page (*https://oreil.ly/4SA4J*). Unless you have a Kubernetes cluster handy, we also recommend minikube be installed on your machine, to provide a Kubernetes environment. Follow the instructions at the minikube website (*https://oreil.ly/vuCs1*) to install it.

Why do we need all these tools? You will see in this book that being reactive adds constraints to your application but also to your infrastructure. Kubernetes provides the primitives we need to deploy applications, create replicas, and keep our system on track. On the other side, Quarkus provides the set of features we need to implement reactive applications, including nonblocking I/O, reactive programming, reactive APIs, and messaging capabilities. Quarkus also provides integration with Kubernetes for easing the deployment and configuration of applications.

Table P-2 lists the tools we are going to use in the book.

Table P-2. Tools used in this book

Tool	Website	Description
Java 11	*https://adoptopenjdk.net*	Java Virtual Machine (JVM) and Java Development Kit (JDK)
Apache Maven	*https://maven.apache.org/download.cgi*	Build automation tool, based on the project object model (POM)
Quarkus	*https://quarkus.io*	A Kubernetes-native stack that optimizes Java for containers
Docker	*https://www.docker.com/get-started*	Container creation and execution
Kubernetes	*https://kubernetes.io*	A container orchestration platform, also known as K8s
minikube	*https://minikube.sigs.k8s.io/docs/start*	A local distribution of Kubernetes
GraalVM	*https://www.graalvm.org*	Provides, among others tools, a compiler to create native executables from Java code
Node.js	*https://nodejs.org/en*	A JavaScript runtime engine

Conventions Used in This Book

The following typographical conventions are used in this book:

Italic
> Indicates new terms, URLs, email addresses, filenames, and file extensions.

`Constant width`
> Used for program listings, as well as within paragraphs to refer to program elements such as variable or function names, databases, data types, environment variables, statements, and keywords.

`Constant width bold`
> Shows commands or other text that should be typed literally by the user.

`Constant width italic`
> Shows text that should be replaced with user-supplied values or by values determined by context.

> This element signifies a tip or suggestion.

> This element signifies a general note.

 This element indicates a warning or caution.

O'Reilly Online Learning

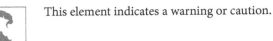 For more than 40 years, *O'Reilly Media* has provided technology and business training, knowledge, and insight to help companies succeed.

Our unique network of experts and innovators share their knowledge and expertise through books, articles, and our online learning platform. O'Reilly's online learning platform gives you on-demand access to live training courses, in-depth learning paths, interactive coding environments, and a vast collection of text and video from O'Reilly and 200+ other publishers. For more information, visit *http://oreilly.com*.

How to Contact Us

Please address comments and questions concerning this book to the publisher:

O'Reilly Media, Inc.
1005 Gravenstein Highway North
Sebastopol, CA 95472
800-998-9938 (in the United States or Canada)
707-829-0515 (international or local)
707-829-0104 (fax)

We have a web page for this book, where we list errata, examples, and any additional information. You can access this page at *https://oreil.ly/ReactiveSysJava*.

Email *bookquestions@oreilly.com* to comment or ask technical questions about this book.

For news and information about our books and courses, visit *http://oreilly.com*.

Find us on Facebook: *http://facebook.com/oreilly*

Follow us on Twitter: *http://twitter.com/oreillymedia*

Watch us on YouTube: *http://youtube.com/oreillymedia*

Acknowledgments

Writing a book is never easy. It's a long and demanding task, taking lots of energy and eating quite a lot of family time. Therefore, our first thanks go to our families who supported us during this marathon.

We are also grateful to be working with exceptional people at Red Hat. Countless people helped us during this journey; it's impossible to cite all of them. A special thank you to Georgios Andrianakis, Roberto Cortez, Stuart Douglas, Stéphane Epardaud, Jason Greene, Sanne Grinovero, Gavin King, Martin Kouba, Julien Ponge, Erin Schnabel, Guillaume Smet, Michal Szynkiewicz, Ladislav Thon, and Julien Viet. Their work is not only brilliant, but also breathtaking. It's a privilege for us to work with such top-notch developers.

Finally, we thank all the reviewers who have provided fantastic and constructive feedback: Mary Grygleski, Adam Bellemare, Antonio Goncalves, Mark Little, Scott Morrison, Nick Keune, and Chris Mayfield.

## PART I

Reactive and Quarkus Introduction

## CHAPTER 1

Reactive in a Nutshell

Reactive is an overloaded word. You may have searched for *reactive* with a search engine to understand what it's all about. If you haven't, no worries—you've saved yourself a lot of confusion. There are many *reactive things*: Reactive Systems, Reactive Programming, Reactive extensions, Reactive messaging. Every day new ones pop up. Are all these "reactives" the same reactive? Are they different?

These are the questions we are going to answer in this chapter. We are going to sneak a peek at the reactive landscape to identify and help you understand the various nuances of *reactive*, what they mean, the concepts associated with them, and how they relate to one another. Because yes, without spoiling too much, all these "reactives" are related.

 As noted in the preface, we use the noun *Reactive*, with an uppercase *R*, to aggregate all the various facets of the reactive landscape, such as reactive programming, reactive systems, reactive streams, and so on.

What Do We Mean by Reactive?

Let's start at the beginning. Forget about software and IT for a few minutes, and use an old-fashioned approach. If we look for *reactive* in the *Oxford English Dictionary* (*https://oreil.ly/nL7Fp*), we find the following definition:

reactive (adjective)

Showing a response to a stimulus. 1.1 Acting in response to a situation rather than creating or controlling it. 1.2 Having a tendency to react chemically. 1.3 (Physiology) Showing an immune response to a specific antigen. 1.4 (Of a disease or illness) Caused by a reaction to something. 1.5 (Physics) Relating to reactance.

Among these definitions, two are relevant in our context. The first definition, *showing a response to a stimulus*, refers to some kind of reaction. Being reactive means reacting to stimuli, whatever they are. Subdefinition 1.1 says that being reactive is also about facing unexpected and uncontrolled situations. You will see throughout this book that cloud native applications, and distributed systems in general, face plenty of these kinds of situations. While these definitions are interesting, they don't apply to software. But we can take these definitions into account to make a new one specific to software:

> 1.6 (Software) An application reacting to stimuli, such as user events, requests, and failures.

Yet, as you will see in this book, today's *reactive* goes beyond this. Reactive is an approach to designing, implementing, and reasoning about your system in terms of events and flows. Reactive is about building *responsive*, *resilient*, and *elastic* applications. Reactive is also about resource utilization through efficient management of resources and communication. To put it another way: Reactive is about designing and building better distributed systems—more robust and more efficient. We call them *reactive systems*.

Reactive Software Is Not New

But wait, the definition (1.6) we just gave is not groundbreaking. On the contrary, you may feel some déjà vu, no? Isn't the nature of software to *react* to user inputs and operating system signals? How does software behave when you hit a keystroke? It reacts. So, why are there so many books, talks, and debates about Reactive if it's just regular software?[1] Please be patient; there is a bit more to it.

But you are right; Reactive is *not* new. It's actually pretty old. We can track the foundation of the ideas behind reactive software to just after the appearance of computers in the '50s. The DYSEAC (*https://oreil.ly/ehP7l*), a first-generation computer (in operation in 1954), was already using hardware interrupts as an optimization, eliminating waiting time in polling loops. This computer was one of the first systems to use reactive and event-driven architecture!

Reacting to events implies being event-driven. *Event-driven software* receives and produces events. The received events determine the flow of the program. A fundamental aspect of being event-driven is asynchronicity: you don't know when you are going to receive events.[2] That is precisely definition 1.1 from the previous section. You cannot plan when you will receive events, are not in control of which events you

---

1 You can find a plethora of talks about Reactive on YouTube (*https://oreil.ly/SyGxB*).

2 Asynchronous is the opposite of synchronous. Being *asynchronous* means happening at a different point in time, while being *synchronous* means happening at the same time.

---

will get, and you need to be prepared to handle them. That's the essence of being reactive: being asynchronous.

The Reactive Landscape

From this idea of being asynchronous and event-driven, many forms of *Reactive* have emerged. The reactive landscape is broad and crowded. Figure 1-1 depicts an excerpt of this landscape and the relationships among the main *reactive things*.

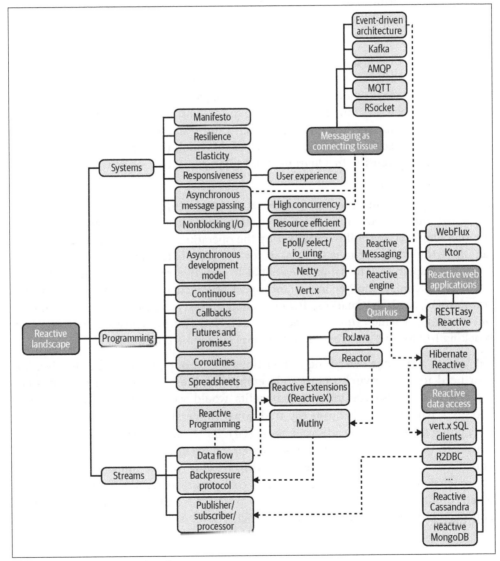

Figure 1-1. The reactive landscape

But don't forget our objective: building better distributed systems—reactive systems. The other "reactives" are here to help us implement these systems.

The reasons for Reactive, and reactive systems in particular, come from distributed systems. As you will see in Chapter 3, building distributed systems is hard. In 2013, distributed system experts wrote the first version of "The Reactive Manifesto" (*https://oreil.ly/6z8mt*) and introduced the concept of reactive systems.

Yes, you can build distributed systems without applying reactive principles. Reactive provides a blueprint to ensure that no significant known concerns were overlooked while architecting and developing your system. On the other hand, you can apply these principles on nondistributed systems.

A reactive system is first and foremost responsive. It must handle requests in a timely fashion even under load or when facing failures. To achieve this responsiveness, the manifesto proposes using asynchronous message passing as the primary way to communicate between the components forming the system. You will see in Chapter 4 how this communication method enables elasticity and resilience, two essential attributes of solid distributed systems. The objective of this book is to show you how to build such reactive systems with Quarkus. So, building reactive systems is our primary goal.

Infusing asynchronous message passing at the core of distributed systems does not come without consequences. Your application needs to use asynchronous code and nonblocking I/O, the ability provided by the operating system to enqueue I/O interactions without having to actively wait for the completion. (We cover nonblocking I/Os in Chapter 4). The latter is essential to improve resource utilization, such as CPU and memory, another important aspect of Reactive. Today, many toolkits and frameworks, such as Quarkus, Eclipse Vert.x (*https://vertx.io*), Micronaut (*https://micronaut.io*), Helidon (*https://helidon.io*), and Netty (*https://netty.io*), are using nonblocking I/O for this very reason: doing more with limited resources.

Yet having a runtime leveraging nonblocking I/O is not enough to be reactive. You also need to write asynchronous code embracing the nonblocking I/O mechanics. Otherwise, the resource utilization benefits would vanish. Writing asynchronous code is a paradigm shift. From the traditional (imperative), do x; do y;, you are now going to shape your code as on event(e) do x; on event(f) do y;. In other words, to be reactive, not only is your system an event-driven architecture, but also your code is going to become event-driven. One of the most straightforward approaches to implementing such code is callbacks: you register functions invoked when events are received. Like futures, promises, and coroutines, every other approach is based on callbacks and offers higher-level APIs.

You may wonder why spreadsheets are in the landscape. Spreadsheets are reactive. When you write a formula in a cell and change a value read (in another cell) by the formula, the result of this formula is updated. The cell reacts to the update of a value (event), and the outcome (reaction) is the new result. Yes, your manager may be a better reactive developer than you are! But don't worry, this book will change this.

Reactive programming, addressed in Chapter 5, is also an approach to writing asynchronous code. It uses data streams to structure your code. You observe the data transiting in these streams and react to it. Reactive programming provides a powerful abstraction and APIs to shape event-driven code.

But using data streams comes with an issue. If you have a fast producer directly connected to a slow consumer, you may flood the consumer. As you will see, we can buffer or use a message broker in between, but imagine flooding a consumer without them. That would be against the responsiveness and anti-fragile ideas promoted by Reactive. To help us with that particular issue, Reactive Streams (*https://oreil.ly/5c275*) proposes an asynchronous and nonblocking backpressure protocol where the consumer signals to the producer its availability. As you can imagine, this may not be applicable everywhere, as some data sources cannot be slowed down.

The popularity of Reactive Streams has increased over the past few years. For example, RSocket (*https://rsocket.io*) is a network protocol based on Reactive Streams. R2DBC (*https://r2dbc.io*) proposes asynchronous database access using Reactive Streams. Also, RxJava (*https://oreil.ly/QNEOJ*), Project Reactor (*https://oreil.ly/eUHAL*), and SmallRye Mutiny (*https://oreil.ly/A17fF*) adopted reactive streams to handle backpressure. Finally, Vert.x allows mapping the Vert.x backpressure model to Reactive Streams.[3]

That concludes our quick tour of the reactive landscape. As we said, it's crowded with many terms, and many tools. But never lose sight of the overall objective of Reactive: to build better distributed systems. That's the primary focus of this book.

Why Are Reactive Architectures So Well-Suited for Cloud Native Applications?

The cloud—public, private, or hybrid—has put Reactive in the spotlight. The cloud is a distributed system. When you run your application on the cloud, that application faces a high degree of uncertainty. The provisioning of your application can be slow, or fast, or even fail. Communication disruptions are common, because of network

---

3 See Vert.x Reactive Streams Integration (*https://oreil.ly/t2noI*) for more details.

failures or partitions. You may hit quota restrictions, resource shortages, and hardware failures. Some services you are using can be unavailable at times or moved to other locations.

While the cloud provides outstanding facilities for the infrastructure layer, it covers only half of the story. The second half is your application. It needs to be designed to be a part of a distributed system. It needs to understand the challenges of being part of such a system.

The reactive principles we cover in this book help to embrace the inherent uncertainty and challenges of distributed systems and cloud applications. It won't hide them—to the contrary, it embraces them.

As microservices and serverless computing (*https://oreil.ly/IH6wY*) are becoming prominent architectural styles, the reactive principles become even more important. They can help ensure that you design your system on a solid foundation.

Reactive Is Not a Silver Bullet

As with everything, Reactive has pros and cons. It's not a magic weapon. No solution works everywhere.

Remember microservices in the late 2010s? They quickly became exceedingly popular, and many organizations implemented them in areas for which they may not have been well-suited. This often traded one set of problems for another. Much like microservice architectures, reactive architectures have areas in which they are well-suited. They shine for distributed and cloud applications but can be disastrous on more monolithic and computation-centric systems. If your system relies on remote communication, event processing, or high efficiency, Reactive will be interesting. If your system uses mostly in-process interactions, handles just a few requests per day, or is computation-intensive, then Reactive won't bring anything but complexity.

With Reactive, you put the notion of events at the core of your system. If you are used to the traditional synchronous and imperative way of building applications, the path to become reactive can be steep. The need to become asynchronous disrupts most traditional frameworks. We are moving away from the well-known Remote Procedure Call (RPC) and HTTP endpoints. So, with that disclaimer, it's time to start our journey!

## CHAPTER 2

Introduction to Quarkus

Before continuing with understanding Reactive, let's take a few moments to learn more about Quarkus. So what is Quarkus?

Quarkus is a Kubernetes-native Java stack. It has been tailored for Kubernetes, containers, and the cloud, but works perfectly well on bare metal and virtual machines.[1] Quarkus applications require less memory and start faster than applications using traditional frameworks. They also have the capability to be compiled into native executables, which make them consume even less memory and start instantly.

One exciting, and central, aspect of Quarkus is the reactive engine. When running in containers or virtualized environments, a reactive engine is essential to reducing memory and CPU consumption. The engine makes any Quarkus application efficient while also enabling the creation of reactive applications and systems.

In this chapter, you will see the main characteristics of Quarkus and learn to create an application, deploy it to Kubernetes, and create native builds. In Chapter 6, we cover the reactive engine in detail and show how to develop on Quarkus with a unified reactive and imperative programming model.

Java on the Cloud

Java is now 25 years old! That's hard to imagine sometimes. From the era of three-tier and client/server architecture, Java has evolved with many changes in architecture over the years. However, when a language is 25 years old, there will be pieces lingering that may not be suited to modern development.

---

1 In this book, *container* refers to a form of operating system virtualization, not to Java EE containers.

What do we mean by that? When the initial versions of Java came out, *clouds*, *containers*, *microservices*, *serverless*, and any other term associated with computing today had not been imagined yet. There is no way we can expect the Java language created in the era of three-tier and client/server architecture to perform as we need in containers today.

Yes, many advancements have occurred over the years in Java, especially over the last couple of years with a new and faster release cadence. At the same time, Java prides itself on not breaking backward compatibility for developers and users. A large cost of that approach is that Java still retains pieces that were conceived without the benefits and knowledge of containers and what they provide.

For many applications, Java will continue to work fine, and as is, for many more years to come. However, over the last few years, with the explosion of microservices, and most recently the evolution to serverless, Java does not fit these deployment models naturally.

Only a few years ago, Java's lack of suitability in containers became apparent for all as we found out Java ignored cgroups (*https://oreil.ly/Mbux3*). For containers, this created a huge problem. Java, unable to see the amount of memory allocated to a container, could only see the memory of the entire physical machine.

What Are cgroups?

The term *cgroups* is shorthand for *control groups*, a kernel feature allowing the allocation of specific amounts of resources, such as CPU time, memory, and bandwidth, to processes. In our situation, cgroups are used to limit the amount of resources a container can use from the entire system.

In an environment where each container needs to work within a constrained amount of memory, Java didn't *play nice*. Java was greedy. In addition, Java would create application threads based on the number of CPU cores. This caused many more threads to be allocated in a memory- and CPU-constrained container.

Is it a big deal? You might get lucky with your Java applications deployed in containers, if deploying to a Kubernetes node with other containers staying well within their memory limits. Then one day there's a load spike, along with a spike in the memory consumed by the Java Virtual Machine (JVM), and then *boom*! Kubernetes kills the container for using too much memory.

This specific problem with Java and cgroups has been fixed since Java 10, and since Java Development Kit (JDK) 8u131 options are available for enabling the same behavior. Check out the "Java Inside Docker" article (*https://oreil.ly/L5Yh7*) on the Red Hat Developer's site by Rafael Benevides with all the details.

You might be thinking that Java should now be *good* in containers or in the cloud, right? Though this fix is available with an appropriate JDK version, many enterprises are using JDK 8 or older, and quite possibly not using a JDK 8 with the flags available. And Java's issue in the cloud is more than cgroups alone.

Containers not being killed for grabbing more memory than the container expected is great. However, Java in containers raises concerns about the speed with which applications start receiving requests and the amount of memory they consume while running. Neither of these are great for Java applications, compared with other languages running in containers. Maybe startup speed isn't a concern for many applications running today, but it can impact microservices needing to scale quickly for large traffic spikes, or the cold start time for serverless applications.

What do we mean by *start receiving requests*? While it's common for frameworks used in building applications to log their startup time, it refers to the amount of time taken for a *framework* to start. The time does not represent the time taken by an *application* before being able to start receiving requests. This time is a critical indicator with containers and the cloud!

The time to start receiving requests can also be called *time to first request*. Whether a framework can start in half a second doesn't mean much, if another 2–3 seconds passes before any traffic can be received and processed by the application. In such an example, it could be anywhere from 2.5 to 3.5 seconds before a new application instance can begin receiving user requests.

Granted, time to start receiving requests and memory consumption may not be a concern for a monolithic application with a few hundred, or even thousand, internal users. Monolithic applications can be developed with Quarkus, though the benefits we talk of for Quarkus will not be as prominent when developing monoliths. However, for microservices, and especially serverless, both these factors impact the costs of running a service and the availability to users.

 Frameworks can often have low startup times by delaying work until receiving the first request. The remainder of any startup tasks are performed before processing the first request. *Lazy initialization* is another name for this behavior, offering a false indication on when an application is really ready. The time to *start receiving requests* is the best measure of application startup time. Having a low *time to first request* is essential in serverless workloads, as well as any kind of mechanism using a *scale-to-zero* approach, where the services are started only when needed. In more common architectures, such fast startup time reduces the recovery time after a crash.

How can we measure startup time? Many approaches are possible, including modification of endpoints to output a timestamp when they're accessed. To make our lives a bit simpler, we're going to use a Node.js script developed by John O'Hara from Red Hat.[2] The script uses the application start command, and the URL to access it, to start the application in another process. The script waits for the URL to return 200, meaning success, before computing the time to first request.

For ease of use, we included the contents of the GitHub repository (*https://github.com/cescoffier/reactive-systems-in-java*) along with the code in the *chapter-2/startup-measurement* directory. Ensure that you have Node.js installed, and run npm install request to install the script dependencies.

Right now you might be thinking that this discussion about startup speed and memory consumption is a very *hand wavy* topic that's too subjective. We totally agree, which is why we're now going to use a traditional Java EE stack, in this case Thorntail (*https://thorntail.io*), to illustrate these concepts in practice. We chose Thorntail for the comparison as the first microservice framework from Red Hat, while Quarkus is the latest. Though the Thorntail project is no longer maintained, sadly, the good news is Quarkus incorporates lots of ideas from Thorntail.

One last thing before we get coding and running applications. *Memory* can be a somewhat vague term, as there are many types of memory. When we're talking about memory, we're referring to *resident set size* (RSS) (*https://oreil.ly/o4TzC*), and not the JVM heap size, as heap is only part of the total memory that a Java application consumes. When running an application on the JVM, the total allocated memory can include the following:

- Heap space
- Class metadata
- Thread stacks
- Compiled code
- Garbage collection

RSS represents the amount of memory that a process is occupying from main memory (RAM). RSS includes all the memory that the JVM requires to run an application, providing a more accurate value for the amount of memory actually occupied. As we're running a single application in a single JVM process, we can easily ensure that we're not measuring memory consumption of nonapplication processes.

---

2 You can find the script to measure startup time on GitHub (*https://github.com/cescoffier/reactive-systems-in-java*).

All performance numbers are from our MacBook computer. As such, the results you see in this chapter may differ slightly, depending on your particular hardware configuration. If you happen to have an Apple M1, you could see even better results!

Okay, time to run some code and see what we're talking about with startup speed and memory consumption.

Thorntail Example

We start by creating a *traditional* application with Thorntail to provide a comparison of the memory, or RSS, and time-to-first-request metrics. For anyone not familiar with Thorntail, the project focused on the idea of a customizable WildFly server (*https://wildfly.org*). Thorntail takes only the bits you need for a specific application, removing everything else.

The Thorntail application requires a Java API for RESTful Web Services (*https://oreil.ly/eYjXF*) (JAX-RS) application, and a simple resource endpoint for us to make requests against. The Thorntail example needs a JAX-RS application, and a JAX-RS resource with a single method returning a greeting for an HTTP GET request. All the source code for the Thorntail example can be found in the */chapter-2/thorntail-hello* directory.

There's nothing special about the classes. They're the bare minimum required to provide an HTTP endpoint with JAX-RS to make requests against. Let's build the Thorntail application and then start it, as shown in Example 2-1.

Example 2-1. Build and run the Thorntail Hello World application

```
> mvn verify
> java -jar target/thorntail-hello-world-thorntail.jar
```

Once the application has started, hit the *http://localhost:8080/hello* endpoint with curl or a browser. After you've made a few requests, or more if you prefer, it's time to take a look at the RSS memory used by the process. Accessing the endpoint before measuring RSS is important because an application may not have loaded all classes during startup, meaning we could see a misleading figure.

To be able to find out the memory used, we need the ID of the process the Thorntail application is running in. On Linux-based systems, including Mac, we can use ps -e | grep thorntail, which lists all the active processes and restricts the results to those containing thorntail in the name. With the process ID in hand, we can now find out how much RSS the process is using (as seen in Example 2-2).

Example 2-2. Measure the RSS usage of the Thorntail application

```
> ps -o pid,rss,command -p 4529 | awk '{$2=int($2/1024)"M";}{ print;}'      ❶

PID   RSS COMMAND
4529 441M java -jar target/thorntail-hello-world-thorntail.jar
```

❶ ps retrieves the RSS and command, and awk converts the RSS value to megabytes.

You will see something like the preceding terminal output, showing the process ID, RSS converted to megabytes (M), and the command. Full details on how to find RSS for a process can be found on the Quarkus website.[3]

We can see that a "Hello World" style application with a single endpoint returning a string uses 441 megabytes (MB). Whoa! That's a lot of memory for a single JAX-RS endpoint returning a fixed string!

We should caution we're running these tests on OpenJDK 11 without any customization for limiting the amount of memory the JVM captures, or any other tuning available to the JVM. We can limit what the JVM is able to grab and see how that affects the overall RSS (Example 2-3).

Example 2-3. Start the Thorntail application to configure the heap size

```
> java -Xmx48m -XX:MinHeapFreeRatio=10 -XX:MaxHeapFreeRatio=20 \
    -jar target/thorntail-hello-world-thorntail.jar
```

Now we get the output in Example 2-4.

Example 2-4. Measure the RSS usage

```
> ps -o pid,rss,command -p 5433 | awk '{$2=int($2/1024)"M";}{ print;}'
PID   RSS COMMAND
5433 265M java -Xmx48m -XX:MinHeapFreeRatio=10 -XX:MaxHeapFreeRatio=20 \
    -jar target/thorntail-hello-world-thorntail.jar
```

That dropped the memory usage down to 265 MB! We saved nearly 200 MB of RSS by limiting the amount of heap the JVM grabbed to 48 MB. Maybe 48 MB isn't quite the sweet spot in terms of throughput, but that's something to verify with your own applications, to find the balance between reduced memory consumption and increased throughput.

---

3 See Platform Specific Memory Reporting on the Quarkus website (*https://oreil.ly/eYjXF*).

We've shown the RSS usage, and now we need to calculate the time to first request. Ensure that all previous instances of the Thorntail application are stopped before continuing. Let's check out time to first request, as shown in Example 2-5.

Example 2-5. Measure the time to first request of the Thorntail application

```
> node time.js "java \
    -jar [fullPathToDir]/thorntail-hello/target/
      thorntail-hello-world-thorntail.jar" \
    "http://localhost:8080/hello"
```

We see a bunch of 404 messages fly past in the console until the application returns a 200 response, and then we see the time taken. In our case, it was 6,810 milliseconds (ms)! That's not exactly fast in the world of microservices and functions. You can run it a few times to see whether the time varies much or not really at all. With a 7-second startup time, scaling microservices can't meet traffic spikes quick enough, causing user delays and possibly errors. From a serverless perspective, we're even worse off as we'd expect a serverless function to be started, run, and stopped well before 7 seconds elapsed.

 The time to first request captured with *time.js* may be fractionally longer than it actually is, as a very small amount of time will be included as the child process spawns but before the JVM starts. We're not too worried about such a small amount, as the impact applies to each runtime we test in the same manner.

So, we've seen what a traditional application consumes for RSS, and how long it can take to reach time to first request. Now it's time to see how Quarkus compares.

Quarkus Example

We're going to create an identical Hello World endpoint, though it doesn't say "Hello from Thorntail!" With Quarkus, we don't need the JAX-RS application class; we need only the JAX-RS resource that has the same content as the Thorntail version, except for the message.[4] The source code for the Quarkus example can be found in the */chapter-2/quarkus-hello* directory.

In "Create Your First Quarkus Application" on page 21, we cover how to create a Quarkus application. Now build and run the Quarkus Hello World application, as shown in Example 2-6.

---

4 Quarkus offers multiple ways to implement HTTP endpoints. JAX-RS is one of them. You can also use controller classes with Spring MVC annotation or reactive routes if you prefer more programmatic approaches.

Example 2-6. Build and start the Quarkus Hello World application

```
> mvn verify
> java -jar target/quarkus-hello-world-1.0-SNAPSHOT-runner.jar
```

As with Thorntail, we're not optimizing the JVM to see what raw RSS usage we see. Hit *http://localhost:8080/hello* a few times as we did with Thorntail. Hopefully, you're seeing the message "Hello from Quarkus!" Otherwise, you're still running the Thorntail application.

Go find the process ID for the Quarkus application and check out the RSS (Example 2-7).

Example 2-7. Measure the RSS usage of the Quarkus Hello World application

```
> ps -o pid,rss,command -p 6439 | awk '{$2=int($2/1024)"M";}{ print;}'
PID   0M COMMAND
6439 133M java -jar target/quarkus-hello-world-1.0-SNAPSHOT-runner.jar
```

Here we see Quarkus using 133 MB of RSS, over 300 MB less than the 441 MB with Thorntail! That's an astonishing improvement for what is essentially the same application.

If we limit the maximum heap size to 48 MB, as we did for Thorntail, how much of an improvement do we get? Review Example 2-8. Don't forget to use the endpoint once the application is started.

Example 2-8. Constrain the heap usage and measure the RSS usage

```
> java -Xmx48m -XX:MinHeapFreeRatio=10 -XX:MaxHeapFreeRatio=20 \
    -jar target/quarkus-hello-world-1.0-SNAPSHOT-runner.jar
> ps -o pid,rss,command -p 7194 | awk '{$2=int($2/1024)"M";}{ print;}'
PID   0M COMMAND
7194 114M java -Xmx48m -XX:MinHeapFreeRatio=10 -XX:MaxHeapFreeRatio=20 \
    -jar target/quarkus-hello-world-1.0-SNAPSHOT-runner.jar
```

That got it down to 114 MB, but let's see how far we can push Quarkus into smaller heap sizes! Refer to Example 2-9. Once again, don't forget to use the endpoint once started.

Example 2-9. Constrain the heap usage of the Quarkus application even more and measure the RSS usage

```
> java -Xmx24m -XX:MinHeapFreeRatio=10 -XX:MaxHeapFreeRatio=20 \
    -jar target/quarkus-hello-world-1.0-SNAPSHOT-runner.jar
> ps -o pid,rss,command -p 19981 | awk '{$2=int($2/1024)"M";}{ print;}'
PID   0M COMMAND
```

```
19981 98M java -Xmx24m -XX:MinHeapFreeRatio=10 -XX:MaxHeapFreeRatio=20 \
    -jar target/quarkus-hello-world-1.0-SNAPSHOT-runner.jar
```

With a max heap of 24 MB, we're down to 98 MB of RSS! More importantly, the application still works! See how low you can reduce the maximum heap before Quarkus is unable to start. Although for regular applications, and even microservices, you wouldn't be setting the maximum heap so low, being able to set it this low is critical for serverless environments.

Setting the heap size to a very low value may penalize the performance of the application, especially if the application does a lot of allocations. Don't aim for the smallest value as possible, but verify the value according to your expected performance and deployment density gain. Note that the Quarkus architecture tries to avoid having such a penalty. However, we highly recommend you check with your application.

Time for startup speed (see Example 2-10).

Example 2-10. Measure the time to first request for the Quarkus application

```
> node time.js "java \
    -jar [fullPathToDir]/quarkus-hello/target/
      quarkus-hello-world-1.0-SNAPSHOT-runner.jar" \
    "http://localhost:8080/hello"
```

If your hardware is similar to ours, you should see a time to first request of around 1,001 ms! That's nearly seven times faster than the traditional application!

All this is really great, but what's the point? Recalling our earlier discussion about Java in containers, let's see the impact when running in containers. Assuming we have a node with 2 GB of RAM available, how many containers of each application can fit? Take a look at Figure 2-1.

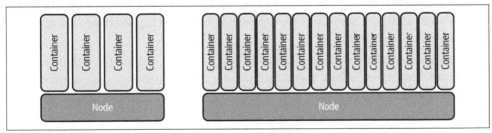

Figure 2-1. Java memory in containers: Quarkus allows increasing the deployment density

Container density is a key characteristic of cloud deployments with Kubernetes. Given a specific node size, such as 2 GB of RAM, the more containers that can run in that single node, the greater container density we can provide. Improving container density enables better utilization of the resources available. From the example in Figure 2-1, will more throughput be achieved with 4 instances or 14? If each of the 14 containers supports less throughput, or requests per second, compared with one of the traditional containers, it doesn't matter. A minor reduction in throughput in a container is more than offset by supporting 14 containers instead of 4.

Container density is an important metric in determining the number of instances that are required. What a developer needs to determine is their expected, or desired, throughput to be supported. Maybe fewer containers with larger memory requirements are fine for today's needs, but keep in mind that things change, and you could easily need more than four to support your users!

You've now seen the amount of RSS memory and time to first request with traditional applications on the JVM, and how Quarkus can significantly reduce these aspects for an application. Quarkus wants to tackle the challenge of improving Java in containers with a new approach. This approach improves the startup speed and the memory consumption of Java in a container.

The next section explains the details of how Quarkus makes this possible, and more importantly, how it differs from a traditional framework approach.

The Quarkus Way

We're sure you want to know all the intricate details of how Quarkus starts faster and consumes less memory than a traditional framework, right? We need to slow down a bit first, by explaining how traditional frameworks work, so you can understand what changes with Quarkus.

Some well-known features of traditional frameworks are depicted in Figure 2-2:

- Annotations within code defining expected behavior, with many examples of this we've all used over the years. Typical ones include `@Entity`, `@Autowired`, `@Inject`, and many, many more.

- Configuration files of various kinds. These files do everything from defining how classes should be wired together to configuring persistent data sources, and everything in between.

- Classes used only during startup for creating runtime metadata and classes for the application to function.

- Utilizing reflection in determining methods to invoke, setting values into objects, and dynamically loading classes by name only.

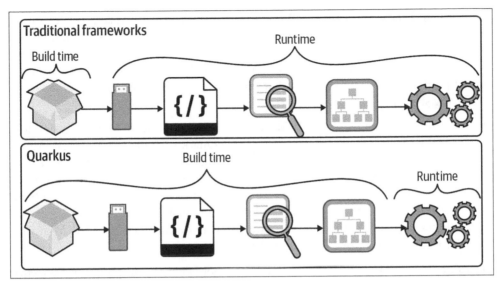

Figure 2-2. The Quarkus way

We're certainly not saying that Quarkus doesn't have annotations, configuration files, or any other features of traditional frameworks. We *are* saying Quarkus handles them in a very different manner.

Why would these features of traditional frameworks be considered "bad"? That's a good question, and the answer requires some understanding of how these frameworks handle the preceding features. When there's any type of configuration to be parsed or annotations to be discovered, framework classes are required to perform this work. Depending on how complex the process might be, anywhere from dozens to hundreds of classes could be needed to perform the task. In addition, each class would typically be holding state within itself representing intermediate states as startup occurs, or a final desired state after everything is processed.

There's nothing particularly special about this; frameworks have worked this way for years, decades even. What you may not realize, though, is that any classes used to perform these startup tasks are still present, even if the JVM process has been running for six months without a restart! While any memory those classes grabbed should be eventually garbage collected, provided the classes properly released their hold on the memory when work was complete, the class metadata for them is still present in the JVM, even on the latest Java versions. It may not seem like much, but a couple of hundred classes that are no longer needed can impact the amount of memory required by the JVM.

This problem impacts all JVMs today, without special handling by a framework. All the classes used during startup, and never again, can be garbage collected by the JVM only if all objects of the class can be garbage collected, all references to the class are removed, and most importantly, all other classes in the same classloader are also no longer referenced. To facilitate the garbage collection of startup classes, a framework would need to utilize a classloader for startup classes and another classloader for runtime classes. It can be difficult to enable garbage collection for startup classes when thread pools are used, especially `ForkJoinPool`, and when thread-local variables are set during startup.

Why should we retain classes in JVM memory if they will never be used again? Ideally, we shouldn't, as it's wasteful. This is where Quarkus shines. Quarkus extensions are designed and built to separate the various pieces of the traditional framework startup processing into smaller chunks of work. Doing this enables the build process, with Maven or Gradle, to take advantage of those smaller chunks and execute them during the build, instead of waiting until the runtime start. Utilizing startup classes *during build time* means those classes don't need to be included in the JVM at runtime! This saves us memory and startup time.

How does it help to do this at build time, and where does the output go that's needed during runtime? Extensions use bytecode recorders to do everything from setting static values on classes for runtime, to creating new classes to hold metadata that's needed for runtime. What do we mean by that? Earlier we talked about frameworks doing a lot of work during startup, and Quarkus is able to create the output of that work during build time and write bytecode equating to the same result as with traditional frameworks at startup. At runtime, instead of performing the startup work, the JVM loads the class written by a Quarkus extension into memory as if all that startup work just happened without the cost of the memory and classes to do the work.

Looking at some steps a traditional framework performs at startup, we can see in Figure 2-3 how Quarkus handles them differently.

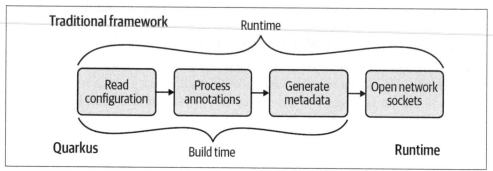

Figure 2-3. Framework startup phases in traditional frameworks versus Quarkus

While Quarkus reads the configuration at build time, some properties, such as locations and credentials, are still configured and read at runtime. However, everything application-centric that can be decided at build time is handled during the build process. So far, we've been using build time to describe when Quarkus completes these typically startup-related tasks, but there is another term: *ahead-of-time* (AOT) compilation. You've seen that Quarkus differs from traditional frameworks in the way it approaches optimizing your application code and dependencies. Yes, this approach reduces the variability that is generally handled at runtime.

However, modern workloads deployed in the cloud or in containers do not need such variability, as almost everything is known at build time. We hope you now have a clearer understanding of what Quarkus offers with this innovative approach, and why it is bringing excitement to Java development in the cloud again.

Create Your First Quarkus Application

There are quite a few ways to create a Quarkus application for the first time:

- Manually creating the project *pom.xml* or *build.gradle* file, adding Quarkus dependencies, setting up and configuring the plug-ins, and defining the source folders. Pretty messy and tedious, in our view!

- Using Maven and the Quarkus plug-in to construct the project skeleton.

- Browsing to *https://code.quarkus.io* and selecting the dependencies that are needed. This is the simplest, quickest way to get started, and the method we'll use.

It's time to dive into creating a project! Head over to *https://code.quarkus.io*, and you will be presented with the page in Figure 2-4. We've circled some key parts to explain them in detail.

At the very top of the page is the Quarkus version of the generated project. Just below it to the left, you can customize the group and artifact names that will be set for the project. These can be changed later if desired as well; you're not stuck with *org.acme* if you forget to customize it.

To the right, users can decide whether they want starter code added to the project. The default is yes, so if you select any extensions with the *CODE* marker, such as *RESTEasy JAX-RS*, starter code for that extension will be generated for the project. Below the top part of the page is the list of all available Quarkus extensions. A lot of extensions are available; the screenshot shows only the ones that would fit on a single page. Use each checkbox to select specific extensions to include in your project.

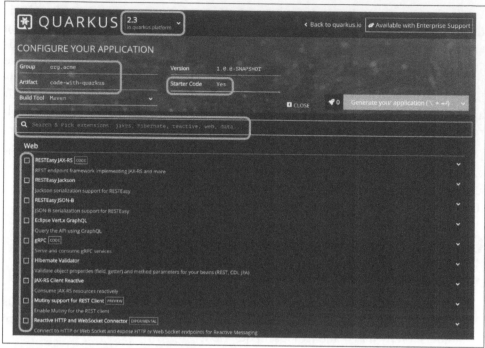

Figure 2-4. Quarkus project selection

Lastly, if you don't want to scroll through all the extensions, start typing terms into the search box above all the extensions. As you type, the list of extensions below it will filter, showing only the extensions matching your search criteria. As extensions are selected, they appear under the Selected Extensions area next to "Generate your application."

Figure 2-5 shows how the screen looks when we're about to generate the application.

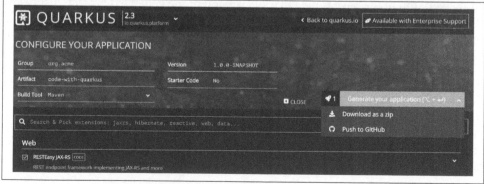

Figure 2-5. Quarkus project generation

You can see we've chosen not to generate any starter code, and the RESTEasy JAX-RS extension is selected. We're sticking with plain JAX-RS for now. We will explore a more reactive JAX-RS in Chapter 8.

As we hover over "Generate your application," we can decide to download the project as a ZIP file or publish it to a GitHub repository. Right now, we will download as a ZIP file. The file will be automatically downloaded, with a name matching the artifact name. Once the download is finished, extract the ZIP file to a directory.

With that done, we open a terminal window and change to the directory where the generated project was extracted. Let's dive into using live reload (Example 2-11) and experience real Developer Joy!

Example 2-11. Run the application in dev mode

```
> mvn quarkus:dev
```

The preceding command starts Quarkus in live reload, enabling us to quickly iterate with code and instantly see the impact. A successful start will have the terminal output, shown in Example 2-12.

Example 2-12. Output the Quarkus application

```
__  ____  __  _____   ___  __ ____  _____
 --/ __ \/ / / / _ | / _ \/ //_/ / / / __/
 -/ /_/ / /_/ / __ |/ , _/ ,< / /_/ /\ \
 --_____/_/ |_/_/|_/_/|_|\____/___/
INFO  [io.quarkus] (Quarkus Main Thread) code-with-quarkus 1.0.0-SNAPSHOT on JVM \
    (powered by Quarkus 2.2.0.Final) started in 0.937s. \
    Listening on: http://localhost:8080
INFO  [io.quarkus] (Quarkus Main Thread) Profile dev activated.
  Live Coding activated.
INFO  [io.quarkus] (Quarkus Main Thread) Installed features: [cdi]
```

We're off and running. Open *http://localhost:8080* in a browser, and you will see `Resource not found`. Oh, no! What went wrong?

Actually, nothing went wrong. Eagle-eyed readers might have noticed the startup log listed only `cdi` as an installed feature. What about RESTEasy? We selected the extension for it when creating the project. Have a look inside *pom.xml*, and you will see the dependencies (Example 2-13).

Example 2-13. Quarkus extension dependencies of generated project (chapter-2/code-with-quarkus/pom.xml)

```
<dependency>
  <groupId>io.quarkus</groupId>
```

```
    <artifactId>quarkus-resteasy</artifactId>
  </dependency>
  <dependency>
    <groupId>io.quarkus</groupId>
    <artifactId>quarkus-arc</artifactId>
  </dependency>
  <dependency>
    <groupId>io.quarkus</groupId>
    <artifactId>quarkus-junit5</artifactId>
    <scope>test</scope>
  </dependency>
```

RESTEasy is definitely there as a dependency, so what's going on? During the build process, Quarkus recognized there wasn't actually any code present utilizing REST-Easy, making the feature uninstalled and available for removal to save memory. Let's fix that now.

With Quarkus still running, create the *org.acme* package within */src/main/java*. Now create a class named MyResource within the package and the content in Example 2-14.

Example 2-14. JAX-RS MyResource (chapter-2/code-with-quarkus/src/main/java/org/acme/MyResource.java)

```
import javax.ws.rs.GET;
import javax.ws.rs.Path;
import javax.ws.rs.Produces;
import javax.ws.rs.core.MediaType;

@Path("/")
@Produces({MediaType.TEXT_PLAIN})
public class MyResource {
  @GET
  public String message() {
    return "Hi";
  }
}
```

 You may wonder why in the preceding snippet none of the import lines are Quarkus specific. Quarkus provides a cohesive full-stack framework by leveraging a growing list of over 50 best-of-breed libraries. In the preceding example, we use JAX-RS, a simple but efficient and flexible approach to building HTTP and REST APIs.

Refresh *http://localhost:8080*. Wow, we now see Hi in the browser; what happened? Take a look in the terminal window (Example 2-15).

Example 2-15. Automatic restart of the application after a code change

```
INFO  [io.qua.dep.dev.RuntimeUpdatesProcessor] (vert.x-worker-thread-7) \
    Changed source files detected, recompiling \
    [{pathToProject}/code-with-quarkus/src/main/java/org/acme/MyResource.java]
INFO  [io.quarkus] (Quarkus Main Thread) code-with-quarkus stopped in 0.037s
__  ___  __  ___   __  __ ___  ____
 --/ __ \/ / / / _ | / / _ \/ //_/ / / / __/
 -/ /_/ / /_/ / __ |/ , _/ ,< / /_/ /\ \
--_____/_/ |_/_/|_/_/|_|\____/___/
INFO  [io.quarkus] (Quarkus Main Thread) code-with-quarkus 1.0.0-SNAPSHOT on JVM \
    (powered by Quarkus 1.11.1.Final) started in 0.195s. \
    Listening on: http://localhost:8080
INFO  [io.quarkus] (Quarkus Main Thread) Profile dev activated. Live Coding activated
INFO  [io.quarkus] (Quarkus Main Thread) Installed features: [cdi, resteasy]
INFO  [io.qua.dep.dev.RuntimeUpdatesProcessor] (vert.x-worker-thread-7) \
    Hot replace total time: 0.291s
```

We can see Quarkus noticed modifications to *MyResource.java*, stopped, and then restarted itself. Looking at the installed features, we see it now includes resteasy. How cool is that? Even better, the server stopped and restarted in just over 300 ms.

Why don't we explore live reload some more to have a better feel of the real Developer Joy! With mvn quarkus:dev still running, open *http://localhost:8080/welcome* in a browser (Figure 2-6).

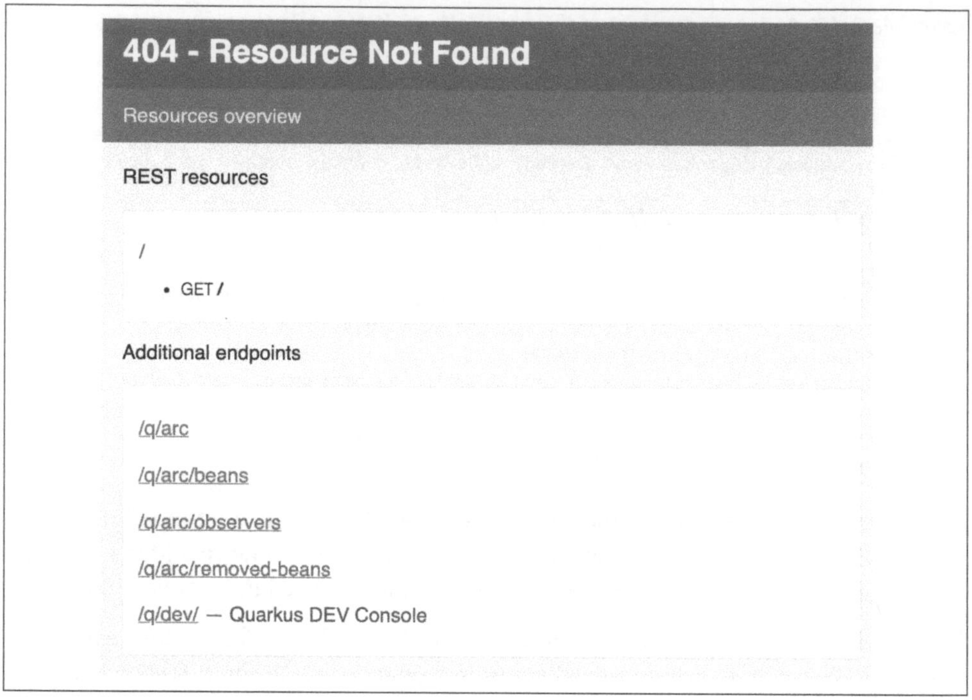

Figure 2-6. Resource not found

We got an error. Oh no!

Don't fear too much; we did expect it because we don't have anything to respond to the */welcome* endpoint yet. However, Quarkus offers us some links to help diagnose the problem based on what it knows about the application. We are shown the list of valid endpoints—in this case, there is only an HTTP GET on /.

Under "Additional endpoints," there are endpoints to assist while developing applications. In this example, we have endpoints related to *ArC*, which is the bean container based on Contexts and Dependency Injection (CDI) for Quarkus, as well as a link to the developer console. Clicking the developer console link will bring you to its main page (Figure 2-7).

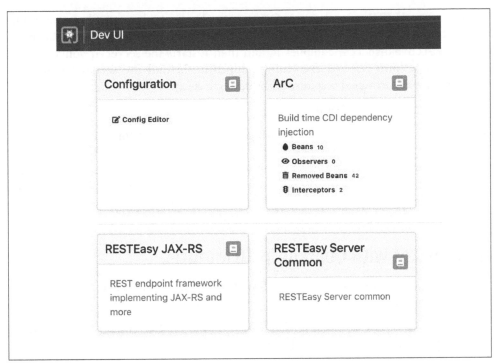

Figure 2-7. Quarkus Dev console

There isn't a lot there now, but we need to remember that the only extension we've added is RESTEasy. As we enhance an application with more extensions, more options and abilities will be available from the developer console. We went down a side track there, so let's get back to resolving our failed page load! With the */welcome* page open to the failure in the browser, go back to the source and create a new class called `WelcomeResource` (Example 2-16).

Example 2-16. JAX-RS `WelcomeResource` (chapter-2/code-with-quarkus/src/main/ java/org/acme/WelcomeResource.java)

```
@Path("/welcome")
public class WelcomeResource {
  @GET
  public String welcomeMessage() {
    return "Welcome to Quarkus!";
  }
}
```

With the class written, head back to the browser and click Refresh.

Triggering an HTTP request causes Quarkus to check whether any files were modified since the last request, as we're running with live reload. Quarkus notices the presence of `WelcomeResource`, compiles it, and then restarts the server. If you're like us, you may not have realized everything happening behind the scenes because the browser gave the expected response without much delay.

Are you exhausted yet? We are.

That was a lot of information on creating a Quarkus project for the first time with *https://code.quarkus.io*, and experiencing the ease of development that live reload with Quarkus brings. It does have drawbacks, including less chance to get a coffee during a compile and restart. We will continue to explore everything that live reload can do as we work through the chapters, but take it for a spin yourself, adding new extensions and seeing what can be done without stopping it!

Kubernetes with Quarkus in 10 Minutes

In the previous section, we had lots of fun changing code and seeing the application update on the fly. We hope you had fun; we know we did!

While that's great for developing the code, can we use live coding in production? Well, maybe you could, but we really don't think you want to do that!

For deploying to production, we want to use immutable containers, which requires container orchestration, which for most means Kubernetes. "The New Kids on the Block: Cloud Native and Kubernetes Native Applications" on page 46 covers cloud native and Kubernetes applications in further detail.

Why is Quarkus great for the cloud and, in particular, Kubernetes? Quarkus applications are designed to run efficiently in containers and have built-in health checks and monitoring capabilities. Quarkus also provides a great user experience, including the ability to deploy in a Kubernetes cluster in a single command, without having to write Kubernetes resource descriptors.

Kubernetes introduces its own specific jargon, which may be confusing. This section introduces its main concepts.

What are the steps to take our Quarkus application from the previous section and deploy it to Kubernetes? Let's extend the application we generated in the previous section. The first thing we do is add the extension for Kubernetes to our application, as shown in Example 2-17.

Example 2-17. Kubernetes extension dependency (chapter-2/code-with-quarkus/pom.xml)

```
<dependency>
  <groupId>io.quarkus</groupId>
  <artifactId>quarkus-kubernetes</artifactId>
</dependency>
```

With this new dependency, the build can generate the necessary resource files for deploying the application to Kubernetes, as well as enable us to deploy the application. What a time-saver! Let's see how it works!

Before we can see how it works, we need to choose the preferred containerization mechanism. With Quarkus, we can choose between Docker, Jib (*https://oreil.ly/Ybxcs*), and Source-to-Image (S2I). We will choose Jib, as all dependencies are cached in a layer separate from the application, making subsequent container builds much faster. Let's add the Jib container dependency, as shown in Example 2-18.

Example 2-18. Jib container extension dependency (chapter-2/code-with-quarkus/pom.xml)

```
<dependency>
  <groupId>io.quarkus</groupId>
  <artifactId>quarkus-container-image-jib</artifactId>
</dependency>
```

We're nearly there! But first, we need a Kubernetes cluster! The easiest is to use minikube, but you can also use Docker Desktop, or MicroK8s (*https://microk8s.io/*). In this book, we will use minikube, as it's one of the most straightforward solutions. Minikube is not a complete Kubernetes cluster but provides enough features for us.

Follow the instructions from the minikube documentation (*https://oreil.ly/Vn7Jf*) to download and install minikube. With minikube installed, start it (Example 2-19).

Example 2-19. Start minikube

```
> minikube start
```

The default configuration of minikube will be used unless we have specific configuration options set. Right now, the default is fine, which is two CPUs and 4 GB RAM for a virtual machine. If this is the first time minikube is being run, there will be a short delay while minikube downloads the necessary images.

Quarkus provides an additional extension for use with minikube, to tailor the Kubernetes resources specifically for minikube. A big advantage to this approach is not requiring a Kubernetes Ingress to access services inside Kubernetes; instead, we can access them through a NodePort service. This allows us to see localhost-accessible

URLs for our services when running `minikube services list`. To activate localhost-accessible URLs, we need another dependency (Example 2-20).

Example 2-20. Minikube extension dependency (chapter-2/code-with-quarkus/pom.xml)

```
<dependency>
  <groupId>io.quarkus</groupId>
  <artifactId>quarkus-minikube</artifactId>
</dependency>
```

Before deploying our application, let's play a bit with Kubernetes to understand some concepts. You can interact with Kubernetes clusters by using the `kubectl` command; see Example 2-21.

Example 2-21. Retrieve the nodes

```
> kubectl get nodes
NAME       STATUS    ROLES    AGE     VERSION
minikube   Ready     master   2m45s   v1.18.3
```

This command prints the *nodes* managed by Kubernetes. You should not be surprised to see that we have a single node here, named `master`. That's your machine, or virtual machine, depending on your operating system.

Unlike other systems such as Docker, Kubernetes doesn't run containers directly. Instead, it wraps one or more containers into a higher-level structure called a *pod*. Pods are used as the unit of replication. If your application is getting too many requests, and a single pod instance can't carry the load, you can ask Kubernetes to instantiate new replicas. Even when not under heavy load, it is a good idea to have multiple replicas of a pod, to allow load balancing and fault-tolerance. You can get the list of pods by using `kubectl get pods` (Example 2-22).

Example 2-22. Use the `kubectl` command to list the running pods

```
> kubectl get pods
No resources found in default namespace.
```

Not a big surprise, our cluster is empty.

In "Java on the Cloud" on page 9, we talked a lot about wanting to reduce the amount of memory for services written in Java within a container. To be able to determine that in minikube, we need to install an add-on before deploying our service (Example 2-23).

Example 2-23. Add the metric server to the minikube cluster

```
> minikube addons enable metrics-server
```

To create pods, we need a *deployment*. Deployments have two primary purposes:

- Indicate which containers need to run in the pod
- Indicate the number of instances of the pod that should be running at a time

Generally, to create a deployment, you need the following:

- A container image accessible to your Kubernetes cluster
- A YAML document describing your deployment[5]

Quarkus provides facilities to avoid having to create the image and write the deployment manually, such as the Kubernetes, minikube, and Jib container extensions we mentioned earlier.

With all the pieces in place, it's time for us to build and deploy the application to Kubernetes in minikube! Open a terminal window and change to the directory of the project. Because we don't want to run our own Docker daemon for building the containers, we can run `eval $(minikube -p minikube docker-env)` to expose the Docker daemon from minikube to the local terminal environment.

 `eval $(minikube -p minikube docker-env)` must be run in every terminal window we use to access minikube. Without, it any Docker commands we execute will use the local Docker daemon, which we don't want.

Next we build and deploy the container (as shown in Example 2-24).

Example 2-24. Deploy a Quarkus application to Kubernetes

```
> mvn verify -Dquarkus.kubernetes.deploy=true ❶
```

❶ Package the application, create the container image, create the deployment descriptor, and deploy it to our cluster.

Execute the `kubeclt get pods` command to verify (Example 2-25).

---

5 YAML (Yet Another Markup Language) is the most used format to describe Kubernetes resources. Wikipedia provides a gentle introduction (*https://oreil.ly/mZOTT*).

Example 2-25. List running pods with kubectl

```
> kubectl get pods
code-with-quarkus-66769bd48f-l65ff   1/1      Running   0          88s
```

Yeah! Our application is running!

Quarkus creates a deployment for us, as shown in Example 2-26.

Example 2-26. List the installed deployments

```
> kubectl get deployments
NAME                   READY   UP-TO-DATE   AVAILABLE   AGE
code-with-quarkus      1/1     1            1           6m23s
```

You can check the created deployment in *target/kubernetes/minikube.yml*, or review Example 2-27.

Example 2-27. The generated deployment

```
apiVersion: apps/v1
kind: Deployment
metadata:
  # ...
  name: code-with-quarkus
spec:
  replicas: 1 ❶
  #...
  template:
    metadata:
      # ...
    spec:
      containers:
        image: your_name/code-with-quarkus:1.0.0-SNAPSHOT ❷
        imagePullPolicy: IfNotPresent
        name: code-with-quarkus
        ports:
        - containerPort: 8080
          name: http
          protocol: TCP
        # ...
```

❶ The number of replicas

❷ The container image name

As you can see, the deployment YAML indicates the number of replicas and the set of containers running in the pod (here, a single one).

If you look carefully at the generated descriptor, you will see service:

```
apiVersion: v1
kind: Service
metadata:
  # ...
  name: code-with-quarkus
spec:
  ports:
  - name: http
    nodePort: 31995            ❶
    port: 8080
    targetPort: 8080
  selector:
    app.kubernetes.io/name: code-with-quarkus
    app.kubernetes.io/version: 1.0.0-SNAPSHOT
  type: NodePort
```

❶ Random local port number we can access the service on

A *service* is a channel of communication delegating to a set of pods (selected using labels). In our example, the service is named code-with-quarkus. This name can be used by other applications to discover the functionality we expose. This service delegates the port 8080 on pods with matching labels (*app.kubernetes.io/name* and *app.kubernetes.io/version*). The good news is that our pod is configured with these labels. As a result, calling this code-with-quarkus on port 8080 delegates to port 8080 of our container.

> Quarkus generates multiple descriptors. The *minikube.yml* descriptor is tailored for minikube. The *kubernetes.yml* descriptor is more generic. The main difference is the type of service that gets created.

So, let's invoke our service! We need to ask minikube to give us the service URL, as shown in Example 2-28.

Example 2-28. Retrieve the service URL

```
> minikube service code-with-quarkus --url

🦊  Starting tunnel for service code-with-quarkus.
|-----------|---------------------|-------------|-----------------------------|
| NAMESPACE |        NAME         | TARGET PORT |            URL              |
|-----------|---------------------|-------------|-----------------------------|
| default   | code-with-quarkus   |             | http://127.0.0.1:31995      |
|-----------|---------------------|-------------|-----------------------------|
http://127.0.0.1:31995
```

! Because you are using a Docker driver on darwin, the terminal needs
  to be open to run it.

Open a browser and use the URL of the service to access it, or curl if you prefer. If deployment worked, we see Hi as a response on the root path. Add /welcome to see Welcome to Quarkus! We deployed a Quarkus service to Kubernetes!

We've verified that our Quarkus service deployed and works as expected, but what about the memory situation? Let's check it out in Example 2-29.

Example 2-29. Measure resource usage using kubectl top

```
> kubectl top pods
NAME                                   CPU(cores)   MEMORY(bytes)
code-with-quarkus-66769bd48f-l65ff     1m           80Mi
```

Wow, only 80 MB is really nice and compact! That's a large improvement over traditional frameworks in containers.

You've just seen how to take a Quarkus application and add the ability to deploy it to Kubernetes or, in this case, to minikube. There are certainly potential gotchas in defining the Kubernetes resources we need for deployment, but that's why we use the Kubernetes extension with Quarkus to handle all that for us. We prefer not to hand-code YAML or JSON, inadvertently making an error with indentation, and then watching deployment fail!

Going Native

What does *going native* mean? We're referring to the ability to build native executables for an environment. Many applications we use every day on our machines are *native executables*, meaning the code of the application was compiled down to low-level instructions for a specific operating system, in our case macOS.

Developing Java applications has always required the presence of a JVM for execution. However, the ability to build a native executable from Java code has recently been made possible with releases from the GraalVM (*https://www.graalvm.org*) project. In this section, we explain how to utilize the GraalVM project with Quarkus to generate a native executable for your Java code!

In "The Quarkus Way" on page 18, we discussed how Quarkus utilizes AOT compilation to perform actions during build time instead of on application start.

Quarkus extensions achieve this by breaking all the work into three separate phases:

Augmentation
> Build steps process descriptors and annotations, and augment the application classes by generating bytecode containing any required metadata. This phase is always executed within the build process on a JVM.

Static initialization
> Runs any steps intended to have their resulting output captured in bytecode. There are restrictions on what these steps can do, as they should not open ports for listening or start threads.

Runtime initialization
> These steps are run as part of the application's main method during startup. Tasks should be kept to a minimum to take the most advantage of AOT.

Static and runtime initialization both occur at startup when executing on a JVM. However, with native executables we have an extra benefit. With initialization separated into two phases, we're able to perform static initialization during the native executable build process. This allows the output from the static initialization phase to be serialized directly into the native executable, allowing any classes used in this phase to be dropped from the native executable as they're no longer needed. This provides benefits in native executable startup time and reduction in memory requirements.

As part of the native executable build process with GraalVM, all execution paths are evaluated. Any classes, methods, or fields deemed to not be on the execution path are removed from the resulting native executable. This is why reflection, dynamic class loading, and other features of JVM usage are disallowed without special flags, because the goal is to *not* retain every piece of code within a native executable. If we were to attempt to build a native executable for the earlier Thorntail example, it would require flags to be set to allow reflection, dynamic class loading, and possibly others. The design of Thorntail is not suitable for a native executable build, whereas Quarkus has the goal of code reduction in mind from the beginning.

Let's see what's needed to actually build a native executable.[6] Creating the project with *https://code.quarkus.io* means a Maven profile was already added to the project for us. Example 2-30 shows what that looks like.

---

6 GraalVM is not the first tool to build native executables from Java code. Dalvik, Avian, GNU Compiler for Java (GCJ,) and Excelsior JET predate GraalVM.

Example 2-30. Native image generation Maven profile (chapter-2/code-with-quarkus/pom.xml)

```
<profile>
  <id>native</id>
  <activation>
    <property>
      <name>native</name>
    </property>
  </activation>
  <properties>
    <quarkus.package.type>native</quarkus.package.type>
  </properties>
</profile>
```

We now have the ability to build a native executable for Quarkus, but without GraalVM installed we won't get very far! Check the "Building a Native Executable" guide (*https://oreil.ly/HFtW1*) for all the details on installing GraalVM for building native executables.

Once GraalVM is installed, let's build a native executable; see Example 2-31.

Example 2-31. Compile a Quarkus application into a native executable

```
> mvn verify -Pnative
```

Unfortunately, building a native executable does take longer than usual JVM builds. For this reason, we suggest not building a native executable regularly, and recommend doing these builds as part of a CI pipeline.

Running these builds is our new opportunity for coffee breaks!

> As the number of classes grows in an application, a native executable build takes longer to complete. This longer time is caused by the larger number of execution paths requiring evaluation.

With the native executable built, we can run it with `./target/code-with-quarkus-1.0.0-SNAPSHOT-runner`. Relish in the speed with which it starts, and be sure to verify that the two endpoints we created still work.

We've now built a native executable for our local environment, but unless we're using a Linux operating system, our native executable won't work inside a container! As native executables are specific to an operating system, we need to specially build one for use in a Linux container.

To build a native executable for containers, we need to utilize Docker (*https:// docker.com*). Once Docker is installed, ensure that it's started. As the current terminal has been switched to use the Docker daemon inside minikube, we need to open a new terminal so we can use local Docker for a build. Navigate to the project directory and run Example 2-32.

Example 2-32. Compile a Quarkus application into a Linux 64-bit native executable

```
> mvn verify -Pnative -Dquarkus.native.container-build=true
```

What we've done is utilized our local Docker environment to build a native executable for a Linux operating system. If we tried to run the native executable, and our local operating system is not Linux, we see an error (Example 2-33).

Example 2-33. Format error when we start an application not compiled for the host operating system

```
zsh: exec format error: ./target/code-with-quarkus-1.0.0-SNAPSHOT-runner
```

We need to go back to the previous terminal now, as we want to interact with the Docker daemon in minikube. Let's run a Docker build inside minikube, as shown in Example 2-34.

Example 2-34. Build a container running a Quarkus application compiled into a native executable

```
> docker build -f src/main/docker/Dockerfile.native \
    -t <_your_docker_username_>/code-with-quarkus:1.0.0-SNAPSHOT .
```

 Don't forget to replace *<your_docker_username>* with your local Docker username.

We now have a container available inside minikube, so let's create the application deployment; see Example 2-35.

Example 2-35. Deploy the Quarkus application into minikube

```
> kubectl apply -f target/kubernetes/minikube.yml
```

We used the minikube-specific Kubernetes YAML from an earlier build to create the deployment. This version creates the *NodePort* service we need to access a service from our local environment, but also modifies the `imagePullPolicy` of the container to `IfNotPresent` instead of `Always`. This last change prevents minikube from trying to check for a newer container image from Docker Hub, which is good because it wouldn't find one there!

With the deployment done, grab the URL from `minikube service list` and test out the endpoints again. Everything should be good, and we get the same messages as before.

Now for the interesting part! Earlier we installed the metrics server into minikube to track memory utilization, and now it's time to see what our native executable looks like. Though we've made requests and the deployment is present, it can be a few minutes before the metrics are available. Keep trying until they appear. You should see something similar to Example 2-36.

Example 2-36. Measure resource usage in Kubernetes

```
> kubectl top pods
NAME                                 CPU(cores)    MEMORY(bytes)
code-with-quarkus-fd76c594b-48b98    0m            7Mi
```

That's fantastic! Only 7 MB of RAM used!

This is where the combination of Quarkus and native executables really shines. We can also check the logs of the pod to see how quickly the container started; we would expect it to be around 10–20 ms.

 We attempted to build a native image for Thorntail to provide a comparison. However, we experienced issues building a usable native image and were stopped by an `UnsatisfiedLinkError` (*https://oreil.ly/hxcqo*).

Summary

We've covered a great deal about Quarkus in a short amount of time, and there's still plenty more to go through in the remainder of the book. Quarkus is a Kubernetes-native Java stack, focused on minimizing memory requirements with AOT, and amping up the memory reduction even further when we want a native executable. With the Kubernetes and container extensions, Quarkus takes the hassle out of handwriting YAML deployment files, doing it all for us!

In this chapter, you learned about the following:

- Understanding the problems with Java in containers
- Understanding how Quarkus differs from traditional frameworks in moving runtime startup tasks to buildtime with AOT

- Creating a Quarkus project with *https://code.quarkus.io*
- Using Kubernetes and minikube extensions to generate the required deployment configuration
- Building a native executable for Quarkus with GraalVM
- Using the Kubernetes extension to deploy Quarkus applications to a container environment

In the next chapters, we will briefly take a step back to detail distributed systems, reactive systems, reactive programming, and how they relate to each other.

## PART II

Reactive and Event-Driven Applications

## CHAPTER 3

The Dark Side of Distributed Systems

Now that you have a better understanding of Reactive and had a brief overview of Quarkus, let's focus on why you would want to use them and, more specifically, build reactive systems. The reason emanates from the cloud and, more generally, the need to build *better* distributed systems. The cloud has been a game changer. It's making the construction of distributed systems easier. You can create virtual resources on the fly and use off-the-shelf services. However, *easier* does not mean *straightforward*. Building such systems is a considerable challenge. Why? Because the cloud is a distributed system, and distributed systems are complicated. We need to understand the kind of animal we are trying to tame.

What's a Distributed System?

There are many definitions of distributed systems. But let's start with a loose one, written by professor emeritus Andrew Tanenbaum, and see what we can learn:

> A distributed system is a collection of independent computers that appears to its users as a single coherent system.

This definition highlights two important aspects of distributed systems:

- A distributed system is composed of *independent* machines that are autonomous. They can be started and stopped at any time. These machines operate concurrently and can fail independently without affecting the whole system's uptime (in theory, at least).
- Consumers (users) should not be aware of the system's structure. It should provide a consistent experience. Typically, you may use an HTTP service, which is served by an API gateway (Figure 3-1), delegating requests to various *machines*.

For you, the caller, a distributed system behaves as a single coherent system: you have a single entry point and ignore the underlying structure of the system.

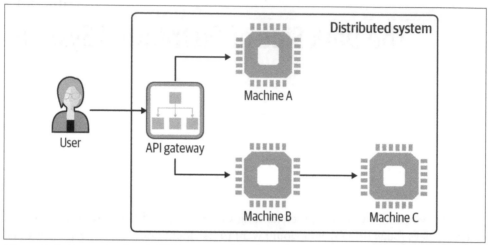

Figure 3-1. Example of an HTTP service delegating calls to other machines/services

To achieve this level of coherence, the autonomous machines must collaborate one way or another. This collaboration and the need for good communications that arise from it are the heart of distributed systems but also their primary challenge. But that definition does not explain why we are building distributed systems. Initially, distributed systems were workarounds. The resources of each machine were too limited. Connecting multiple machines was a smart way to extend the whole system's capacity, making resources available to the other members of the network. Today, the motivations are slightly different. Using a set of distributed machines gives us more business *agility*, eases evolution, reduces the time to market, and from an operational standpoint, allows us to scale more quickly, improves resilience via replication, and so on.

Distributed systems morphed from being a workaround to being the norm. Why? We can't build a single machine powerful enough to handle all the needs of a major corporation, while *also* being affordable. If we could, we'd all use the giant machine and deploy independent applications on it. But this necessity for distribution draws new operational and business boundaries based on physical system boundaries. Microservices, serverless architecture, service-oriented architecture (SOA), REST endpoints, mobile applications—all are distributed systems.

This distribution is stressing, even more, the need for collaboration among all the components forming the system. When an application (for instance, implemented in Java), needs to interact locally, it just uses a method call. For example, to collaborate with a `service` exposing a `hello` method, you use `service.hello`. We stay inside the same process. Calls can be synchronous; no network I/O is involved.

However, the dispersed nature of distributed systems implies interprocess communication, and most of the time, crossing the network (Figure 3-2). Dealing with I/O and traversing the network makes these interactions considerably different. A lot of middleware tried to make the distribution transparent, but, don't be mistaken, complete transparency is a lie, as explained in "A Note on Distributed Computing" (*https://oreil.ly/iCz3c*) by Jim Waldo et al. It always backfires one way or another. You need to understand the unique nature of remote communications and realize how distinctive they are in order to build robust distributed systems.

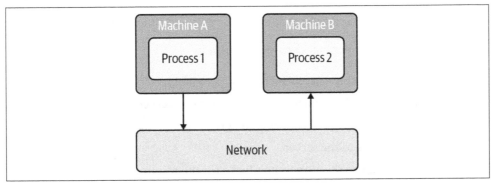

Figure 3-2. Remote interactions leave one process space and cross into another process space via a network connection

The first difference is the duration. A remote call is going to take much more time than a local call. That time is several degrees of magnitude higher. When everything is fine, sending a request from New York City to Los Angeles takes around 72 ms.[1] Calling a local method takes less than a nanosecond.

A remote call also leaves the process space, so we need an exchange protocol. This protocol defines all the aspects of the exchange, such as who is initiating the communication, how the information is written to the wire (serialization and deserialization), how the messages are routed to the destination, and so on.

When you develop your application, most of these choices are hidden from you but present under the hood. Let's take a REST endpoint you want to call. You will use HTTP and most probably some JSON representation to send data and interpret the response. Your code is relatively simple, as you can see in Example 3-1.

---

1 You can check the latency between the main American cities at the Current Network Latency site (*https://oreil.ly/ws4Xd*).

Example 3-1. Invoke an HTTP service using a Java built-in client (chapter-3/http-client-example/src/main/java/http/Main.java)

```
HttpClient client = HttpClient.newHttpClient();
HttpRequest request = HttpRequest.newBuilder()
        .uri(URI.create("https://httpbin.org/anything"))
        .build();

HttpResponse<String> response = client.send(request,
        HttpResponse.BodyHandlers.ofString());

System.out.println(response.body());
```

Let's describe what's happening when you execute it:

1. Your application creates an HTTP request (`request`).
2. It establishes an HTTP connection with the remote server.
3. It writes the HTTP request following the protocol.
4. The request travels to the server.
5. The server interprets the request and looks for the resource.
6. The server creates an HTTP response with the representation of the resource state in JSON.
7. It writes the response following the protocol.
8. The application receives the response and extracts the body (as `String` in this example).

It's the role of middleware (HTTP server and client, JSON mappers…) to make these interactions easy for us developers. In our previous example, steps 2 to 8 are all hidden in the send method. But we need to be aware of them. Especially today, with the cloud, distributed systems and distributed communications are everywhere. It becomes rare to build an application that is not a distributed system. As soon as you call a remote web service, print a document, or use an online collaboration tool, you are creating a distributed system.

The New Kids on the Block: Cloud Native and Kubernetes Native Applications

The role of the cloud can't be overstated, and it's a significant factor in the popularization of distributed systems. If you need a new machine, database, API gateway, or persistent storage, the cloud can enable the delivery of these on-demand computing services. As a reminder, though, for as much as the cloud improves efficiencies, you must never forget that running your application on the cloud is equivalent to running on someone else's machine. Somewhere there are CPUs, disks, and memory used to execute your application, and while cloud providers are responsible for maintaining these systems and have built a reputation around reliability, the hardware is outside your control.

Cloud providers provide fantastic infrastructure facilities, making running applications much more straightforward. Thanks to dynamic resources, you can create many instances of your application and even autotune this number based on the current load. It also offers failover mechanisms such as routing requests to a healthy instance if another instance crashed. The cloud helps to reach high availability by making your service always available, restarting unhealthy parts of your systems, and so on. This is a first step toward elastic and resilient systems.

That being said, it's not because your application can run in the cloud that it will benefit from it. You need to tailor your application to use the cloud efficiently, and the distributed nature of the cloud is a big part of it. *Cloud native* is an approach to building and running applications that exploit the cloud computing delivery model. Cloud native applications should be easy to deploy on virtual resources, support elasticity through application instances, rely on location transparency, enforce fault-tolerance, and so on. The Twelve-Factor App (*https://12factor.net*) lists some characteristics to become a *good cloud citizen*:

Codebase
  One codebase tracked in version control, many deploys.

Dependencies
  Explicitly declare and isolate dependencies.

Config
  store config in the environment.

Backing services
  Treat backing services as attached resources.

Build, release, run
  Strictly separate build and run stages.

Processes
  Execute the app as one or more stateless processes.

Port binding
  Export services via port binding.

Concurrency
  Scale out via the process model.

Disposability
> Maximize the robustness with fast startup and graceful shutdown.

Dev/prod parity
> Keep development, staging, and production as similar as possible.

Logs
> Treat your logs as event streams.

Admin processes
> Run admin/management tasks as one-off processes.

Implementing these factors helps to embrace the cloud native ideology. But achieving cloud native is not an easy task. Each factor comes with technical challenges and architectural constraints.

In addition, each cloud provider provides its own set of facilities and APIs. This heterogeneity makes cloud native applications nonportable from one cloud provider to another. Very quickly, you end up in some kind of vendor lock-in, because of a specific API or services, or tooling, or even description format. It may not be an issue for you right now, but having the possibility to move and combine multiple clouds improves your agility, availability, and user experience. Hybrid cloud applications, for example, run on multiple clouds, mixing private and public clouds, to reduce response time and prevent global unavailability.

Fortunately, both public and private clouds tend to converge around Kubernetes, a container orchestration platform. Kubernetes abstracts the differences between providers using *standard* deployment and runtime facilities.

To use Kubernetes, you package and run your application inside a container. A *container* is a box in which your application is going to run. So, your application is somewhat isolated from the other applications running in their own box.

To create containers, you need an image. A *container image* is a lightweight, executable software package. When you deploy a container, you actually deploy an image, and this image is instantiated to create the container.

The image includes everything needed to run an application: code, runtime, system libraries, and configuration. You can create container images by using various tools and descriptors such as *Dockerfile*. As you have seen in Chapter 2, Quarkus offers image creation facilities without having to write a single line of code.

To distribute your image, you push it to an image registry such as Docker Hub (*https://hub.docker.com*). Then you can pull it and finally instantiate it to start your application (Figure 3-3).

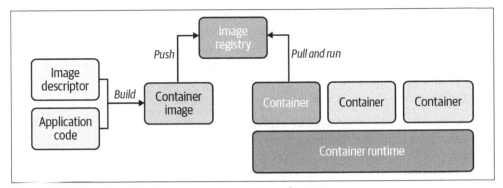

Figure 3-3. Creation, distribution, and execution of containers

While containerization is a well-known technique, when you start having dozens of containers, their management becomes complicated. Kubernetes provides facilities to reduce this burden. It instantiates containers and monitors them, making sure your application is still running.[2] As you can imagine, this can be useful for implementing the responsiveness and resilience characteristics from reactive systems.

 Though Kubernetes facilitates reactive systems through responsiveness and resilience, that does not mean you cannot implement a reactive system outside of Kubernetes. It's definitely possible. In this book, we use Kubernetes to avoid having to implement the underlying infrastructure features such as deployment, replication, and fault detection.

Under the hood, Kubernetes pulls container images, instantiates containers, and monitors them. To achieve this, Kubernetes needs to have access to *nodes* to run the containers. This set of nodes forms a *cluster*. Thinking of a machine as a node allows us to insert a layer of abstraction. Whether these machines are Amazon Elastic Compute Cloud (EC2) instances, physical hardware from a data center, or virtualized is irrelevant. Kubernetes controls these nodes and decides which part of the system will run where.

Once Kubernetes has access to your container image, you can instruct Kubernetes to instantiate the image so that it becomes a running container. Kubernetes decides on which node the container is executed. It may even move it later to optimize resource utilization, another characteristic that fits with reactive architectures.

---

2 Kubernetes provides health checks that constantly verify the state of the application. In addition, Prometheus (*https://prometheus.io*) is becoming the standard framework for metric collection.

Just as applications need to be cloud native to benefit from the cloud, they need to be Kubernetes native to benefit from Kubernetes. That includes supporting Kubernetes service discovery, exposing health checks used for monitoring, and, more importantly, running efficiently in a container. You will see in the next chapter how these three characteristics are essential from a Reactive point of view. You can wrap almost any application in a container. But it may not be a good idea.

When running in a container, your application lives in a shared environment. Multiple containers share the resources from the *host*, the machine executing them. They share the CPU, the memory, and so on. If one container is too greedy, it penalizes the other containers, which may starve. Of course, you can use quotas, but how would the greedy container behave under resource restrictions? So, yes, containers provide isolation, *and* enable resource sharing.

One role of containers and Kubernetes is to increase the deployment density: running more using the finite set of available resources. Deployment density is becoming essential to many organizations because of the economic benefits. It allows reducing costs, either by reducing the monthly cloud bill or by running more applications on the current in-house infrastructure.

Table 3-1 summarizes concepts presented so far around containers and Kubernetes.

Table 3-1. Important concepts around containers and Kubernetes

Name	Description	Associated command
Container image	Lightweight, executable software package	`docker build -f my-docker-file -t my-image:version`
Container	A box in which your application is going to run	`docker run my-image:version`
Pod	The unit of replication in Kubernetes, composed of one or more containers	`kubectl get pods`
Deployment	Describes the content of a pod and number of pod instances we need	`kubectl get deployments`
Service	A channel of communication delegating to a set of pods, selected by labels	`kubectl get services`

If you missed it, check out "Kubernetes with Quarkus in 10 Minutes" on page 28, where we deployed a Quarkus service to Kubernetes!

The Dark Side of Distributed Systems

Our system is simple, but even such a basic system can illustrate the hard reality of distributed systems. Cloud providers and Kubernetes provide excellent infrastructure facilities, but the laws of distributed systems still rule the system you are building. The technical complexity around provisioning and delivery has been replaced with fundamental issues from the nature of distributed systems. The size and complexity of modern applications make them undeniable.

At the beginning of this chapter, you saw a first definition of distributed systems. It was capturing the need for collaboration and communication to provide a consistent experience. Leslie Lamport (*http://www.lamport.org*), a computer scientist and Turing Award winner, gives a different definition that describes the dark nature of distributed systems: "A distributed system is one in which the failure of a computer you didn't even know existed can render your own computer unusable."

In other words, failures are inevitable. They are an inherent component of distributed systems. No matter how your system is built, it is going to fail. As a corollary, the bigger the distributed system, the higher the level of *dynamism* (the fluctuating availability of the surrounding services) and the greater the chance of failure.

What kind of failures can we encounter? There are three types:

Transient failure
Occurs once and then disappears, like a temporary network disruption

Intermittent failure
Occurs, then vanishes and then reappears, like a failure happening once in a while for no apparent reason

Permanent failure
Continues to exist until the faulty component (either software or hardware) is fixed

Each type of failure can have two kinds of consequences. First, it can crash the application. We call these *fail-stop* failures. There are *bad*, of course, but we can easily detect them and repair the system. Second, a failure may introduce unpredictable responses at random times. We call them *Byzantine failures*. They are much harder to detect and to circumvent.

Fallacies of Distributed Computing in a Kubernetes World

As developers, imagining and planning for all the types of failure and consequences can be challenging. How would you detect them? How would you handle them gracefully? How can you continue to provide a consistent experience and service if anything can fall apart? Building and maintaining distributed systems is a complex topic full of pitfalls and landmines. The "Eight Fallacies of Distributed Computing" (*https://oreil.ly/0g3lL*) list, created by L. Peter Deutsch along with others at Sun Microsystems, walks us through many false assumptions around distributed systems:

1. The network is reliable.
2. Latency is zero.
3. Bandwidth is infinite.
4. The network is secure.
5. Topology doesn't change.
6. There is one administrator.
7. Transport cost is zero.
8. The network is homogeneous.

These fallacies were published in 1997, long before the era of the cloud and Kubernetes. But these fallacies are still relevant today—even more relevant. We won't discuss all of them but focus on the ones related to the cloud and Kubernetes:

The network is reliable

The developer often assumes that the network is reliable on the cloud or Kubernetes. Indeed, it's the role of the infrastructure to handle the network and make sure things work. Health checks, heartbeats, replications, automatic restart—a lot of mechanisms are built in at the infrastructure layer. The network will do its best, but sometimes, bad things happen, and you need to be prepared for that. Data centers can fall apart; parts of the system can become unreachable, and so on.[3]

Latency is zero

The second fallacy seems obvious: a network call is slower than a local call, and the latency of any given call can vary significantly, even from one invocation to the next. We already discussed this. The latency is not limited to that aspect; it can change over time for various reasons.

---

3 In 2018, a power loss incident in AWS US-East-1 caused many Amazon service disruptions.

Bandwidth is infinite and the network is homogeneous

You may reach the bandwidth limit, or parts of the system may use a faster network than some other parts because they are running on the same *node*. Estimating latency is not trivial. Many capacity-planning techniques and time-out computation are based on network latency.

Topology doesn't change

On the cloud or on Kubernetes, services, applications, and containers move. Kubernetes can move containers from one node to another anytime. Containers are frequently moving because of the deployment of new applications, updates, rescheduling, optimization, and so on. Mobility is a great benefit as it allows optimizing the whole system, but interacting with services always on the move can be challenging. You may interact with multiple instances of your service, while, for you, it acts as one. Some instances can be close to you (and provide a better response time), while some may be farther or just slower because of limited resources.[4]

There is one administrator

Managing systems has drastically changed over the past few years. The old-school system administration processes and maintenance downtimes are becoming less common. DevOps philosophies and techniques such as continuous delivery and continuous deployment are reshaping the way we manage applications in production. Developers can easily deploy small incremental changes throughout the day. DevOps tools and site reliability engineers (SREs) work hard to provide an almost constant availability, while a continuous stream of updates provides new features and bug fixes. The administration role is shared among SREs, software engineers, and software. For example, Kubernetes operators (*https://oreil.ly/cX8nN*) are programs deployed on Kubernetes and responsible for installing, updating, monitoring, and repairing parts of the system automatically.

Transport cost is zero

Considering the network to be free is not only a fallacy, but also an economic mistake. You must pay attention to the cost of network calls and look for optimization. For example, crossing cloud regions, transferring large amounts of data, or (especially) communicating to separate cloud providers can be expensive.

So, not that simple, right? When you build a distributed system, consider all these issues and take them into account in your architecture and application code. Those

---

4 Kubernetes may move containers to achieve a higher deployment density, but also be instructed to move interacting applications on the same node to reduce the response time.

are just some of the issues. Another one is the inability to reach a consensus.[5] In addition, the CAP theorem prevents a distributed data store from simultaneously providing more than two out of the following three guarantees:[6]

Consistency
Every read receives the most recent write.

Availability
Every request receives a response.

Partition tolerance
The system continues to operate despite an arbitrary number of messages being dropped (or delayed) by the network.

Can things get even darker? Oh yes, distributed systems can be wonderfully imaginative to drive us crazy.

A Question of Timing: The Synchronous Communication Drawback

Time is an often misunderstood issue. When two computers communicate and exchange messages, we make the natural assumption that the two machines are both available and reachable. We often trust the network between them. Why wouldn't it be entirely operational? Why can't we invoke remote services as we would for a local service?

But that may not be the case, and not considering this possibility leads to fragility. What happens if the machine you want to interact with is not reachable? Are you prepared for such a failure? Should you propagate the failure? Retry?

In a hypothetical microservices-based example, it's common to use synchronous HTTP as the main communication protocol between services. You send a request and expect a response from the service you invoked. Your code is synchronous, waiting for the response before continuing its execution. Synchronous calls are simpler to reason about. You structure your code sequentially, you do one thing, then the next one, and so on. This leads to *time-coupling*, one of the less considered and often-misunderstood forms of coupling. Let's illustrate this coupling and the uncertainty that derives from it.

---

5 See "Distributed Consensus Revised" (*https://oreil.ly/qRVeD*) by Heidi Howard for a discussion on the problem of consensus in modern distributed system.

6 "Perspectives on the CAP Theorem" (*https://oreil.ly/p33qM*) by Seth Gilbert and Nancy A. Lynch explains the technical implications of the CAP theorem in *future* distributed systems.

In the *chapter-3/quarkus-simple-service* directory of the GitHub repository (*https://oreil.ly/vZR3j*), you will find a simple Hello World Quarkus application. This application is similar to the one built in Chapter 2. It contains a single HTTP endpoint, as shown in Example 3-2.

Example 3-2. JAX-RS simple service (chapter-3/quarkus-simple-service/src/main/java/org/acme/reactive/SimpleService.java)

```
package org.acme.reactive;

import javax.ws.rs.GET;
import javax.ws.rs.Path;
import javax.ws.rs.Produces;
import javax.ws.rs.core.MediaType;

@Path("/")
@Produces(MediaType.TEXT_PLAIN)
public class SimpleService {

    @GET
    public String hello() {
        return "hello";
    }
}
```

Hard to have code simpler than this, right? Let's deploy this application to Kubernetes. Make sure minikube is started. If it's not, start it as shown in Example 3-3.

Example 3-3. Start minikube

```
> minikube start
...
> eval $(minikube docker-env) ❶
```

❶ Don't forget to connect the Docker socket to minikube.

Verify that everything is fine by running the kubectl get nodes command (Example 3-4).

Example 3-4. Get the node names and roles

```
> kubectl get nodes
NAME       STATUS   ROLES                  AGE   VERSION
minikube   Ready    control-plane,master   30s   v1.20.2
```

Now, navigate in the *chapter-3/simple-service* directory and run Example 3-5.

Example 3-5. Deploy a Quarkus application to Kubernetes

```
> mvn verify -Dquarkus.kubernetes.deploy=true
```

Wait for the pod to be *ready*, as shown in Example 3-6.

Example 3-6. Get the list of running pods

```
> kubectl get pods
NAME                                      READY   STATUS    RESTARTS   AGE
quarkus-simple-service-7f9dd6ddbf-vtdsg   1/1     Running   0          42s
```

Then expose the service by using Example 3-7.

Example 3-7. Retrieve the URL of the service

```
> minikube service quarkus-simple-service --url
🦊  Starting tunnel for service quarkus-simple-service.
|-----------|------------------------|-------------|------------------------|
| NAMESPACE |          NAME          | TARGET PORT |          URL           |
|-----------|------------------------|-------------|------------------------|
| default   | quarkus-simple-service |             | http://127.0.0.1:63905 |
|-----------|------------------------|-------------|------------------------|
http://127.0.0.1:63905
❗ Because you are using a Docker driver on darwin, the terminal needs to be open to
    run it.
```

Don't forget that the port is assigned randomly, so you will need to replace the port in the following commands.

Finally, let's invoke our service by running Example 3-8 in another terminal.

Example 3-8. Invoke the service

```
> curl http://127.0.0.1:63905
hello%
```

So far, so good. But this application contains a *mechanism* to simulate distributed system failures to illustrate the problem of synchronous communication. You can look at the implementation in *chapter-3/quarkus-simple-service/src/main/java/org/acme/reactive/fault/FaultInjector.java*. It's basically a *Quarkus route* (a kind of interceptor) that monitors the HTTP traffic and allows simulating various failures. It intercepts the incoming HTTP request and outgoing HTTP response and introduces delays, losses, or application failures.

When we call our service in a synchronous way (expecting a response, such as with curl or a browser), three types of failure can happen:

- The request between the caller and the service can be lost. This results in the service not being invoked. The caller waits until a time-out is reached. This simulates a transient network partition. This type of failure can be enabled by using the INBOUND_REQUEST_LOSS mode.

- The service receives the request but fails to handle it correctly. It may return an incorrect response or maybe no response at all. In the best case, the caller would receive the failure or wait until a time-out is reached. This simulates an intermittent bug in the called service. This type of failure can be enabled by using the SERVICE_FAILURE mode.

- The service receives the request, processes it, and writes the response, but the response is lost on its way back, or the connection is closed before the response reaches the caller. The service got the request, handled it, and produced the response. The caller just doesn't get it. As in the first type of failure noted previously, the response is in a transient network partition but happening after the service invocation. This type of failure can be enabled using the OUT BOUND_RESPONSE_LOSS mode.

 Don't forget to update the port in the previous and following commands, as minikube randomly picks a port.

To illustrate how the system behaves when facing failures, let's inject some request losses (Example 3-9).

Example 3-9. Configure the system to lose 50% of the incoming requests

```
> curl http://127.0.0.1:63905/fault?mode=INBOUND_REQUEST_LOSS
Fault injection enabled: mode=INBOUND_REQUEST_LOSS, ratio=0.5
```

This command configures FaultInjector to randomly lose 50% of the incoming requests. The caller waits for a response that will never arrive half of the time, and will eventually time out. Try the command in Example 3-10 until you experience a time-out.

Example 3-10. Invoke the service with a configured time-out

```
> curl --max-time 5 http://127.0.0.1:63905/  ❶
hello%
> curl --max-time 5 http://127.0.0.1:63905/
curl: (28) Operation timed out after 5004 milliseconds with 0 bytes received
```

❶ `--max-time` 5 configures a time-out of 5 seconds. Again, do not forget to update the port.

To simulate the second type of failure, execute the command in Example 3-11.

Example 3-11. Configure the system to inject faulty responses

```
> curl http://127.0.0.1:63905/fault?mode=SERVICE_FAILURE
```

You have now a 50% chance of receiving a faulty response; see Example 3-12.

Example 3-12. Invoke the faulty application

```
> curl http://127.0.0.1:63905
hello%
> curl http://127.0.0.1:63905
FAULTY RESPONSE!%
```

Finally, let's simulate the last type of failure. Execute the commands in Example 3-13.

Example 3-13. Configure the system to lose responses

```
> curl http://127.0.0.1:63905/fault?mode=OUTBOUND_RESPONSE_LOSS
> curl http://127.0.0.1:63905
curl: (52) Empty reply from server
```

Now, the caller has a 50% chance of getting no response. The connection is closed abruptly before the response reaches the caller. You don't get a valid HTTP response.

The purpose of these examples is to illustrate the strong coupling and uncertainty arising from synchronous communication. This type of communication, often used because of simplicity, hides the distributed nature of the interaction. However, it makes the assumption that everything (including the services and the network) is operational. But that's not always the case. As a caller using synchronous communication, you must gracefully handle faulty responses and the absence of response.

So, what can we do? We immediately think about a time-out and retries. With `curl`, you can specify a time-out (`-max-time`) and retries (`--retry`), as shown in Example 3-14.

Example 3-14. Invoke the application by using a time-out and `retry`

```
> curl --max-time 5 --retry 100 --retry-all-errors http://127.0.0.1:63905/
curl: (28) Operation timed out after 5003 milliseconds with 0 bytes received
Warning: Transient problem: time-out Will retry in 1 seconds. 100 retries left.
hello%
```

There is a good chance that we can reach our service with 100 tries. However, bad luck and random numbers may decide otherwise, and even 100 may not be enough. Note that during the time that the caller (you) is waiting, that's a rather bad user experience.

Yet, do we know for sure that if we get a time-out, the service was not invoked? Maybe the service or the network was just slow. What would be the ideal duration of the time-out? It depends on many factors: where the service is located, the latency of the network, and the load of the service. Maybe there isn't a single instance of this service but several, all with different characteristics.

Retries are even more sneaky. As you can't know for sure whether the service was invoked, you can't assume it was not. Retrying may reprocess the same request multiple times. But you can retry safely only if the service you are calling is idempotent.

Idempotence

Idempotence is used to describe the reliability of messages in a distributed system, specifically about the reception of duplicated messages. Because of retries or message broker features, a message sent once can be received multiple times by consumers.

A service is *idempotent* if processing the same event multiple times results in the same state and output as processing that event just a single time. The reception of a duplicated event does not change the application state or behavior.

Most of the time, an idempotent service detects these events and ignores them. Idempotence can be implemented using unique identifiers. Each event has a unique ID. Duplicated events have the same ID. Then, the service needs *storage* to save all processed IDs. When a duplicated event arrives, the service checks in this storage, and if the event is a duplicate, ignores it. Otherwise, the service processes the event.

Setting up this kind of storage is not as simple as it looks. There are many concerns to address, because the storage is ruled by the CAP theorem. You will need to understand the characteristics you need and pick the right infrastructure. Possibilities include an in-memory data grid such as Infinispan (*https://infinispan.org*) or Hazelcast (*https://hazelcast.com*), an inventory service such as Apache ZooKeeper or etcd), or a dedicated database such as Redis. However, never forget that all these solutions come with trade-offs.

So, what can we do? It's essential to understand the impact of the time and decouple our communication. Complex exchanges involving multiple services cannot expect all the participants and the network to be operational for the complete duration of that exchange. The dynamic nature of the cloud and Kubernetes stresses the limit of synchronous communications. Bad things happen: partitions, data loss, crashes…

In Chapter 4, you will see how Reactive addresses this issue. By using message passing, and spatial and time decoupling, a reactive system not only is more elastic and resilient, but also improves the overall responsiveness. In other words, reactive systems are distributed systems done right. Also, in Chapter 5, you will see the approaches Reactive is proposing to embrace the asynchronous nature of distributed systems and how we can elegantly develop event-driven and asynchronous code. The result not only is concurrent and efficient applications, but also paves the road to new classes of applications such as data streaming, API gateways, and so on.

Summary

Distributed systems are challenging. To build distributed systems, you need to understand their nature and always plan for the worst-case scenario. Hiding the nature of distributed systems to seek simplicity does not work. It results in fragile systems.

This chapter covered the following:

- The erratic nature of distributed systems
- The evolution of distributed systems from a workaround to the norm
- Use of the cloud and Kubernetes to simplify the construction of distributed systems
- Potential failures of distributed communications caused by network disruptions, or slowness

But we won't stop on a failure! Time to rebound! Let's look a bit more into Reactive and see how it proposes to address these issues.

## CHAPTER 4

Design Principles of Reactive Systems

In Chapter 3, we looked at the challenges behind distributed systems. It's now time to see what Reactive has to offer. Reactive can be seen as a set of principles for building distributed systems, a kind of checklist to verify that no major known concern was overlooked while architecting and building a system. These principles focus on the following:

Responsiveness
    The ability to handle requests when facing failures or peaks of load

Efficiency
    The ability to do more with fewer resources

In this chapter, we cover the principles promoted by reactive systems.

Reactive Systems 101

In 2013, a group of distributed systems experts gathered and wrote the first version of "The Reactive Manifesto." They assembled in this whitepaper their experience building distributed systems and cloud applications. While in 2013 the cloud was not precisely what it is today, the dynamic creation of ephemeral resources was already a well-known mechanism.

"The Reactive Manifesto" defines *reactive systems* as distributed systems having four characteristics:

Responsive
    Able to handle requests in a timely fashion

Resilient
    Able to manage failures gracefully

Elastic
> Able to scale up and down according to the load and resources

Message driven
> Using asynchronous message-based communication among the components forming the system

These four characteristics are represented in Figure 4-1.

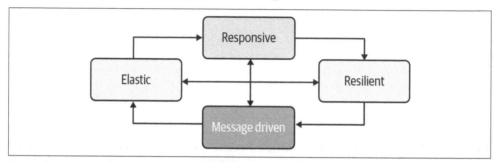

Figure 4-1. Reactive systems characteristics

If you're seeing this picture for the first time, you may be confused by all the arrows. It can look like a well-tailored marketing campaign. It's not, and let's explain why these pillars make a lot of sense when building cloud native and Kubernetes-native applications. Let's start with the bottom of the figure.

Instead of trying to make distributed systems simpler than they are, reactive systems embrace their asynchronous nature. They use *asynchronous message passing* to establish the connective tissue among the components. Asynchronous message passing ensures loose coupling, isolation, and location transparency. In a reactive system, interactions rely on messages sent to abstract destinations. These messages carry everything—data as well as failures. Asynchronous message passing also improves resource utilization. Employing nonblocking communication (we cover that part later in this chapter) allows idle components to consume almost no CPU and memory. Asynchronous message passing enables elasticity and resilience, as depicted by the two bottom arrows in Figure 4-1.

Elasticity means that the system can adapt itself, or parts of itself, to handle the fluctuating load. By looking at the messages flowing among the components, a system can determine which parts reach their limits and create more instances or route the messages elsewhere. Cloud infrastructure enables creating these instances quickly at runtime. But elasticity is not only about scaling up; it's also about scaling down. The system can decide to scale down underused parts to save resources. At runtime, the system adjusts itself, always meeting the current demand, avoiding bottlenecks, overflows, and overcommitted resources. As you can imagine, elasticity requires observability, replication, and routing features. Observability is covered in Chapter 13. In general, the last two are provided by the infrastructure such as Kubernetes or cloud providers.

Resilience means handling failure gracefully. As explained in Chapter 3, failures are inevitable in distributed systems. Instead of hiding them, reactive systems consider failures first-class citizens. The system should be able to handle them and react to them. Failures are contained within each component, isolating components from one another. This isolation ensures that parts of the system can fail and recover without jeopardizing the whole system. For instance, by replicating components (elasticity), the system can continue to handle incoming messages even if some elements are failing. The implementation of resilience is shared between the application (which needs to be aware of failures, contain them, and, if possible, handle them gracefully) and the infrastructure (which monitors the systems and restarts fallen components).

The last characteristic is the whole purpose of reactive systems: being *responsive*. Your system needs to stay responsive—to respond in a timely fashion—even under fluctuating load (elasticity) and when facing failure (resilience). Relying on message passing enables these characteristics and much more, such as flow control by monitoring the messages in the system and applying backpressure when necessary.

In a nutshell, reactive systems are exactly what we want to build: distributed systems able to handle the uncertainty, failures, and load efficiently. Their characteristics meet the requirement for cloud native and Kubernetes-native applications perfectly. But don't be mistaken; building a reactive system is still making a distributed system. It's challenging. However, by following these principles, the resulting system will be more responsive, more robust, and more efficient. The rest of this book details how we can easily implement such systems with Quarkus and messaging technologies.

Commands and Events

Now that we've covered many of the foundational principles, you might be confused. In Chapter 1, we said that being reactive is related to being event driven, but in the previous section, we explicitly mentioned asynchronous message passing. Does that mean the same thing? Not completely.

But first, we need to discuss the differences between commands and events. As complicated as a distributed system design can be, the concepts of commands and events are fundamental. Nearly all interactions between individual components involve one or the other.

Commands

Every system issues commands. *Commands* are actions that a user wishes to perform. Most HTTP-based APIs pass commands: the client asks for an action to happen. It's important to understand that the action has not yet happened. It may happen in the future, or not; it may complete successfully or fail. In general, commands are sent to a specific recipient, and a result is sent back to the client.

Take the simple HTTP application we used in Chapter 3. You emitted a simple HTTP request. As we've said, that was a command. The application receives that command, handles it, and produces a result.

Events

Events are actions that have successfully completed. An event represents a *fact*, something that happened: a keystroke, a failure, an order, anything important to the organization or system at hand. An event can be the result of work done by a command.

Let's go back to the preceding HTTP request example. Once the response has been written, it becomes an event. We have seen an HTTP request and its response. That event can be written in a log or broadcast to interested parties so they can be aware of what happened.

Events are immutable. You cannot delete an event. Admittedly, you can't change the past. If you want to refute a previously sent fact, you need to fire another event invalidating the fact. The carried facts are made irrelevant only by another fact establishing the current knowledge.

Messages

But, how to publish these events? There are many ways. These days, solutions like Apache Kafka or Apache ActiveMQ (we cover both in Chapter 11) are popular. They act as brokers between the producers and consumers. Essentially, our events are written into *topics* or *queues*. To write these events, the application sends a message to the broker, targeting a specific destination (the queue or the topic).

A *message* is a self-contained data structure describing the event and any relevant details about the event, such as who emitted it, at what time it was emitted, and potentially its unique ID. It's generally better to keep the event itself business-centric and use additional metadata for the technical aspects.

On the other side, to consume events, you subscribe to the queue or topic containing the events you are interested in and receive the messages. You unwrap the event and can also get the associated metadata (for example, when the event happened, where it happened, and so forth). The processing of an event can lead to the publication of other events (again, packaged in messages and sent to a known destination) or to the execution of commands.

Brokers and messages can also convey commands. In this case, the message contains the description of the action to execute, and another message (potentially multiple messages) would carry the outcome if needed.

Commands Versus Events: An Example

Let's take a look at an example to highlight the differences between commands and events. Imagine an ecommerce shop, like the one depicted in Figure 4-2. The user picks a set of products and finalizes the order (process to payment, get the delivery date, etc.).

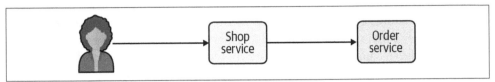

Figure 4-2. Simplified architecture of an ecommerce shop

The user sends a command (using an HTTP request, for example) to the shop service with the items the user wishes to receive. In a traditional application, once `ShopSer vice` receives the command, it would call `OrderService` and invoke an `order` method with the username, the list of items (basket), and so on. Calling the `order` method is a command. That makes `ShopService` dependent on `OrderService` and reduces the component autonomy: `ShopService` cannot operate without `OrderService`. We are creating a distributed monolith, a distributed application that would collapse as soon as one of its parts fails.[1]

Let's see the difference if, instead of using a command between `ShopService` and `OrderService`, we publish an event. Once the user finalizes the order, the application still sends a command to `ShopService`. However, this time, `ShopService` *transforms* that command into an event: *a new order has been placed*. The event contains the user, the basket, and so on. The event is a fact written in a log, or wrapped into a message and sent to a broker.

On the other side, `OrderService` observes the *a new order has been placed* event, by reading where these events are stored. When `ShopService` emits the event, it receives it and can process it.

With this architecture, `ShopService` does not depend on `OrderService`. In addition, `OrderService` does not depend on `ShopService`, and it would process any observed event, regardless of the emitter. For example, a mobile application can emit the same event when the user validates an order from a mobile phone.

---

1 "Don't Build a Distributed Monolith" (*https://oreil.ly/CtY3x*) by Ben Christensen is an interesting talk about distributed monoliths and why you should avoid them.

Multiple components can consume events (Figure 4-3). For example, in addition to OrderService, StatisticsService keeps track of the most ordered items. It consumes the same event, without having to modify ShopService to receive them.

A component observing events can derive new ones from them. For instance, StatisticsService could analyze the order and compute recommendations. These recommendations could be seen as another fact, and so communicate as an event. ShopService could observe these events and process them to influence item selection. However, StatisticsService and ShopService are independent of each other. The knowledge is cumulative and occurs by receiving new events and deriving, as done by StatisticsService, new facts from the received events.

As depicted in Figure 4-3, we can use *message queues* to transport our events. These events are wrapped into messages, sent to known destinations (orders and recommendations). OrderService and StatisticsService consume and process the messages independently.

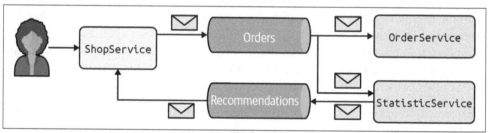

Figure 4-3. Architecture of the ecommerce shop with events and message queues

It's important for these destinations to persist the events as an ordered sequence. By keeping that sequence, the system can go back in time and reprocess the events. Such a *replay* mechanism, popular in the Kafka world, has multiple benefits. You can restart with a clean state after a disaster by reprocessing all the stored events. Then, if we change the recommendation algorithm from the statistic services, for example, it would be able to re-accumulate all the knowledge and derive new recommendations.

While the event emission sounds explicit in this example, that's not always the case. For instance, events can be created from database writes.[2]

---

2 This pattern is called Change Data Capture (*https://oreil.ly/Umhs9*). Frameworks such as Debezium (*https://debezium.io*) are a key element of reactive systems when using databases, as the events are emitted without any impact on the application code.

Commands and events are the basis of most of the interactions. While we use mostly commands, events come with significant benefits. Events are facts. Events tell a story, the story of your system, a narrative that describes your system's evolution. In reactive systems, events are wrapped into messages, and these messages are sent to destinations, transported by message brokers such as AMQP or Kafka (Figure 4-4). Such an approach solves two important architectural issues arising from the distributed systems. First, it naturally handles real-world asynchronicity. Second, it binds together services without relying on strong coupling. At the edge of the system, this approach uses commands most of the time, often relying on HTTP.

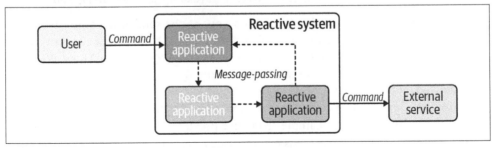

Figure 4-4. Overview of a reactive system

This asynchronous message-passing aspect of reactive systems forms the connective tissue. It not only grants the applications forming the system more autonomy and independence, but also enables resilience and elasticity. You may wonder how, and you will get the beginning of our response in the next section.

Destinations and Space Decoupling

The reactive applications, forming a reactive system, communicate using messages. They subscribe to destinations and receive the messages sent by other components to these destinations. These messages can carry commands or events, though as described in the previous section, events provide interesting benefits. These destinations are not bound to specific components or instances. They are virtual. Components must know only the name (generally business related, such as orders) of the destination, not who's producing or consuming. It enables location transparency.

Location Transparency

Location transparency refers to the use of *names* to identify resources, rather than their actual location. For example, you would use *https://www.oreilly.com/* and not the 23.43.200.127 IP address. The main benefit of location transparency is that it no longer matters where the resource is located. In reactive systems, *destinations* provide location transparency. Reactive systems use these identifiable destinations instead of the exact location of the consumer.

If you are using Kubernetes, you may consider location transparency as already managed for you. Indeed, you can use Kubernetes *services* to implement location transparency. You have a single endpoint delegating to a group of selected *pods*. But this location transparency is somewhat limited and often tied to HTTP or request/reply protocols. Other environments can use service discovery infrastructure such as HashiCorp Consul (*https://consul.io*) or Netflix Eureka (*https://oreil.ly/H9Ygn*).

Using messages sent to a destination allows you, as the sender, to ignore who precisely is going to receive the message. You don't know if someone is currently available or if multiple components or instances are waiting for your message. This number of consumers can evolve at runtime; more instances can be created, moved, or destroyed, and new components deployed. But for you, as a sender, you don't need to know. You just use a specified destination. Let's illustrate the advantages of this *addressability* by using the example from the previous section. ShopService emits order placed events carried inside messages sent to the orders destination (Figure 4-3). It is likely possible that during a quiet period, only a single instance of OrderService runs. If there are not many orders, why bother having more? We could even imagine having no instance, and instantiating one when we receive an order.

Serverless platforms are offering this *scale-from-zero* ability. However, over time, your shop gets more customers, and a single instance may not be enough. Thanks to location transparency, we can start other instances of `OrderService` to share the load (Figure 4-5). `ShopService` is not modified and ignores this new topology.

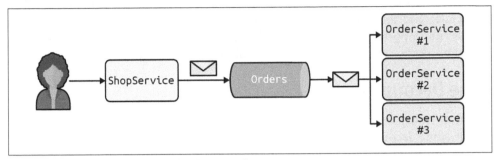

Figure 4-5. Elasticity provided by the use of message passing

The way the load is shared among the consumers is also irrelevant for the sender. It can be a round-robin, a load-based selection, or something more clever. When the load returns to normal, the system can reduce the number of instances and save resources. Note that this kind of elasticity works perfectly for stateless services. For stateful services, it may be harder, as the instances may have to share the state. However, solutions exist (though not without caveats), like the Kubernetes `StatefulSet` (*https://oreil.ly/kVRID*) or an in-memory data grid (*https://oreil.ly/wNUIQ*), to coordinate state among instances of the same service. Message passing also enables replication. Following the same principle, we can shadow the active `OrderService` instance and take over if the primary instance fails (Figure 4-6). This approach avoids service disruption. That kind of failover may also require state sharing.

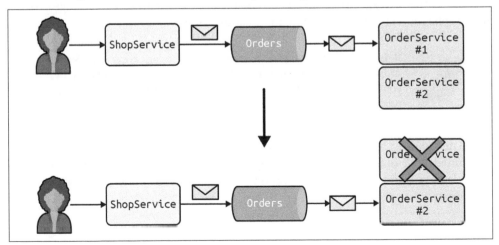

Figure 4-6. Resilience provided by the use of message passing

By using message passing, our system becomes not only asynchronous, but also elastic and resilient. When you architect your system, you list the destinations that implement the communication pattern you want. In general, you would use one destination per type of event, but that's not necessarily the case. However, avoid at all costs having a destination per component instance. It introduces coupling between the sender and the receiver, discarding the benefits. It also reduces the extensibility. Finally, it's important to keep the set of destinations stable. Changing a destination would break the components using it or would force you to handle redirections.

Time Decoupling

Location transparency is not the only benefit. Asynchronous message passing also enables time decoupling.

Modern message backbones, such as AMQP 1.0 (*https://amqp.org*), Apache Kafka (*https://kafka.apache.org/*), and even Java Message Service (JMS), enable time decoupling. With these event brokers, events are not lost if there are no consumers. The events are stored and delivered later. Each broker has its own way. For instance, AMQP 1.0 uses persistent messages and durable subscribers to ensure message delivery. Kafka stores records in a durable, fault-tolerant, ordered log. The records can be retrieved so long as they remain stored within the topic.

If our ShopService emits the finalized orders as events, it does not need to know whether OrderService is available. It knows that it's going to be processed eventually. If, for example, no instances of OrderService are available when ShopService emits the event, it's not lost. When an instance gets ready, it receives the pending orders and processes them. The user is then notified asynchronously with an email.

Of course, the message broker must be available and reachable. Most message brokers have replication abilities preventing unavailability issues and message loss.

 It is becoming common to store events in an event log. Such ordered and append-only structure represents the full history of your system. Every time the state changes, the system appends the new state to the log.

Time decoupling increases the independence of our components. Time decoupling, combined with other features enabled by asynchronous message passing, achieves a high level of independence among our components and keeps coupling to a minimum.

The Role of Nonblocking Input/Output

At this point, you may wonder what the difference is between an application using Kafka or AMQP and a reactive system. Message passing is the essence of reactive systems, and most of them rely on some sort of message broker. Message passing enables resilience and elasticity, which lead to responsiveness. It promotes space and time decoupling, making our system much more robust.

But reactive systems are not only exchanging messages. Sending and receiving messages must be done efficiently. To achieve this, Reactive promotes the use of nonblocking I/Os.

Blocking Network I/O, Threads, and Concurrency

To understand the benefits of nonblocking I/O, we need to know how blocking I/Os work. Let's use a client/server interaction to illustrate. When a client sends a request to a server, the server processes it and sends back a response. HTTP, for instance, follows this principle. For this to happen, both the client and the server need to establish a connection before the interaction starts. We will not go into the depths of the seven-layer model (*https://oreil.ly/kcTBH*) and the protocol stack involved in this interaction; you can find plenty of articles online about that topic.

 Examples from this section can be run directly from your IDE. Use *chapter-4/non-blocking-io/src/main/java/org/acme/client/Echo-Client.java* to invoke the started server. Be sure to avoid running multiple servers concurrently as they all use the same port (9999).

To establish that connection between the client and the server, we use `sockets`, as shown in Example 4-1.

Example 4-1. A single-threaded echo server using blocking I/O (chapter-4/non-blocking-io/src/main/java/org/acme/blocking/BlockingEchoServer.java)

```
int port = 9999;

// Create a server socket
try (ServerSocket server = new ServerSocket(port)) {
    while (true) {

        // Wait for the next connection from a client
        Socket client = server.accept();

        PrintWriter response = new PrintWriter(client.getOutputStream(), true);
        BufferedReader request = new BufferedReader(
                new InputStreamReader(client.getInputStream()));
```

```
        String line;
        while ((line = request.readLine()) != null) {
            System.out.println("Server received message from client: " + line);
            // Echo the request
            response.println(line);

            // Add a way to stop the application.
            if ("done".equalsIgnoreCase(line)) {
                break;
            }
        }
        client.close();
    }
}
```

The client and server have to bind themselves to a socket forming the connection. The server listens to its socket for the client to connect. Once established, the client and server can both write and read data from the socket bound to that connection.

Traditionally, because it's simpler, applications are developed using a synchronous development model. Such a development model executes instructions sequentially, one after the other. So when such applications interact across the network, they expect to continue using a synchronous development model even for I/O. This model uses synchronous communication and blocks the execution until the operation completes. In Example 4-1, we wait for a connection and handle it synchronously. We read and write using synchronous APIs. It's simpler, but it leads to the use of blocking I/O.

With blocking I/O, when the client sends a request to the server, the socket processing that connection and the corresponding thread that reads from it is blocked until some read data appears. The bytes are accumulated in the network buffer until everything is read and ready for processing. Until the operation is complete, the server can do nothing more but wait.

The consequence of this model is that we cannot serve more than one connection within a single thread. When the server receives a connection, it uses that thread to read the request, process it, and write the response. That thread is blocked until the last byte of the response is written on the wire. A single client connection blocks the server! Not very efficient, right?

To execute concurrent requests with this approach, the only way is to have multiple threads. We need to allocate a new thread for each client connection. To handle more clients, you need to use more threads and process each request on a different *worker* thread; see Example 4-2.

Example 4-2. Principles behind multithreaded server using blocking I/O

```
while (listening) {
    accept a connection;
    create a worker thread to process the client request;
}
```

To implement this principle, we need a thread pool (*worker pool*). When the client connects, we accept the connection and offload the processing to a separate thread. Thus, the server thread can still accept other connections, as shown in Example 4-3.

Example 4-3. A multithreaded echo server using blocking I/O (chapter-4/non-blocking-io/src/main/java/org/acme/blocking/BlockingWithWorkerEchoServer.java)

```
int port = 9999;
ExecutorService executors = Executors.newFixedThreadPool(10); ❶

// Create a server socket
try (ServerSocket server = new ServerSocket(port)) {
    while (true) {

        // Wait for the next connection from a client
        Socket client = server.accept();

        executors.submit(() -> {                                    ❷
            try {
                PrintWriter response =
                new PrintWriter(client.getOutputStream(), true);
                BufferedReader request = new BufferedReader(
                        new InputStreamReader(client.getInputStream()));

                String line;
                while ((line = request.readLine()) != null) {
                    System.out.println(Thread.currentThread().getName() +
                            " - Server received message from client: " + line);
                    // Echo the request
                    response.println(line);

                    // Add a way to stop the application.
                    if ("done".equalsIgnoreCase(line)) {
                        break;
                    }
                }
                client.close();
            } catch (Exception e) {
                System.err.println("Couldn't serve I/O: " + e.toString());

            }
        });
    }
}
```

❶ Create a worker thread pool to handle the request.

❷ Offload the processing of the request to a thread from the thread pool. The rest of the code is unchanged.

That's the model used, by default, in traditional Java frameworks such as Jakarta EE or Spring.[3] Even if these frameworks may use nonblocking I/O under the hood, they use *worker* threads to handle the requests. But this approach has many drawbacks, including:

- Each thread requires a stack of memory allocated to it. With the increasing number of connections, spawning multiple threads and switching between them will consume not only memory but also CPU cycles.

- At any given point in time, multiple threads could be waiting for the client requests. That's a massive waste of resources.

- Your concurrency (the number of requests you can handle at a given time—10 in the previous example) is limited by the number of threads you can create.

On public clouds, the blocking I/O approach inflates your monthly bill; on private clouds, it reduces the deployment density. Therefore, this approach is not ideal if you have to handle many connections or implement applications dealing with a lot of I/O. In the realm of distributed systems, that's often the case. Luckily, there's an alternative.

How Does Nonblocking I/O Work?

The alternative is *nonblocking I/O*. The difference is evident from its name. Instead of waiting for the completion of the transmission, the caller is not blocked and can continue its processing. The magic happens in the operating system. With nonblocking I/O, the operating system queues the requests. The system processes the actual I/O in the future. When the I/O completes, and the response is ready, a *continuation*, often implemented as a callback, happens and the caller receives the result.

Continuations

The term *continuation* comes from functional programming. *Continuation-passing style* (*CPS*) is a style of programming in which control is passed explicitly in the form of a continuation. It contrasts with the imperative style, which is the usual style of programming that executes each instruction in order.

---

3 We are referring to the traditional Spring Framework. Reactive Spring is based on nonblocking I/O.

To better understand the benefits and see how these continuations work, we need to look under the hood: how is nonblocking I/O implemented? We already mentioned a queue. The system enqueues I/O operations and returns immediately, so the caller is not blocked while waiting for the I/O operations to complete. When a response comes back, the system stores the result in a structure. When the caller needs the result, it interrogates the system to see whether the operation completed (Example 4-4).

Example 4-4. An echo server using nonblocking I/O (chapter-4/non-blocking-io/src/ main/java/org/acme/nio/NonBlockingServer.java)

```java
InetSocketAddress address = new InetSocketAddress("localhost", 9999);
Selector selector = Selector.open();
ServerSocketChannel channel = ServerSocketChannel.open();
channel.configureBlocking(false);

channel.socket().bind(address);
// Server socket supports only ACCEPT
channel.register(selector, SelectionKey.OP_ACCEPT);

while (true) {
    int available = selector.select(); // wait for events
    if (available == 0) {
        continue;   // Nothing ready yet.
    }

    // We have the request ready to be processed.
    Set<SelectionKey> keys = selector.selectedKeys();
    Iterator<SelectionKey> iterator = keys.iterator();
    while (iterator.hasNext()) {
        SelectionKey key = iterator.next();
        if (key.isAcceptable()) {
            // -- New connection --
            SocketChannel client = channel.accept();
            client.configureBlocking(false);
            client.register(selector, SelectionKey.OP_READ);
            System.out.println("Client connection accepted: "
                + client.getLocalAddress());
        } else if (key.isReadable()) {
            // -- A client sent data ready to be read and we can write --
            SocketChannel client = (SocketChannel) key.channel();
            // Read the data assuming the size is sufficient for reading.
            ByteBuffer payload = ByteBuffer.allocate(256);
            int size = client.read(payload);
            if (size == -1 ) { // Handle disconnection
                System.out.println("Disconnection from "
                    + client.getRemoteAddress());
                channel.close();
                key.cancel();
            } else {
```

```
        String result = new String(payload.array(),
            StandardCharsets.UTF_8).trim();
        System.out.println("Received message: " + result);
        if (result.equals("done")) {
            client.close();
        }
        payload.rewind(); // Echo
        client.write(payload);
      }
    }
    // Be sure not to handle it twice.
    iterator.remove();
  }
}
```

Nonblocking I/O introduces a few new concepts:

- We don't use InputStream or OutputStream (which are blocking by nature), but Buffer, which is a temporary storage.

- Channel can be viewed as an endpoint for an open connection.

- Selector is the cornerstone of nonblocking I/O in Java.

Selector manages multiple channels, either server or client channels. When you use nonblocking I/O, you create Selector. Each time you deal with a new channel, you register this channel on the selector with the events you are interested in (accept, ready to read, ready to write).

Then your code polls Selector with only one thread to see if the channel is ready. When the channel is ready to read or write, you can start to read and write. We don't need to have a thread for every channel at all, and a single thread can handle many channels.

The selector is an abstraction of the nonblocking I/O implementation provided by the underlying operating system. Various approaches, depending on the operating systems, are available.

First, select was implemented in the 1980s. It supports the registration of 1,024 sockets. That was certainly enough in the '80s, but not anymore.

poll is a replacement for select introduced in 1997. The most significant difference is that poll no longer limits the number of sockets. However, as with select, the system tells you only how many channels are ready, not which ones. You need to iterate over the set of channels to check which ones are ready. When there are few channels, it is not a big problem. Once the number of channels is more than hundreds of thousands, the iteration time is considerable.

Then, `epoll` appeared in 2002 in the Linux Kernel 2.5.44. `Kqueue` appeared in FreeBSD in 2000 and `/dev/poll` in Solaris around the same time. These mechanisms return the set of channels that are ready to be processed—no more iteration over every channel! Finally, Windows systems provide IOCP, an optimized implementation of `select`.

What's important to remember is that regardless of how the operating systems implement it, with nonblocking I/O, you need only a single thread to handle multiple requests. This model is much more efficient than blocking I/O, as you don't need to create threads to handle concurrent requests. Eliminating these extra threads makes your application much more efficient in terms of memory consumption (about 1 MB per thread) and avoids wasting CPU cycles because of context switches (1–2 microseconds per switch).[4]

Reactive systems recommend the use of nonblocking I/O to receive and send messages. Thus, your application can handle more messages with fewer resources. Another advantage is that an idle application would consume almost no memory or CPUs. You don't have to reserve resources up front.

Reactor Pattern and Event Loop

Nonblocking I/O gives us the possibility to handle multiple concurrent requests or messages with a single thread. How could we handle these concurrent requests? How do we structure our code when using nonblocking I/O? The examples given in the previous section are not scaling well; we can quickly see that implementing a REST API with such a model will be a nightmare. Besides, we would like to avoid using worker threads, as it would discard the advantages of nonblocking I/O. We need something different: the reactor pattern.

The *reactor pattern*, illustrated in Figure 4-7, allows associating I/O events with *event handlers*. The *reactor*, the cornerstone of this mechanism, invokes the event handlers when the expected event is received.

The purpose of the reactor pattern is to avoid creating a thread for each message, request, and connection. This pattern receives events from multiple channels and sequentially distributes them to the corresponding event handlers.

---

4 "Measuring Context Switching and Memory Overheads for Linux Threads" (*https://oreil.ly/hv2Uy*) by Eli Bendersky provides interesting data about the cost of threads on Linux.

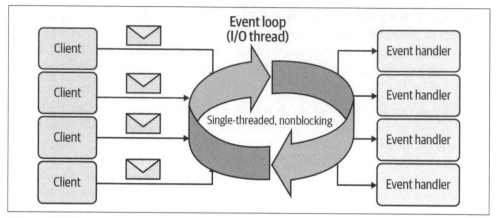

Figure 4-7. The reactor pattern

Implementation of the reactor pattern uses an *event loop* (Figure 4-7). It's a thread iterating over the set of channels, and when data is ready to be consumed, the event loop invokes the associated event handler sequentially, in a single-threaded manner.

When you combine nonblocking I/O and the reactor pattern, you organize your code as a set of event handlers. That approach works wonderfully with reactive code as it exposes the notion of events, the essence of Reactive.

The reactor pattern has two variants:

- The *multireactor* pattern uses multiple event loops (generally one or two per CPU core), which increase the concurrency of the application. Multireactor pattern implementations, such as Eclipse Vert.x, call the event handlers in a single-threaded manner to avoid deadlock or state visibility issues.

- The *proactor* pattern can be seen as an asynchronous version of the reactor pattern. Long-running event handlers invoke a continuation when they complete. Such mechanisms allow mixing nonblocking and blocking I/O (Figure 4-8).

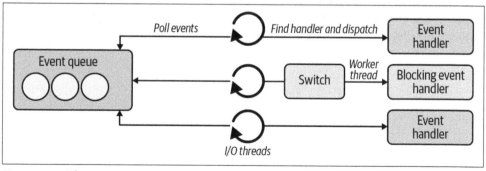

Figure 4-8. The proactor pattern

You can integrate nonblocking event handlers, as well as blocking ones, by offloading their execution to separate threads when it's inevitable. When their execution completes, the proactor pattern invokes the continuation. As you will see in Chapter 6, this is the pattern used by Quarkus.

Anatomy of Reactive Applications

In the last few years, many frameworks have popped up, offering reactive application support. Their goal is to simplify the implementation of reactive applications. They achieve this by providing higher-level primitives and APIs to handle events and abstract nonblocking I/O.

Indeed, and you may have recognized this already, using nonblocking I/O is not that simple. Combining this with a reactor pattern (or a variant) can be convoluted. Fortunately, alongside frameworks, libraries and toolkits are doing the heavy lifting. Netty is an asynchronous event-driven network application framework leveraging nonblocking I/O to build highly concurrent applications. It's the most used library to handle nonblocking I/O in the Java world. But Netty can be challenging. Example 4-5 implements the *echo* TCP server using Netty.

Example 4-5. An echo server using Netty (chapter-4/non-blocking-io/src/main/java/org/acme/netty/NettyEchoServer.java)

```
public static void main(String[] args) throws Exception {
    new NettyServer(9999).run();
}

private final int port;

public NettyServer(int port) {
    this.port = port;
}

public void run() throws Exception {
    // NioEventLoopGroup is a multithreaded event loop that handles I/O operation.
    // The first one, often called 'boss', accepts an incoming connection.
    // The second one, often called 'worker', handles the traffic of the accepted
    // connection once the boss accepts the connection and registers the
    // accepted connection to the worker.
    EventLoopGroup bossGroup = new NioEventLoopGroup();

    EventLoopGroup workerGroup = new NioEventLoopGroup();
    try {
        // ServerBootstrap is a helper class that sets up a server.
        ServerBootstrap b = new ServerBootstrap();
        b.group(bossGroup, workerGroup)
                // the NioServerSocketChannel class is used to instantiate a
                // new Channel to accept incoming connections.
```

```
                .channel(NioServerSocketChannel.class)
                .childHandler(new ChannelInitializer<SocketChannel>() {
                    // This handler is called for each accepted channel and
                    // allows customizing the processing. In this case, we
                    // just append the echo handler.
                    @Override
                    public void initChannel(SocketChannel ch) {
                        ch.pipeline().addLast(new EchoServerHandler());
                    }
                });

            // Bind and start to accept incoming connections.
            ChannelFuture f = b.bind(port).sync();

            // Wait until the server socket is closed.
            f.channel().closeFuture().sync();
        } finally {
            workerGroup.shutdownGracefully();
            bossGroup.shutdownGracefully();
        }
    }

    private static class EchoServerHandler extends ChannelInboundHandlerAdapter {

        @Override
        public void channelRead(ChannelHandlerContext ctx, Object msg) {
            // Write the received object, and flush
            ctx.writeAndFlush(msg);
        }
    }
}
```

The Vert.x toolkit, based on top of Netty, provides higher-level features to build reactive applications such as HTTP clients and servers, messaging clients, etc. Typically, the same *echo* TCP server using Vert.x looks like Example 4-6.

Example 4-6. An echo server using Vert.x (chapter-4/non-blocking-io/src/main/java/org/acme/vertx/VertxEchoServer.java)

```
Vertx vertx = Vertx.vertx();
// Create a TCP server
vertx.createNetServer()
        // Invoke the given function for each connection
        .connectHandler(socket -> {
            // Just write the content back
            socket.handler(buffer -> socket.write(buffer));
        })
        .listen(9999);
```

Most Java frameworks offering Reactive capabilities are based on Netty or Vert.x. As shown in Figure 4-9, they all follow the same type of blueprint.

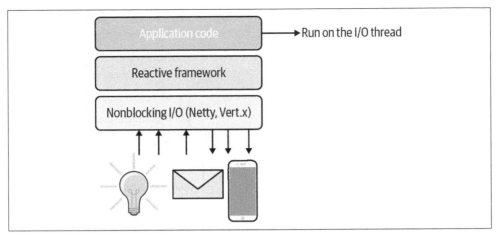

Figure 4-9. The common architecture of reactive frameworks

At the bottom, you have the nonblocking I/O. Generally, frameworks use Netty or Vert.x. This layer handles client connections, outbound requests, and response writing. In other words, it manages the I/O part. Most of the time, this layer implements the reactor pattern (or a variant), and so provides an event-loop-based model.

Then, in the second layer, you have the *reactive framework* per se. The role of this layer is to provide high-level APIs that are easy to use. You use these APIs to write your application code. Instead of having to handle nonblocking I/O channels, this layer provides high-level objects such as HTTP requests, responses, Kafka messages, and so on. Much easier!

Finally, in the top layer, you have your application. Your code does not need to touch nonblocking I/O concepts, thanks to the reactive framework. It can focus on incoming events and handle them. Your code is *just* a collection of event handlers. It can use the features provided by the reactive framework to interact with other services or middleware.

But there is a catch. The event handler from your code is invoked using the *event loop* thread (an I/O thread). If your code blocks this thread, no other concurrent events can be processed. It would be a disaster in terms of responsiveness and concurrency. The consequence of such an architecture is clear: your code must be nonblocking. It must never block the I/O threads, as they are rare and are used to handle multiple concurrent requests. To achieve this, you could offload the processing of some events to a worker thread (using the proactor pattern). While it can discard some of the benefits of nonblocking I/O, it is sometimes the most rational choice (Figure 4-10). Nevertheless, we should not abuse this as it would discard the reactive benefits and make the application slow. The multiple context switches required to handle an event on a worker thread penalizes the response time.

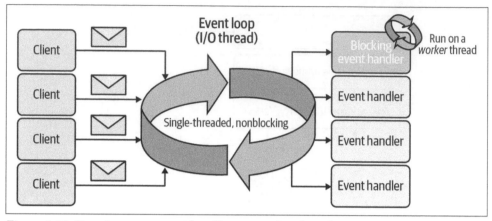

Figure 4-10. Running some event handlers on worker threads

Typically, our applications from Chapter 2 and Chapter 3 rely on such a mechanism.

Another possibility is to rely only on nonblocking code, relying on asynchronous APIs provided by the reactive framework. These APIs would be nonblocking, and if the business logic involved I/O, it uses nonblocking I/O. Every time an *event handler* executes an asynchronous operation, another handler (the continuation) is registered, and when the expected event arrives, the event loop invokes it. Thus, the processing is divided into smaller handlers running asynchronously. That model is the most efficient and embraces the concepts entirely behind Reactive.

Summary

Reactive systems are about building better distributed systems. They don't aim to hide the nature of distributed systems but, on the contrary, embrace it.

In this chapter, you learned the following:

- The four pillars of reactive systems (asynchronous message passing, elasticity, resilience, and responsiveness)
- How asynchronous message passing enables elasticity and resilience, and increases the autonomy of each individual component
- The role of commands and events in a distributed system
- How nonblocking I/O improves resource utilization in reactive applications

But this last point has a significant drawback, as we need to write nonblocking code. What a coincidence! The next chapter is precisely about that!

CHAPTER 5

Reactive Programming: Taming the Asynchronicity

In the previous chapter, we introduced reactive systems and how they elegantly handle the challenges of distributed systems. Although never forget that nothing comes for free in the IT world. One of the characteristics of reactive systems is the use of nonblocking I/O. Nonblocking I/O improves the concurrency, responsiveness, and resource utilization of reactive applications. To fully benefit from nonblocking I/O, you must design and develop the code in a nonblocking manner, and that is a not-so-easy challenge.

This chapter explores approaches to writing nonblocking and asynchronous Java code such as callbacks and reactive programming. We also cover flow control and Reactive Streams, which is an essential part of modern reactive applications.

Asynchronous Code and Patterns

How does nonblocking lead to asynchronous code? Remember the design of nonblocking I/O from the preceding chapter. It allows using a few threads to handle concurrent network interactions. That particular architecture reduces memory consumption but also CPU usage. As a consequence, the application code gets executed by one of these I/O threads, and there are scarce resources. If your code unconsciously blocks one of these threads, it would reduce your application's concurrency and increase the response time, as fewer threads are available to handle the requests. In the worst-case scenario, all the I/O threads get blocked, and the application cannot handle requests anymore. In other words, the benefits from nonblocking I/O would vanish.

Let's illustrate this with an example. Imagine a `greeting` service, which takes a name as a parameter and produces a greeting message. With a synchronous model, you would invoke that service as shown in Example 5-1.

Example 5-1. Example of synchronous code

```
String greetings = service.greeting("Luke");
System.out.println(greetings);
```

You call the service, synchronously get the result, and use it on the next line.

Now, let's imagine that the `greeting` service is a remote service. You could still call it synchronously, but, in this case, you are going to block the thread until the response is received, as depicted in Figure 5-1.

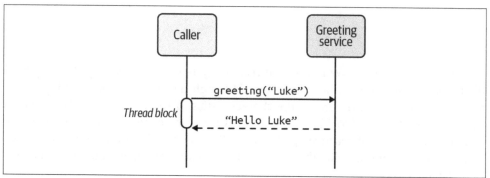

Figure 5-1. Synchronous invocation

If your code runs on the I/O thread, you block that thread. As a consequence, the service cannot handle any other requests while waiting for the response. Blocking the I/O thread discards all the advantages of nonblocking I/O.

What can we do? That's simple: we must not block the thread. We call the method, and it returns immediately, not *waiting* for the response. But, there is a small problem with this approach: how would you get this response? You need to pass some continuation, invoked when the response is received, as shown in Example 5-2.

Example 5-2. Example of asynchronous code

```
service.greeting("Luke", greeting -> {
    System.out.println(greeting);
});
```

In this code snippet, we pass a continuation implemented using a *callback*, a function invoked with the received result. It embraces well the event-driven nature of this code: `on result, call that function`. With this asynchronous model, we release the I/O thread. When the response is received, it calls the function with that response and continues the execution. During that time, this I/O thread can be used to handle more requests (Figure 5-2).

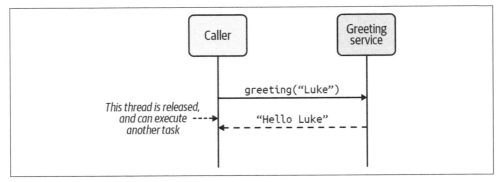

Figure 5-2. Asynchronous invocation

Let's have a deeper look at the preceding code snippet and add some traces by using the good old System.out statements (Example 5-3).

Example 5-3. Asynchronous code and ordering

```
System.out.println("Before");
service.greeting("Luke", greeting -> {
    System.out.println(greeting);
});
System.out.println("After");
```

What would be the output of this program? For sure, Before is printed first, but what about the greeting message and After? Which one would be first? There is a good chance that After is printed first because invoking the greeting service takes at least a few milliseconds (remember, it's a remote service). This means that with asynchronous code, the next line often is executed before the *continuation*.

What does that mean in practice? Let's imagine you want to call the greeting service twice, once for Luke and once for Leia; see Example 5-4.

Example 5-4. Calling asynchronous methods twice

```
service.greeting("Leia", greeting -> {
    System.out.println("Leia: " + greeting);
});
service.greeting("Luke", greeting -> {
    System.out.println("Luke: " + greeting);
});
```

In this code, we can't anticipate which message is going to appear first. It depends on many factors such as latency, speed, and number of instances of the greeting service. However, both calls run concurrently, which is an attractive benefit.

If you want or need a strict order (for example, to call the service for Leia first and then Luke), we need to compose the asynchronous calls (Example 5-5).

Example 5-5. Sequential composition pattern

```
service.greeting("Leia", greeting1 -> {
    System.out.println("Leia: " + greeting1);
    service.greeting("Luke", greeting2 -> {
        System.out.println("Luke: " + greeting2);
    });
});
```

With this code, we first call the service with Leia, and when we get the response, call it with Luke. The calls don't run concurrently anymore, but at least we know the order. We call this pattern *sequential composition*. It's quite common, as you can imagine.

Let's continue our investigation with another type of useful composition: *parallel composition*. We want to execute the calls concurrently this time, but we need to pass a continuation invoked when both calls are complete (Example 5-6).

Example 5-6. Simplified parallel composition pattern

```
String resultForLeia = null;
String resultForLuke = null;
BiConsumer<String, String> continuation = ...;

service.greeting("Leia", greeting -> {
    resultForLeia = greeting;
    if (resultForLuke != null) {
        continuation.accept(resultForLeia, resultForLuke);
    }
});
service.greeting("Luke", greeting -> {
    resultForLuke = greeting;
    if (resultForLeia != null) {
        continuation.accept(resultForLeia, resultForLuke);
    }
    });
});
```

It starts to be a bit more convoluted, and this code is not totally correct, as you can have race conditions if both callbacks are invoked concurrently. We need to store the results, check if they are non-null, and invoke the continuation function.

We have slightly forgotten another aspect: failures. It's not because it's an asynchronous API that failures don't happen. You cannot use `try/catch` blocks anymore, as the failure can also happen asynchronously; see Example 5-7.

Example 5-7. Would this try/catch work as intended?

```
try {
    service.greeting("Luke", greeting -> {
        System.out.println(greeting);
    });
} catch (Exception e) {
    // does not handle the exception thrown by the remote service
}
```

The `catch` block would catch only synchronous exceptions. If the service produces a failure asynchronously, like the inability to produce the greeting message, this `try/catch` is useless. To handle failures, we need to have a proper construct for it. We can imagine two *simple* ways:

- Use an asynchronous result construct encapsulating both the result and the failure.
- Have a second callback for failures.

With the first approach, you would need something like Example 5-8.

Example 5-8. Use asynchronous result encapsulating both result and failure

```
service.greeting("Luke", greeting -> {
    if (greeting.failed()) {
        System.out.println("D'oh! " + greeting.failure().getMessage());
    } else {
        System.out.println(greeting.result());
    }
});
```

`greeting` is not a `String` anymore but a type encapsulating the operation's outcome.[1] You need to check whether the operation failed or succeeded and act accordingly. You can quickly imagine how this would impact our previous composition examples. At that level, it's not challenging; it's a nightmare!

The second approach uses two callbacks: the first one when the operation succeeded, and the second one when it failed (Example 5-9).

---

[1] The Vert.x 3 main development model uses callbacks. Many operations pass a callback receiving `AsyncResult`. In Vert.x 4, an alternative model using futures has been introduced.

Example 5-9. Use different continuations for each outcome

```
service.greeting("Luke",
    greeting -> {
        System.out.println(greeting);
    },
    failure -> {
        System.out.println("D'oh! " + failure.getMessage());
    }
);
```

This approach clearly distinguishes the two cases, but again, it makes composition harder (Example 5-10).

Example 5-10. Use multiple continuations and compositing actions

```
service.greeting("Leia",
    greeting1 -> {
        System.out.println(greeting1);
        service.greeting("Luke",
            greeting2 -> System.out.println(greeting2),
            failure2 -> System.out.println("D'oh! " + failure2.getMessage())
        );
    },
    failure1 -> {
        System.out.println("D'oh! " + failure1.getMessage());
    }
);
```

It's not simple, right? However, this second approach has an advantage. If we imagine having a `greeting` service accepting multiple names, it is well suited to handle sequential responses (Example 5-11).

Example 5-11. Multiple results for a single operation

```
service.greeting(Arrays.asList("Leia", "Luke"),
    greeting -> {    // Called once for Leia, and once for Luke
        System.out.println(greeting);
    },
    failure -> {
        System.out.println("D'oh! " + failure.getMessage());
    }
);
```

This example starts exhibiting a new construct: streams of data. You will see a lot more of these in this book. These streams can be internal to the application or convey messages coming from a message broker. In this chapter, we consider only streams internal to the reactive applications. We will cover how these streams can be connected to various message brokers in Chapter 11.

In Java, to express your continuation using callbacks, we often use Java 8 Lambdas. They are well integrated in the language, but we have also seen the limit of that approach. Callbacks do not compose well. So we need a higher-level construct. Any seasoned developers would say future!

Using Futures

A *future* is a placeholder for a value resolved later. By nature, it's asynchronous; you don't know when the future will get the value. It's just *later*. When the value gets set, the future allows *reacting* on it—for example, transforming the value, implementing side effects, and so forth.

How does it help our asynchronous code concern? In Java, CompletableFuture, or CompletionStage, the associated interface, can represent the result of an asynchronous action. Your API returns a CompletionStage object, which gets the result when the operation completes. The method returning the CompletionStage object returns immediately, and so does not block the caller thread, and the continuation can be attached to the returned CompletionStage; see Example 5-12.

Example 5-12. Example of CompletionStage (chapter-5/reactive-programming-examples/src/main/java/org/acme/future/Futures.java)

```
CompletionStage<String> future = service.greeting("Luke");
```

> The full examples from this section are located in *chapter-5/reactive-programming-examples/src/main/java/org/acme/future/Futures.java*.

The continuation can be divided into a set of *stages* to process, consume, and transform the results, as shown in Example 5-13.

Example 5-13. Chaining operation with CompletionStage (chapter-5/reactive-programming-examples/src/main/java/org/acme/future/Futures.java)

```
service.greeting("Luke")
        .thenApply(response -> response.toUpperCase())
        .thenAccept(greeting -> System.out.println(greeting));
```

Futures also ease the implementation of sequential composition. With the CompletionStage API, you can use thenCompose to invoke a second operation (as seen in Example 5-14).

Example 5-14. Sequential composition with `CompletionStage` *(chapter-5/reactive-programming-examples/src/main/java/org/acme/future/Futures.java)*

```
service.greeting("Luke")
    .thenCompose(greetingForLuke -> {
        return service.greeting("Leia")
                .thenApply(greetingForLeia ->
                        Tuple2.of(greetingForLuke, greetingForLeia)
                );
    })
    .thenAccept(tuple ->
            System.out.println(tuple.getItem1() + " " + tuple.getItem2())
    );
```

The `allOf` method allows implementing parallel composition; see Example 5-15.

Example 5-15. Parallel composition with `CompletableFuture` *(chapter-5/reactive-programming-examples/src/main/java/org/acme/future/Futures.java)*

```
CompletableFuture<String> luke = service.greeting("Luke").toCompletableFuture();
CompletableFuture<String> leia = service.greeting("Leia").toCompletableFuture();

CompletableFuture.allOf(luke, leia)
        .thenAccept(ignored -> {
            System.out.println(luke.join() + " " + leia.join());
        });
```

Futures make composing asynchronous actions much more straightforward than callbacks. Besides, futures encapsulate both the result and failure. In `Completion Stage`, specific methods handle failure and recover, as you can see in Example 5-16.

Example 5-16. Recover from failure with the `CompletionStage` *API (chapter-5/reactive-programming-examples/src/main/java/org/acme/future/Futures.java)*

```
service.greeting("Leia")
        .exceptionally(exception -> "Hello");
```

When using `CompletionStage`, we start seeing the creation of *pipelines*: a sequence of operations handling events and asynchronous results.

You may be wondering, what's missing? Futures seem to tick all the boxes. But one tick is missing: streams. Futures do not handle streams of data well. They can be used for operations returning single values, but they won't work for functions returning sequences as in Example 5-11.

Project Loom: Virtual Threads and Carrier Threads

If you follow the news around Java, you may have heard about Project Loom (*https://oreil.ly/vuLzu*). Loom adds the concept of *virtual threads* into Java. Unlike regular threads, virtual threads are lightweight. A single carrier thread, a regular OS thread, can execute many virtual threads, potentially millions. Loom (the JVM) manages the scheduling of these virtual threads, while the operating system manages the carrier thread's scheduling.

One benefit is that you can execute blocking code in a virtual thread; it does not block the carrier thread. When a virtual thread executes a blocking call, such as an I/O call, the Loom scheduler, managing the virtual threads, parks that virtual thread and runs another virtual thread. So the carrier thread is not blocked and is used to execute this other virtual thread. That does smell good, right?

In other words, you can write blocking code using a synchronous syntax without having to take care of the continuation. Loom handles that for you! Even better: because virtual threads are lightweight, you don't need thread pools anymore; you can create new ones on the fly.

However, at the time of writing, the Loom project is still incubating.[2] The following code snippets may slightly change as the API is still evolving. Besides, some concurrency or blocking constructs are not yet supported, and you may unintentionally block the carrier threads, which, as you can imagine, can be catastrophic.

But, to give some ideas, let's see how we could use our `greeting` service in a Loom world. First, the `greeting` service implementation can be blocking and use blocking I/O to interact with a remote service. If the call is executed on a virtual thread, it does not block the carrier thread, which can execute another virtual thread. Loom replaces the blocking I/O calls with a nonblocking I/O and parks the virtual thread until the response is received. When the response is available, the parked virtual thread can continue its execution with the result. From the developer point of view, it's all synchronous, but under the hood it's not; see Example 5-17.

Example 5-17. Create a virtual thread

```
Thread.startVirtualThread(() -> {
    // We are running on a virtual thread.
    // The service may use blocking I/O, the virtual thread would be parked.
    String response = service.greeting("Luke");
    // Once the response is received, the virtual thread can continue its execution.
    // The carrier thread has not been blocked.
```

---

2 Check the Project Loom site (*https://oreil.ly/arP4E*) for updates on the general availability.

```
    System.out.println(response);
});
```

As you can see, it's pure synchronous code. As a consequence, the sequential composition is remarkably simple (Example 5-18).

Example 5-18. Sequential composition with Loom

```
Thread.startVirtualThread(() -> {
    String response1 = service.greeting("Luke");
    String response2 = service.greeting("Leia");
    System.out.println("Luke: " + response1);
    System.out.println("Leia: " + response2);
});
```

It's not different from what you would use in a traditional application. Don't forget that the virtual thread is suspended and resumes multiple times. But, again, the carrier thread is not.

Failure management can use `try/catch` as, again, you use synchronous code. If the call to the service fails, the failure is thrown as a regular exception (Example 5-19).

Example 5-19. Exception handling with Loom

```
Thread.startVirtualThread(() -> {
    try {
        String response = service.greeting("Luke");
        System.out.println("Luke: " + response);
    } catch (Exception e) {
        System.out.println("Failed");
    }
});
```

Unfortunately, Loom does not offer any specific construct for parallel composition. You need to use the same approach as for `CompletableFuture`, as shown in Example 5-20.

Example 5-20. Parallel composition with Loom

```
ExecutorService executor = Executors.newUnboundedVirtualThreadExecutor();
CompletableFuture<String> future1 = executor.submitTask(()
    -> service.greeting("Luke"));
CompletableFuture<String> future2 = executor.submitTask(()
    -> service.greeting("Leia"));

Thread.startVirtualThread(() -> {
    CompletableFuture.allOf(future1, future2).thenAccept(v -> {
        System.out.println("Luke: " + future1.join());
```

```
        System.out.println("Leia: " + future2.join());
    });
});
```

Sounds magic, right? But, you see it coming; there is a catch…

While you write synchronous code and do not block the carrier thread, I/Os are still happening on I/O threads. The carrier threads are not I/O threads (Figure 5-3). So, there are multiple thread switches that are not free, even if optimized.

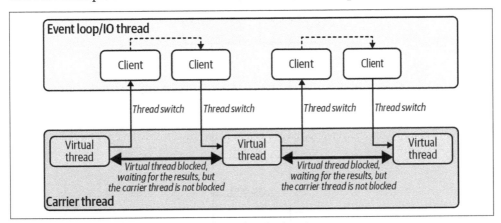

Figure 5-3. Thread switches happening under the hood

Also, the temptation to create a massive number of virtual threads can lead to compli-cated execution. Even if virtual threads are lightweight, storing their stacks in mem-ory may lead to unexpected memory consumption. It's like any software using many threads; they can be hard to understand and tune. That's being said, Loom is promis-ing. Does that make Reactive pointless? It's the opposite. Loom addresses only the development model, not the architecture concepts behind reactive systems. Also, a synchronous model looks attractive but does not accommodate every situation, espe-cially when you need to group events or implement stream-based logic. That's what we cover in the next section: reactive programming.

Reactive Programming

First, what is *reactive programming*? A common definition is:

> Reactive programming combines functional programming, the observer pattern, and the iterable pattern.
>
> —The ReactiveX website (*http://reactivex.io*)

We never found that definition helpful—too many patterns, and it's hard to clearly convey what reactive programming is about. Let's make another definition, much more straightforward: "Reactive programming is about programming with asynchronous streams."

That's it. Reactive programming is about streams and, especially, observing them. It pushes that idea to its limit: everything is a stream. These streams can be seen as a pipe in which *events* flow. We observe the events flowing—such as items, failures, completion, cancellations—and implement side effects (see Figure 5-4).

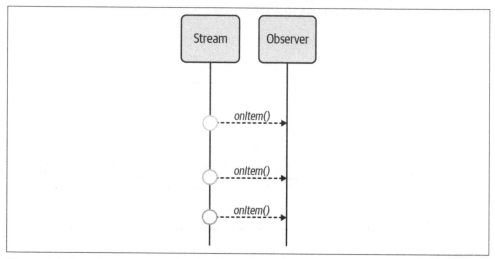

Figure 5-4. Reactive programming is about observing streams

Reactive programming is a specialization of the observer pattern in the sense that you observe an object (the stream) and react. It's asynchronous by nature, as you don't know when the event is going to be seen. Yet, reactive programming goes beyond this. It provides a toolbox to compose streams and process events.

Streams

When using reactive programming, everything—yes, *everything*—is a stream of items. The stock market, user clicks, keystrokes, steps, ticks… All these are streams, and it's easy to see why: they are sequences of individual events. So the stream carries every occurrence of this event, and the observer can react.

But reactive programming also considers asynchronous actions, HTTP requests, RPC method invocations, and database insertions or queries as streams. So, a stream does not need to carry multiple items; it can contain a single one or even none! That is a bit harder to imagine, but it can be powerful.

With reactive programming, you structure your code around streams and build chains of transformation, also called *pipelines*. The events flow from the *upstream* source to the *downstream* subscriber, traversing each operator and getting transformed, processed, filtered, and so on. Each operator observes the upstream and produces a new stream. But, there is an important point to not miss in this chain. You need a final *subscriber* that subscribes to the last stream and triggers the whole computation. When this subscription happens, the direct upstream of the final observer subscribes to its own upstream, which subscribes to its upstream, until it reaches the root.

Let's go back to the idea of a stream. As we've mentioned, we consider a stream as only internal to the reactive applications. These streams are sequences of events ordered in time. The order matters. You observe them in the emission order.

A stream can emit three types of events (Figure 5-5):

Items
The type depends on the stream; it can be a step, a click, or a response from a remote service.

Failures
Indicate that something bad happened, and no more items will be emitted.

Completions
Indicate that there are no more items to emit.

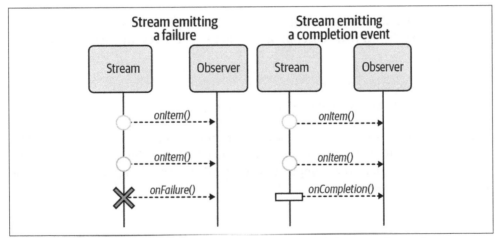

Figure 5-5. Streams can emit three types of events: items, failures, and completions

Item is the most frequent type of event. As an observer, you get notified every time a new item is transiting in the stream. You can react to it, transform it, implement side effects, and so on.

Failure is an error signal. It indicates that something *terrible* happened, and the observed stream cannot recover from it. If not handled properly, failures are a terminal event, and no more items will be emitted after a failure. You may wonder, why do we need to handle failure? Because streams are asynchronous, and if something breaks the source of items, you should be aware of it, and not wait for additional items, as they won't come. As for the other asynchronous development models, you cannot use a try/catch block, so you need to observe failures and react to them. For example, you can log an error or use a fallback item.

Finally, the completion event is emitted only when observing a bounded stream, as unbounded streams never terminate. The event indicates the end of the stream; the source (upstream) is not going to send any more items.

Every time one of these events transit in the observed stream, you, as the observer, get notified. You attach functions handling each of them, as shown in Example 5-21.

Example 5-21. Subscribe to a stream to receive the events (chapter-5/reactive-programming-examples/src/main/java/org/acme/reactive/StreamsExample.java)

```
stream
        .subscribe().with(
            item -> System.out.println("Received an item: " + item),
            failure -> System.out.println("Oh no! Received a failure: " + failure),
            () -> System.out.println("Received the completion signal")
);
```

To observe a stream, you *subscribe* to it. It's a key concept in reactive programming, as streams are lazy by default. Subscribing indicates your interest in the events. Without a subscription:

- You won't receive the items
- You won't tell the stream that it needs to operate

The second point is important. It means that, in general, if no one subscribes to a stream, the stream won't do anything. That may look odd but allows you to save resources and to start the computation only when everything is ready and you actually need the events.

Operators

Although reactive programming is about streams, it would be useless without a toolbox to manipulate these streams. Reactive programming libraries offer countless operators that let you create, combine, filter, and transform the object emitted by streams. As depicted in Figure 5-6, a stream can be used as input to another one.

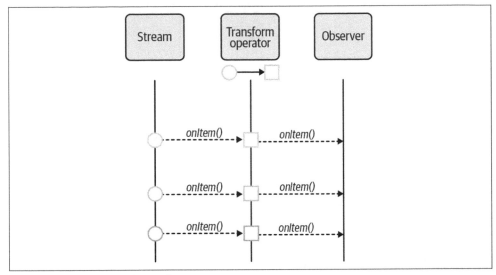

Figure 5-6. Example of transform operator

It's important to understand that operators return new streams. The operator observes the previous stream (named upstream) and creates a new stream by combining their logic and the received events. For example, the transform operator from Figure 5-6 applies a function for each received item[3] and emits the result to its *downstream* subscriber (Example 5-22).

Example 5-22. Transform items (chapter-5/reactive-programming-examples/src/main/java/org/acme/reactive/StreamsExample.java)

```
stream
        .onItem().transform(circle -> toSquare(circle))
        .subscribe().with(
            item -> System.out.println("Received a square: " + item),
            failure -> System.out.println("Oh no! Received a failure: " + failure),
            () -> System.out.println("Received the completion signal")
);
```

As depicted in Figure 5-7 and Example 5-23, operators can also handle failures; for example, to recover or retry.

---

3 In functional programming, transform is often called map.

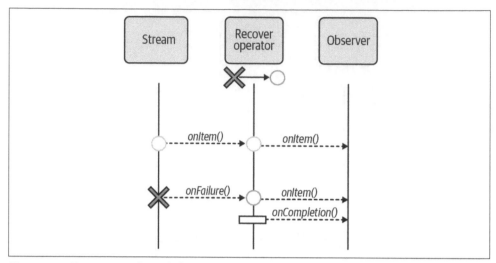

Figure 5-7. Recovering from failures

Example 5-23. Recover from failures (chapter-5/reactive-programming-examples/src/main/java/org/acme/reactive/StreamsExample.java)

```
stream
        .onFailure().recoverWithItem(failure -> getFallbackForFailure(failure))
        .subscribe().with(
            item -> System.out.println("Received a square: " + item),
            failure -> System.out.println("Oh no! Received a failure: " + failure),
            () -> System.out.println("Received the completion signal")
);
```

You may wonder why the `recover` operator emits a completion event after the recovery, as shown in Figure 5-7. When the operator receives the failure event, it knows that the source is not going to emit any more items, as failures are terminal. So, after emitting the *fallback* item, the operator emits the completion event. For the downstream subscriber, it's like the failure did not happen and the stream completed successfully.

Operators are not limited to synchronous or single-in, single-out types of transformations. Operators can transform a single item into a stream, or on the flip side, discard items, as shown in Figure 5-8.

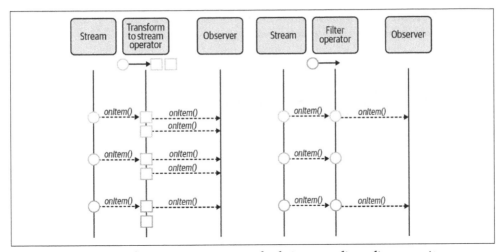

Figure 5-8. Example of operators emitting multiple items or discarding some items

Finally, operators can observe multiple upstreams, to merge them, for example, as shown in Figure 5-9 and demonstrated in Example 5-24.

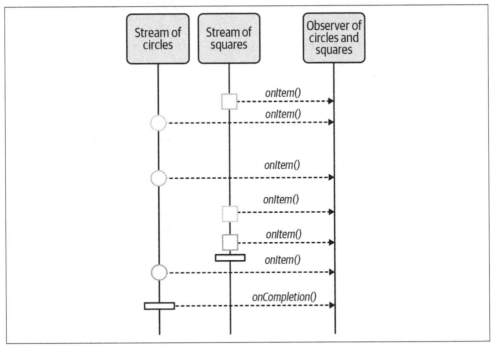

Figure 5-9. Merging multiple streams

Example 5-24. Merge multiple streams (chapter-5/reactive-programming-examples/src/main/java/org/acme/reactive/StreamsExample.java)

```
Multi.createBy().merging().streams(circles, squares)
      .subscribe().with(
      item -> System.out.println("Received a square or circle: " + item),
      failure -> System.out.println("Oh no! Received a failure: " + failure),
      () -> System.out.println("Received the completion signal")
);
```

 In the preceding example, note when the observer received the completion event. The merging operator waits for all the merged streams to complete before sending the completion event, as at that point, no more items will be emitted. That illustrates the coordination role of operators.

Reactive Programming Libraries

Java has many reactive programming libraries. In this book, we are using SmallRye Mutiny, the reactive programming library integrated in Quarkus. We will have a deeper look at Mutiny in Chapter 7. Project Reactor and RxJava, two popular alternatives, propose similar concepts.

Reactive programming is not limited to Java. RX-JS (*https://oreil.ly/pF21o*) is a reactive programming library in JavaScript, often used in combination with Angular. RxPY (*https://oreil.ly/tlGl1*) and RxGo (*https://oreil.ly/Mg4Rj*) offer the same type of constructs for Python and Go applications, respectively.

Reactive Streams and the Need for Flow Control

Using data streams as primary constructs does not come without issues. One of the main problems is the need for flow control. Let's imagine a fast producer and a slow consumer. The producer sends events too quickly for the consumer, which can't keep up. Imagine that this producer emits an item every 10 milliseconds, while a downstream consumer can consume only one per second. Run the code in Example 5-25, and you'll see how it ends: badly.

Example 5-25. Example of backpressure failure (chapter-5/reactive-programming-examples/src/main/java/org/acme/streams/BackPressureExample.java)

```
// Ticks is a stream emitting an item periodically (every 10 ms)
Multi<Long> ticks = Multi.createFrom().ticks().every(Duration.ofMillis(10))
      .emitOn(Infrastructure.getDefaultExecutor());

ticks
    .onItem().transform(BackPressureExample::canOnlyConsumeOneItemPerSecond)
```

```
    .subscribe().with(
        item -> System.out.println("Got item: " + item),
        failure -> System.out.println("Got failure: " + failure)
);
```

If you run that code, you will see that the subscriber gets `MissingBackPressureFai`
`lure`, indicating that the downstream could not keep up (Example 5-26).

Example 5-26. Subscriber getting a `BackPressureFailure`

```
Got item: 0
Got failure: io.smallrye.mutiny.subscription.BackPressureFailure: Could not
emit tick 16 due to lack of requests
```

In Example 5-25, you may wonder about `emitOn`. This operator
controls when a thread is used to emit the events.[4] Backpressure is
required when multiple threads are involved because in a single
thread, blocking the thread would block the source.

So, what can we do to handle this case?

Buffering Items

The first natural solution uses buffers. The consumer can buffer the events, so it does
not fail (Figure 5-10).

Figure 5-10. Buffering to avoid overwhelming downstream consumers

Buffers allow handling small bumps, but they're not a long-term solution. If you
update your code to use a buffer, as in Example 5-27, the consumer can handle more
events but eventually fails.

*Example 5-27. Handle overflow with buffers (chapter-5/reactive-programming-
examples/src/main/java/org/acme/streams/BufferingExample.java)*

```
Multi<Long> ticks = Multi.createFrom().ticks().every(Duration.ofMillis(10))
    .onOverflow().buffer(250)
    .emitOn(Infrastructure.getDefaultExecutor());
```

---

4 More details about `emitOn` can be found in the Mutiny online guides (*https://oreil.ly/qrVdD*).

```
ticks
    .onItem().transform(BufferingExample::canOnlyConsumeOneItemPerSecond)
    .subscribe().with(
        item -> System.out.println("Got item: " + item),
        failure -> System.out.println("Got failure: " + failure)
);
```

Here's the output:

```
Got item: 0
Got item: 1
Got item: 2
Got failure: io.smallrye.mutiny.subscription.BackPressureFailure:
Buffer is full due to lack of downstream consumption
```

You can imagine increasing the buffer's size, but it's hard to anticipate the optimal value. These buffers are local to the application, so, using large buffers also increases your memory consumption and reduces your resource utilization efficiency. Not to mention that unbounded buffers are a terrible idea, as you may run out of memory.

Dropping Items

Another solution consists of dropping items. We can drop the newest received items or oldest ones; see Example 5-28.

Example 5-28. Handle overflow by dropping items (chapter-5/reactive-programming-examples/src/main/java/org/acme/streams/DropExample.java)

```
Multi<Long> ticks = Multi.createFrom().ticks().every(Duration.ofMillis(10))
        .onOverflow().drop(x -> System.out.println("Dropping item " + x))
        .emitOn(Infrastructure.getDefaultExecutor());

ticks
        .onItem().transform(DropExample::canOnlyConsumeOneItemPerSecond)
        .transform().byTakingFirstItems(10)
        .subscribe().with(
            item -> System.out.println("Got item: " + item),
            failure -> System.out.println("Got failure: " + failure)
);
```

Here's the output:

```
// ....
Dropping item 997
Dropping item 998
Dropping item 999
Dropping item 1000
Dropping item 1001
Dropping item 1002
Dropping item 1003
Got item: 9
```

Dropping items provides a sustainable solution to our problem, but we are losing items! As we can see in the preceding output, we may drop the majority of items. In many cases, this is not acceptable.

We need another solution, one that adjusts the overall pace to satisfy the pipeline's slowest element. We need a backpressure protocol.

What Is Backpressure?

In mechanics, backpressure is a way to control the flow of fluid through pipes, leading to a pressure drop. That control can use reducers or bends. While this is great if you are a plumber, it's not clear how it can help us here.

We can see our streams as a flow of fluid, and the set of stages (operator or subscriber) forms a pipe. We want to make the fluid flow as frictionless as possible, without swirls and waves.

An interesting characteristic of fluid mechanics is the way a downstream reduction of the throughput affects the upstream. Essentially, that's what we need: a way for the downstream operators and subscribers to reduce the throughput, not only locally but also upstream.

Don't be mistaken; backpressure is not something new in the IT world and is not limited to Reactive. One of the most brilliant uses of backpressure is in TCP.[5] A reader receiving data can block the writer on the other side of the wire if it does not read the sent data. That way, the reader is never overwhelmed. But the consequences need to be understood: blocking the writer may not be without side effects.

Introducing Reactive Streams

Let's now focus on another backpressure protocol: Reactive Streams. This asynchronous and backpressure protocol is suited to our fast producer/slow consumer problem. With Reactive Streams, the consumer, named Subscriber, requests items from the producer, named Publisher. As depicted in Figure 5-11, Publisher cannot send more than the requested number of items.

---

5 We recommend reading "Using Backpressure to Improve TCP Performance with Many Flows" (*https:// oreil.ly/JEbNh*) by Carlos M. Pazos et al., which explains how TCP backpressure can be used to improve performance.

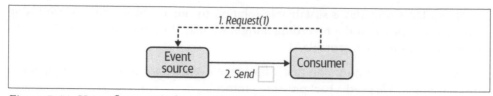

Figure 5-11. Using flow control to avoid overwhelming consumers

When the items are received and processed, the consumer can request more items, and so on. Thus, the consumer controls the flow.

Note that Reactive Streams introduces a strong coupling between a consumer and a producer. The producer must listen to the requests from the consumer.

To implement that protocol, Reactive Streams defines a set of entities. First, Subscriber is a consumer. It subscribes to a stream, called Publisher, which produces items (Figure 5-12). Then Publisher sends, asynchronously, a Subscription object to Subscriber. This Subscription object is a contract. With Subscription, Subscriber can request items and then cancel the subscription when it does not want any more items. Each subscriber subscribing to a publisher gets a different Subscription, and so emits independent requests. The publisher implementation is in charge of the orchestration of the various requests and the emission of the items to the multiple subscribers.

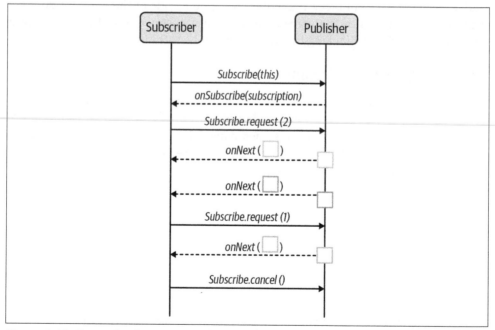

Figure 5-12. Example of interactions between Subscriber and Publisher

`Publisher` cannot send more items than requested to `Subscriber`, and `Subscriber` can request more items at any time.

It is essential to understand that the requests and emissions are not necessarily happening synchronously. `Subscriber` can request three items, and `Publisher` will send them one by one when they are available.

Reactive Streams introduces another entity named `Processor`. `Processor` is a subscriber and a publisher simultaneously. In other words, it's a link in our pipeline, as shown in Figure 5-13.

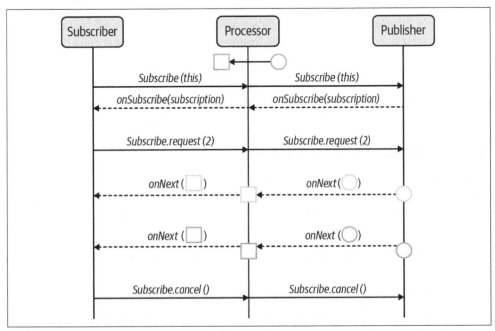

Figure 5-13. Example of interactions between `Subscriber`, `Processor`, *and* `Publisher`

`Subscriber` calls `subscribe` on `Processor`. Before receiving a `Subscription`, `Processor` subscribes to its own upstream source (`Publisher` in Figure 5-13). When that upstream provides `Subscription` to our `Processor`, it can give `Subscription` to `Subscriber`. All these interactions are asynchronous. When this handshake completes, `Subscriber` can start requesting items. `Processor` is responsible for mediating the `Subscriber` requests with its upstream. For example, as illustrated in Figure 5-13, if `Subscriber` requires two items, `Processor` also requests two items to its own upstream. Of course, depending on the `Processor` code, it may not be that simple. What's fundamental is that each `Publisher` and `Processor` enforces the flowing requests to never overload downstream subscribers.

Be Warned: It's a Trap!

If you look at the Reactive Streams API,[6] you will find it *simple*: a few classes, a couple of methods. It's a trap! Behind this apparent simplicity, implementing Reactive Streams entities yourself is a nightmare. The problem is not the interfaces; it's the protocol. Reactive Streams comes with a broad set of rules, and a strict Technology Compatibility Kit (TCK) to verify that your implementation enforces the protocol.

Fortunately, you don't need to implement publishers, subscribers, or processors yourself. Recent reactive programming libraries already implement the protocol for you. Project Reactor, RxJava (versions 2 and 3), and Mutiny implement the specification. For example, Mutiny's `Multi` is a publisher following the Reactive Streams protocol. All the subscription handshakes and request negotiations are done for you.

Also, because all these libraries are using the same core concepts and API, it allows smooth integration: you can consume a Reactor `Flux` by using a Mutiny `Subscriber` and vice versa! Reactive Streams is the integration layer between the various reactive programming libraries, in addition to being a backpressure protocol.

Backpressure in Distributed Systems

Reactive Streams works perfectly within a local node, but what about distributed systems? In such a system, it's important that event producers do not overflow the consumers. We need flow control. Fortunately, we have many alternatives.

First, RSocket is proposing a distributed variant of Reactive Streams. However, because of distributed systems' challenges and potential communication disruptions, the protocol requires a few adaptations.

AMQP 1.0 uses a flow control protocol based on credit (*https://oreil.ly/ZKURr*). As a producer, you get a certain amount of credit. When you run out of credit, you can't send messages anymore. The broker refills your credit according to the consumer pace.

Apache Kafka consumers can also implement backpressure by using pause/resume cycles and explicit polling. In this case, Kafka does not prevent the production of messages. It stores the messages in the broker, and uses it as a large buffer. The consumer polls the messages according to its capacity.

The mechanism presented for AMQP 1.0 and Apache Kafka are not the same as Reactive Streams. Frameworks, such as Quarkus, create bridges between these mechanisms with the Reactive Streams protocol.

---

6 For more information, see the Reactive Streams Javadoc (*https://oreil.ly/mcYRu*).

Summary

In this chapter, you have learned the following:

- Asynchronous code is hard but is required to avoid discarding the benefits of nonblocking I/O.
- Reactive programming is one possibility for writing asynchronous code.
- Reactive programming uses data streams as primary constructs. You write a processing pipeline reacting to events flowing from upstream.
- Reactive Streams is an essential aspect of Reactive. It avoids overwhelming fragile parts of your system.

Small cracks that ripple in your system can lead to dreadful consequences.

Now, you have enough knowledge about Reactive to build your own reactive systems and appreciate the benefits. Wait! You may need some more concrete details, no? That's what we are going to cover in Part III, where we explore how easy it is to build reactive systems with Quarkus.

## PART III

Building Reactive Applications and Systems with Quarkus

## CHAPTER 6

Quarkus: Reactive Engine

In Part II, you learned a lot about Reactive, in all its forms, meanings, and variations! I know, you're probably a bit tired of hearing the word *reactive* right now, but it's a key piece to accurately describing Quarkus. At the core of Quarkus is its reactive engine, which we cover in "A Reactive Engine" on page 120. Without its reactive engine core, Quarkus would not allow implementing reactive applications and provide a seamless integration of reactive programming.

Quarkus unifies two development models: imperative and reactive. In this chapter, we review the main differences and show how Quarkus handles the unification. Quarkus aims for them to be as alike as possible. If the APIs *feel* similar, understanding a complex model such as Reactive becomes seamless.

Before we can get into the reactive engine, we need to revisit the imperative and reactive models. Doing so allows us an opportunity to appreciate how they're unified with Quarkus. For anyone already familiar with imperative and reactive models, how they work, and the benefits and disadvantages of each, feel free to skip ahead to "Unification of Reactive and Imperative" on page 116.

You might worry we're repeating previously covered information. We might be a little, but it's all geared toward reinforcing how the two models impact the way applications are developed—and as a result, how frameworks differ depending on the model they offer.

First up is the imperative model, which most Java developers likely started their careers using.

The Imperative Model

When using the *imperative model*, you may not even be aware of its name. So what is the imperative model? It alters a program's state with a defined sequence of commands. One command is executed after another until all commands are executed.

Figure 6-1 shows a sequence of mathematical commands, executed in succession, until the result (in this case 10 if we start from 0, is produced). As you can see in the imperative model, defining the proper sequence is critical to achieving the desired result, 10.

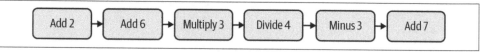

Figure 6-1. Imperative commands with result 10

Figure 6-2 shows the exact same commands, but in a different sequence.

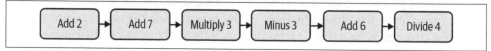

Figure 6-2. Imperative commands with result 7.5

As you see, the sequence of commands, in the imperative mode, is just as important as the commands themselves. Modifying the sequence results in an entirely different program output. An imperative program can be considered the process of getting from A to B, when we already know what A and B need to be. The developer needs to define only the steps between A and B in the correct sequence to achieve the desired result.

In imperative programs, we have a defined input and output, and, in addition, we know the steps needed to get from A to B. For these two reasons, imperative programs are easily reasoned about. When we have a defined input, what we know the output should be, and the defined steps to get there, writing tests is a lot easier because the permutations of what can happen are limited and determinable.

What are some other aspects of the imperative programming model we need to be aware of? As imperative relies on a sequence of commands, resource utilization will always be a primary concern. In the example shown in Figure 6-1, we're not going to need a large amount of resources to perform basic mathematical calculations. However, if we replaced all those operations with database calls retrieving a few hundred records each, the impacts begin adding up quickly.

The impacts we're talking about are related to the threading model for imperative programming. If we have our sequence of database operations using a single I/O thread, the same I/O thread handling the HTTP request (not realistic but useful for illustrative purposes), only one request can be processed at any point in time. We introduced the I/O thread in Chapter 5. Moreover, as the sequence of the imperative program is fixed, each command must complete before the next one can commence. What does that look like?

Though contrived, Figure 6-3 illustrates how each step in the database program must complete before the next can commence. More importantly, any subsequent request can begin only when the one being processed is finished. In this situation, the number of concurrent requests we can process is limited by the number of I/O threads we give the application.

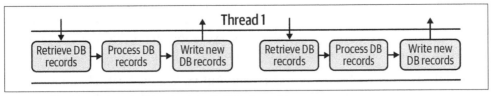

Figure 6-3. Database program on single I/O thread

Now, as depicted in Figure 6-4, we will be generous and provide the same application two I/O threads!

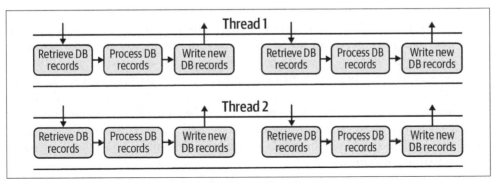

Figure 6-4. Database program on multiple I/O threads

We can process two concurrent requests, but no more than that with only two I/O threads. Being able to handle only a single request per I/O thread is not great, so let's dive deeper into what's going on inside.

Both the *Retrieve DB records* and *Write new DB records* commands have periods of time when the command itself is not performing any work, shown as the lighter section in Figure 6-5. In between sending a request to the database and receiving the response, what is the I/O thread doing? In this situation, absolutely nothing! The I/O thread sits there waiting for the response from the database.

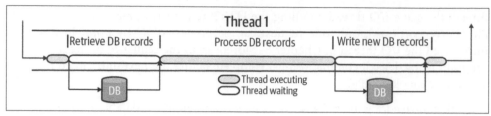

Figure 6-5. Database program I/O thread delays

Why does it do nothing? Could an I/O thread perform other work while waiting? As we mentioned earlier, imperative programming requires an ordered sequence of commands. Because *Retrieve DB records* is still running during the wait period, an I/O thread does not know there is time to perform other work. This is why imperative programming is often tied with synchronous execution, and by default synchronous is the execution model for imperative programming.

Some might wonder whether an I/O thread waiting is a big deal. The time an I/O thread waits for a command to complete could be several seconds or longer. An imperative program taking about a second to complete all its steps may be OK, but it doesn't take many periods of I/O threads waiting to explode the total response time to many seconds.

The expanded time to complete an imperative program has several effects. Increased execution time on an I/O thread leads to a reduction in the number of requests being processed in a given period of time. There are additional impacts on the resources required to buffer in memory any incoming requests that are waiting on I/O threads to become available to begin processing. These resource impacts can cause significant issues with the overall performance of an application. If an application is dealing with a few hundred, or even thousand, users, it may not be noticeable, especially if few are concurrent users. However, tens of thousands of users, many concurrently, will show these problems to their users in failed connections, time-outs, errors, and any number of possible problems.

There are other ways to break the synchronous and blocking nature of an imperative program. We can use `ExecutorService` to move work from the I/O thread onto a separate worker pool thread. Or we can use `@Suspended` and `AsyncResponse` with JAX-RS Resources to delegate work to a worker pool of threads, enabling the HTTP request to be suspended from the I/O thread until a response is set on `AsyncResponse`. Suspending HTTP requests waiting for a response facilitates processing of additional HTTP requests on the I/O thread while others are waiting for a processing response.

Though these approaches work, the complexity of code increases without a significant benefit in throughput as we're still I/O thread limited—not quite to the level of a request per thread when using @Suspended, but not significantly more either. How does the reactive model differ?

The Reactive Model

The *reactive model* is built around the notion of continuations and nonblocking I/O, as we detailed in "Asynchronous Code and Patterns" on page 83. As mentioned previously, this approach significantly increases the level of concurrency, enabling many more requests to be processed in parallel. However, it's not a free ride because it requires additional thought on the part of a developer to develop an application built around these principles.

Taking our previous database example, what would it look like to remove the I/O thread wait times to improve the concurrency? Take a look at Figure 6-6.

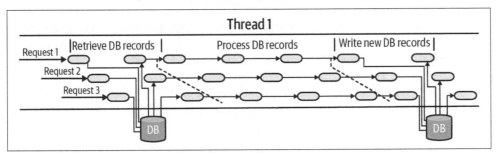

Figure 6-6. Reactive database program on I/O thread

Here, we can see that, instead of an I/O thread waiting, it begins processing another incoming request. It continues to do so until it's been notified that a database response is ready for processing. How do we achieve this separation? We provide a continuation to process the database response. The continuation is added to the queue of methods to execute on the I/O thread after the database response is received. Likewise, the single command to process the database records is split into smaller methods to help with the concurrency.

Figure 6-6 shows how a reactive model utilizing continuations can facilitate the removal of I/O thread wait time and increase the number of requests processed concurrently. As you've seen, we developers need to adjust how programs are developed to *align* with the reactive model. We need to break work into smaller chunks, but most importantly, modify interactions with anything external to the application into separate request and response handling.

In Figure 6-6, we approximated how pieces of a program could be segmented to prevent the I/O thread from waiting or being blocked. Quarkus uses an *event loop*, as discussed in "Reactor Pattern and Event Loop" on page 77, to implement the reactive model. The event loop can visually be represented as shown previously in Figure 4-7.

We've discussed some hugely beneficial aspects of the reactive model, but nothing comes for free. With the reactive model needing to separate code execution, as opposed to the imperative model in which everything is sequential, complexity is introduced in the ability to understand the entirety of a program.

A program is no longer a sequenced set of steps, but a series of handlers executing at different points in time with no predetermined order. Though continuations can be guaranteed to occur after they were triggered, there is no ordering among various asynchronous invocations within a single request, or among multiple requests. This shift requires an alteration in thinking by developers toward event passing, with the triggering of associated event handlers. No longer is it a sequence of commands called one after another in code.

Unification of Reactive and Imperative

What do we mean by Quarkus unifying reactive and imperative? We don't mean being able to ignore the complexities of reactive or expecting imperative to provide high levels of concurrency. We *do* mean the following:

- Quarkus's reactive core nonblocking I/O is key to any extension built on top.
- Quarkus offers a framework of extensions built on the performance of the Eclipse Vert.x toolkit, the reactive engine.
- A developer's choice of imperative or reactive is an API choice, and not a framework one.

Often when choosing to develop an application, an *up-front* choice needs to be made as to whether to use reactive or imperative programming. This decision requires much forethought by developers and architects in terms of the skills required by the team building the application, the current business requirements for the application, as well as the final architecture of the application. We developers find choosing a specific technology stack one of the most difficult decisions to make. We always want to consider the future needs of the application, even if we don't know what those needs are concretely. No matter how we try, there will always be new requirements or unforeseen problems, requiring a change in architecture or even design.

We feel more comfortable about a decision when it doesn't box us in, offering ways to shift and alter the way an application works as needs change. This is a huge advantage with Quarkus. When we choose Quarkus, and the unification of imperative and reactive models, we're free to pick one or the other, a mix of the two, or even switch parts of an application between the models over time.

Quarkus, Vert.x, and Mutiny

The Quarkus reactive core relies on Eclipse Vert.x. The Vert.x toolkit is the reactive core of everything Quarkus does. Without this reactive core, everything else Quarkus does would not be possible. Vert.x provides the layer interacting with nonblocking I/O and a large ecosystem of clients and servers.

In Quarkus, to ease the construction of reactive applications, we use SmallRye Mutiny. Mutiny provides the API model we use.

Vert.x and Mutiny are independent, the first one dealing with the network, and the second the API model. To ease the integration of Vert.x in Quarkus, the SmallRye Mutiny Vert.x Bindings project (*https://oreil.ly/geseu*) provides the complete Vert.x API using the Mutiny types.

How does Quarkus support reactive or imperative models seamlessly? Supporting both models seamlessly is the key foundation to everything Quarkus offers. Built on the foundation of Vert.x, Quarkus has a routing layer enabling either model. This is how the layers work together when we've deployed reactive code, assuming an HTTP request is being processed (Figure 6-7).

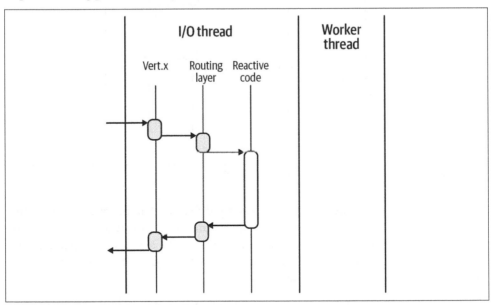

Figure 6-7. Quarkus reactive model

We see in Figure 6-7 how a request is received by the Vert.x HTTP server, passes through the routing layer, and our reactive code executes. All these interactions occur on the I/O thread; a worker thread is not needed. As already mentioned, having code execute on the I/O thread provides the highest level of concurrency.

 In Figure 6-7, only a single HTTP request is being processed. If there were multiple requests, those executions would be interleaved on the I/O thread.

You might be wondering how executing imperative code alters the behavior—take a look at Figure 6-8.

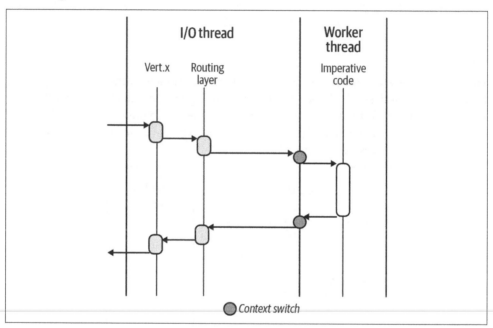

Figure 6-8. Quarkus imperative model

You can see that the model is not significantly different. The biggest change is that our code, now imperative in nature, is executed on a worker thread and not the I/O thread. In this way, Quarkus can execute imperative code, a series of sequential commands, without impacting the concurrency of the I/O thread. Quarkus has *offloaded* the imperative execution to a worker.

The process of offloading to a worker thread comes with a cost, however. Every time we execute on a worker thread, a context switch, before and after execution, is necessary. In Figure 6-8, we represent this switch as a circle on the boundary between the I/O and worker threads. These context switches cost time and resources to perform the switch and store the information in a new thread.

We've seen how the two models operate on Quarkus, but what about when we unify them? For example, if we have a reactive application needing to execute a piece of blocking code, how can we do that without blocking the I/O thread? In Figure 6-9, we see our code executing on both the I/O and worker threads!

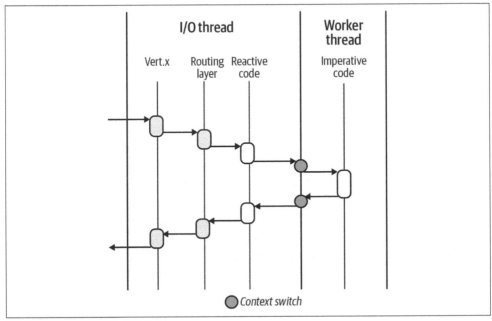

Figure 6-9. Quarkus reactive and imperative model

When reactive code is executed, it's on the I/O thread, but any imperative code is executed on a worker thread. Quarkus handles all of this for developers without them needing to create Executors or Threads, or needing to manage them.

Figure 6-9 is a visualization of the *proactor* pattern we defined in "Reactor Pattern and Event Loop" on page 77. Nonblocking and blocking handlers can coexist, as long as we offload blocking execution onto worker threads and invoke continuations when a blocking handler completes.

The proactor pattern unifies imperative and reactive code in Quarkus. Anyone familiar with developing reactive applications knows that sometimes it's necessary to write code in a blocking, or sequential, manner. Quarkus's unification allows us to delegate such execution onto a worker thread, by using @Blocking, which we cover for HTTP in Chapter 8 and Reactive Messaging in Chapter 10.

Utilizing the reactive model, and thus the I/O thread, for as much work as possible has an added benefit. We minimize the amount of context switching performed when delegating execution to a worker thread. Anytime execution of the same request moves between threads, from the I/O to worker thread, or vice versa, costs are associated with the switch. Any objects associated with the request need to be available from the new thread, costing time and resources to move them, as well as resource costs for additional threads.

We've talked a lot about how the models are unified in Quarkus, but what extensions use these models? RESTEasy Reactive, covered in Chapter 8, and Reactive Messaging, in Chapter 10, both utilize the reactive model. The classic RESTEasy and Spring controller both use the imperative model.

A Reactive Engine

If you have written reactive programs or done any research into Reactive, you are likely aware of the Vert.x toolkit. As mentioned before, the Quarkus reactive engine utilizes Vert.x. In addition to Vert.x, as well as Netty, the routing layer of Quarkus forms the outer layer of the reactive engine. It's the integration piece for extensions, coordinating the offloading of blocking handlers onto worker threads, and the execution of their continuations.

In addition, all the reactive clients are built on top of the reactive engine to utilize the nonblocking handling. Reactive applications are no longer reactive after they use blocking clients, a key aspect often overlooked by developers. Quarkus endeavors to have all clients that an application might need built on the reactive engine, for true reactive integration.

 By default, everything in Quarkus is reactive. Developers must decide whether they want reactive or imperative. What do we mean by *everything*? It includes HTTP handling, event-driven applications with AMQP and Kafka, and *everything* Quarkus offers.

A Reactive Programming Model

SmallRye Mutiny is the reactive programming library of Quarkus. You already learned about it in "Reactive Programming" on page 93, and we will learn even more in Chapter 7, so we won't cover too much detail here.

In short, Mutiny is built around three key aspects:

Event-driven
    Listening to events from the stream and handling them appropriately.

Easily navigable API
    Navigating the API is driven by an event type and the available options for that event.

Only two types

Multi and Uni can handle any desired asynchronous actions.

One point to note is the laziness of the Mutiny types. Events won't begin flowing through the data streams until a subscriber requests them. This is a fantastic feature to prevent streams from consuming resources if nothing is listening, but developers do need to be aware of this, so we don't forget to subscribe!

All Quarkus reactive APIs use Multi and Uni. This approach facilitates the seamless integration of Quarkus extensions with reactive programming and Mutiny. Let's see examples of using Mutiny.

A reactive application with Quarkus using the PostgreSQL reactive client retrieves Fruit objects from the database with Multi, as shown in Example 6-1.

Example 6-1. Reactive Mutiny client

```
client.query("SELECT id, name FROM fruits ORDER BY name ASC").execute()    ❶
    .onItem().transformToMulti(rowSet -> Multi.createFrom().iterable(rowSet))  ❷
    .onItem().transform(row -> convertRowToFruit(row));                      ❸
```

❶ client is an instance of PgPool, the PostgreSQL reactive client built with Mutiny and Vert.x.

❷ When a RowSet item is received, transform the single RowSet into a Multi<Row>.

❸ Convert each Row in Multi to a Fruit instance. The result of the execution is Multi<Fruit>.

Given we're writing about Reactive in this book, all the remaining chapters have examples utilizing Mutiny in many situations. We present reactive HTTP endpoints in Chapter 8 and their consumption in Chapter 12. We cover reactive data access with Quarkus and Mutiny in Chapter 9, including many examples.

Event-Driven Architecture with Quarkus

Though building reactive applications with Quarkus is great, performant, and fun, we want to do more than build a single application. We need a reactive system, as covered in Chapter 4, combining smaller applications into a coordinated distributed system. To support such an architecture, Quarkus must receive and produce events, an event-driven architecture! Quarkus achieves this by using Reactive Messaging, as shown in Example 6-2. Reactive Messaging integrates with various messaging technologies, such as Apache Kafka, AMQP, and others, with annotations for developers to specify whether a method receives or produces events.

Example 6-2. Reactive Messaging

```
@Incoming("prices")
@Outgoing("quotes")                                              ❶
public Quote generatePrice(Price p) {                            ❷
    return new Quote(p, "USD");
}
```

❶　Read messages from the `prices` channel.

❷　Transform each `Price` into a `Quote`.

The offered development model allows consuming, transforming, and generating messages easily. The `@Incoming` annotation denotes the consumption of a *channel*. Reactive Messaging invokes the method for each transiting `Price` from the configured channel. The `@Outgoing` annotation indicates in which channel the results are written.

Full details of Reactive Messaging are covered in Chapter 10.

Summary

This chapter covered the imperative model, a series of sequential commands, and the reactive model, utilizing continuations and nonblocking I/O.

We have seen the following:

- How the two models work with threads (in Figures 6-8, 6-7, and 6-9), providing improved concurrency with the reactive model.
- How Quarkus unifies these models to allow developers to grow their applications, introducing reactive aspects, as it grows and expands without the need to switch frameworks.
- How we can use reactive programming in Quarkus.

In the coming chapters, we explore the various reactive aspects of Quarkus, such as HTTP and RESTEasy Reactive in Chapter 8, and reactive data access in Chapter 9. But first, let's have a deeper look into the Mutiny reactive programming API.

CHAPTER 7

Mutiny: An Event-Driven Reactive Programming API

In Chapter 5, we introduced reactive programming and how it helps implement reactive applications. Then, in Chapter 6, we discussed how Quarkus uses Mutiny to allow implementing reactive applications. This chapter focuses on Mutiny itself.[1]

This chapter presents Mutiny's concepts and common patterns, which will help you understand the next few chapters. Mutiny is the API used for every reactive-related feature from Quarkus. You will see a lot more of it when delving into the construction of reactive applications and systems with Quarkus.

Why Another Reactive Programming Library?

That's a great question! As you have seen in Chapter 5, other popular reactive programming libraries exist. So why another one?

In the past few years, we've observed how developers developed reactive systems and used reactive programming libraries. Through this experience, we observed the challenges faced by the developers. In a nutshell, reactive programming is hard to learn and hard to read. Writing and maintaining reactive code creates a significant burden, slowing the adoption of reactive approaches.

When we look at reactive programming usage, we immediately see a steep learning curve, which makes reactive programming limited to top-notch developers. Indeed, the functional programming roots of reactive programming are both elegant and limiting at the same time. Not every developer has a functional background. We have

---

1 Quarkus integrates Mutiny, which is a separate project that can be embedded anywhere.

seen developers lost in a `map` and `flatMap` jungle, trying to find their way out of a maze made of monads.

> ## Monads?
>
> Monads come from category theory but are massively used in functional programming. A *monad* represents a form of computation. Monads enable the chaining of operations. With monads, each chained operation takes as input the output of the previous one.

Even for seasoned developers, some concepts are abstract and confusing. For example, the difference between `flatMap` and `concatMap`, two prominent operators in traditional reactive programming libraries, leads to many mistakes, including production failures. These reactive programming libraries require a functional background and a good understanding of the available operators. Mastering hundreds of operators requires time.

Another aspect is the API modeling. Existing libraries often implement Reactive Extensions (ReactX) (*http://reactivex.io/*) and provide Java classes with hundreds of methods. Even with modern IDEs, finding the right method is like looking for a needle in a haystack. It's common to scroll through the list of methods to find the right one, not even looking at the method names but at the signature, hoping for the best.

Finally, and this is a more philosophical aspect, existing reactive programming libraries do not reflect the event-driven nature of the reactive principles. While it uses data streams, which are asynchronous constructs, the API does not convey the idea of events. Reactive architectures should help to implement event-based processes, and these approaches fall short and require an additional mental-mapping between the business process and its implementation.

To address these issues, we decided to create Mutiny, a new reactive programming API focusing on readability, maintenance, and putting the notion of *event* at the center.

What Makes Mutiny Unique?

Mutiny is an intuitive, event-driven reactive programming library for Java. Mutiny uses the notion of an *event* to communicate that something happened. This event-driven nature fits perfectly the asynchronous nature of distributed systems, as described in Chapter 3. With Mutiny, you get notified when an event occurs, and you react to it. As a result, Mutiny structures itself around *on* methods such as `onItem` and `onFailure`. Each method lets you express what you want to do when you receive an event. For example, `onItem.transform` receives an item event and transforms it, or `onFailure.recoverWithItem` recovers with a fallback item after a failure event.

We wanted to address the API navigation and avoid the *one class with hundreds of methods* pattern. We introduced the notion of method *groups*. Each group handles a specific type of event. In the `onItem` group, you find all the methods to handle an individual item event, such as to transform it (`onItem.transform`), or invoke a method (`onItem.invoke`). In the `onFailure` group, you find the methods to handle failures and recover, such as `onFailure.recoverWithItem` or `onFailure.retry`. The resulting API is more readable, understandable, and navigable. As a user, you select the group and navigate across a limited number of methods.

Mutiny's API is not concise. We favor readability and understandability over conciseness. Over the years, we heard many times that reactive programming was hard and usable only by senior developers or architects. It was a key obstacle to the reactive adoption. When we designed Mutiny, we wanted to avoid creating an elitist library. This is not to "dumb down" the ideas behind reactive programming, but instead the goal is to strip away mathematical jargon.

Mutiny Usage in Quarkus

To illustrate the common patterns you will see when using Mutiny, we need an example. The application is a simple shop, handling users, products, and orders (Figure 7-1). A user creates orders that contain a list of products. How the application is implemented is not relevant for this chapter. Chapters 8 and 9 will cover how Mutiny integrates on the HTTP and data parts of Quarkus.

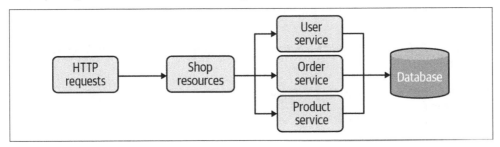

Figure 7-1. Shop application architecture

The application uses nonblocking database clients to avoid blocking when integrating with the database. Thus, the APIs of `OrderService`, `UserService`, and `ProductService` are asynchronous and use Mutiny types. `ShopResource`, implementing the HTTP API, also uses Mutiny to query the services and compose the response.

The code is available in the *chapter-7/order-example* directory, and can be started with `mvn quarkus:dev`. The code uses port 8080 to expose the HTTP API.

Uni and Multi

Mutiny provides two main classes: Uni and Multi.[2] Uni represents an asynchronous action or operation. It can emit a single item or failure, if the represented action fails. Multi represents a stream of items. It can convey multiple items, as well as a terminal failure or completion event.

Let's look at two use cases to better understand the differences. Imagine you want to retrieve a single user (represented by the UserProfile class) from the database. You will use Uni<UserProfile>, as shown in Example 7-1.

Example 7-1. Example of Uni (chapter-7/order-example/src/main/java/org/acme/ShopResource.java)

```
Uni<UserProfile> uni = users.getUserByName(name);
return uni
        .onItem().transform(user -> user.name)
        .onFailure().recoverWithItem("anonymous");
```

You can attach logic to Uni, so you can react when it emits events. In the previous snippet, when UserProfile becomes available, we extract the name of the user. If a failure happened, we recover with a fallback value. The onItem and onFailure groups form the center of the Uni API.

Multi can emit 0, 1, *n*, or an infinite number of items. It can also emit a failure, which is a terminal event. Finally, when there are no more items to emit, Multi emits the completion event. As a result, the API is slightly different. Let's now imagine we need all the users. For this case, you use Multi, as shown in Example 7-2.

Example 7-2. Example of Multi (chapter-7/order-example/src/main/java/org/acme/ShopResource.java)

```
Multi<UserProfile> users = this.users.getAllUsers();
return users
        .onItem().transform(user -> user.name);
```

As for Uni, you can handle events. In the snippet, you extract the name of each user. So, unlike Example 7-1, the code can call the transformation multiple times. While the API is somewhat similar, Multi proposes specific groups to select, drop, and collect items; see Example 7-3.

---

2 The Mutiny name comes from the contraction of Multi and Uni.

Example 7-3. Example of code using Multi (chapter-7/mutiny-examples/src/main/java/org/acme/MultiApi.java)

```
Multi<UserProfile> multi = users.getAllUsers();
multi
        .onItem().transform(user -> user.name.toLowerCase())
        .select().where(name -> name.startsWith("l"))
        .collect().asList()
        .subscribe().with(
                list -> System.out.println("User names starting with `l`" + list)
);
```

As you can see, these two types are inherently event driven. However, the set of events each handles differ. The API reflects these differences. Uni and Multi do not offer the same set of groups, as some are specific to each case (Table 7-1).

Table 7-1. Uni and Multi use cases

	Events	Use cases	Implement Reactive Streams
Uni	Item and failure	Remote invocation, asynchronous computation returning a single result	No
Multi	Item, failure, completion	Data streams, potentially unbounded (emitting an infinite number of items)	Yes

An essential aspect of Uni and Multi is their laziness. Holding a reference on Uni and Multi instances does nothing. In Example 7-3, nothing will happen until someone explicitly subscribes (and so expresses an interest), as shown in Example 7-4.

Example 7-4. Subscription to Uni and Multi (chapter-7/order-example/src/main/java/org/acme/UniMultiExample.java)

```
Uni<UserProfile> uni = users.getUserByName("leia");
Multi<UserProfile> multi = users.getAllUsers();

uni.subscribe().with(
        user -> System.out.println("User is " + user.name),
        failure -> System.out.println("D'oh! " + failure)
);

multi.subscribe().with(
        user -> System.out.println("User is " + user.name),
        failure -> System.out.println("D'oh! " + failure),
        () -> System.out.println("No more user")
);
```

To subscribe (and thereby trigger the operation) you use the subscribe group. In Quarkus, you may not need to subscribe, because if you return Uni or Multi to

Quarkus, it subscribes for you. For instance, you can have the HTTP method shown in Example 7-5.

Example 7-5. Quarkus handles the subscription for HTTP methods (chapter-7/order-example/src/main/java/org/acme/ShopResource.java)

```
@GET
@Path("/user/{name}")
public Uni<String> getUser(@PathParam("name") String name) {
    //tag::uni[]
    Uni<UserProfile> uni = users.getUserByName(name);
    return uni
            .onItem().transform(user -> user.name)
            .onFailure().recoverWithItem("anonymous");
    //end::uni[]
}
```

When a matching HTTP request arrives, Quarkus calls this method and subscribes on the produced Uni. Quarkus will write the HTTP response only when Uni emits an item or failure.

Mutiny and Flow Control

As indicated in Table 7-1, Multi implements the Reactive Streams backpressure protocol. In other words, it implements the Reactive Streams Publisher interface, and Multi's consumers are the Reactive Streams Subscriber. That's not the case for Uni.

When dealing with a stream sending multiple items, so a Multi, having backpressure support makes sense. Under the hood, the subscriber can control the flow and the pace by requesting items when it can handle them. It avoids flooding the subscribers with too many items.

When dealing with Uni, subscribing to it is enough to express your interest and capacity to handle the emitted item. There's no need to send another request signal to express your interest.

But, as you have seen in Chapter 5, not every stream can support flow control. Streams representing events from the physical world, such as user clicks or time, can't be slowed. In this case, there is a risk of sending too many events to the subscriber. That's why Multi provides the onOverflow group. This group monitors the number of items emitted by the upstream source as well as the number of items requested by the downstream subscriber. When there are more incoming items than requests, Multi emits an *overflow* event. The onOverflow group allows configuring the desired behavior when this happens.

To illustrate this, let's imagine a stream producing product recommendations. Every second, it sends a new recommended product. But time cannot be slowed, so we cannot apply backpressure. If the downstream can't keep up, we would have an overflow. To avoid that, if we can't emit the tick item because of the lack of request, we just drop it, as shown in Example 7-6.

Example 7-6. Handle overflow with Multi (chapter-7/order-example/src/main/java/org/acme/ShopResource.java)

```java
public Multi<Product> getRecommendations() {
    return Multi.createFrom().ticks().every(Duration.ofSeconds(1))
            .onOverflow().drop()
            .onItem().transformToUniAndConcatenate(
                x -> products.getRecommendedProduct());
}
```

The onOverflow group provides other possibilities, such as buffering the items.

Observing Events

Once you have a Uni or Multi instance, it's natural to observe the events emitted by these instances. For each type of event, an invoke method is called when it sees a matching event; see Example 7-7.

Example 7-7. Observe events (chapter-7/mutiny-examples/src/main/java/org/acme/MultiObserve.java)

```java
multi
        .onSubscribe().invoke(sub -> System.out.println("Subscribed!"))
        .onCancellation().invoke(() -> System.out.println("Cancelled"))
        .onItem().invoke(s -> System.out.println("Item: " + s))
        .onFailure().invoke(f -> System.out.println("Failure: " + f))
        .onCompletion().invoke(() -> System.out.println("Completed!"))
        .subscribe().with(
            item -> System.out.println("Received: " + item)
);
```

The invoke method does not modify the event; you observe it without changing it. The downstream receives the same event you did. This method is handy when needed to implement side effects or trace your code. For example, we can use it to log when a new user is created or if the creation failed (see Example 7-8).

Example 7-8. Observe Uni events (chapter-7/order-example/src/main/java/org/acme/ShopResource.java)

```
@POST
@Path("/users/{name}")
public Uni<Long> createUser(@QueryParam("name") String name) {
    return users.createUser(name)
            .onItem().invoke(
                l -> System.out.println("User created: " + name + ", id: " + l))
            .onFailure().invoke(t -> System.out.println(
                    "Cannot create user " + name + ": " + t.getMessage())
            );
}
```

If you have the application running, you can run this code by using Example 7-9.

Example 7-9. Invoke the users endpoint

```
> curl -X POST http://localhost:8080/shop/users?name=neo
```

Transforming Events

Most of the time, we need to transform the event. Let's first see how we can transform events synchronously. You receive the event, transform it, and produce the result as a new event. For each type of event, a `transform` method is called when it sees a matching event, as shown in Example 7-10.

Example 7-10. Transform events (chapter-7/mutiny-examples/src/main/java/org/acme/MultiTransform.java)

```
Multi<String> transformed = multi
        .onItem().transform(String::toUpperCase)
        .onFailure().transform(MyBusinessException::new);
```

Unlike `invoke`, `transform` produces a new event. It invokes the passed function and sends the result to the downstream subscriber.

The synchronous nature of `transform` is important. After receiving the event, `transform` calls the transformation logic and emits the result downstream. If the transformation logic takes a long time to complete, `transform` waits until the logic terminates. So, use `transform` when the transformation is fast enough.

For example, the following method retrieves the list of products, capitalizes their names consistently, and builds the representation (`ProductModel`). For each product, `transform` extracts the name and applies the transformation. This synchronous process is fast. It emits the result downstream immediately, as shown in Example 7-11.

Example 7-11. Transform products (chapter-7/order-example/src/main/java/org/acme/ShopResource.java)

```
@GET
@Path("/products")
public Multi<ProductModel> products() {
    return products.getAllProducts()
            .onItem().transform(p -> captializeAllFirstLetter(p.name))
            .onItem().transform(ProductModel::new);
}
```

Chaining Asynchronous Actions

The `transform` method can process events synchronously, but what if we need to invoke an asynchronous process? Imagine that you receive an event, and need to invoke a remote service or interact with a database. You can't use `transform`, as these methods should be asynchronous (otherwise, they would block, which would be against the reactive principles). You need to *wait* until the asynchronous computation completes.

How can we express this using the Mutiny lingo? It would mean transforming an event, but unlike `transform` returning a *plain* result, it returns an asynchronous structure: another `Uni` or `Multi`. What does that look like? Take a look at Example 7-12.

Example 7-12. Chain asynchronous actions (chapter-7/mutiny-examples/src/main/java/org/acme/UniTransformAsync.java)

```
uni
    .onItem().transformToUni(item -> callMyRemoteService(item))
    .subscribe().with(s -> System.out.println("Received: " + s));

uni
    .onItem().transformToMulti(s -> getAMulti(s))
    .subscribe().with(
        s -> System.out.println("Received item: " + s),
        () -> System.out.println("Done!")
);
```

`transformToUni` and `transformToMulti` provide the ability to produce a `Uni` or a `Multi` instance.[3] When you receive an item, Mutiny invokes the function returning `Uni` or `Multi`. Then, it emits the events downstream from this `Uni` or `Multi`. In Example 7-13, we retrieve the list of orders for a specific user (identified by its name).

---

3 The `transformToUni` and `transformToMulti` operations are generally called `flatMap` in traditional reactive programming libraries.

Example 7-13. Retrieve order for a specific user (chapter-7/order-example/src/main/java/org/acme/ShopResource.java)

```
@GET
@Path("/orders/{user}")
public Multi<Order> getOrdersForUser(@PathParam("user") String username) {
    return users.getUserByName(username)
            .onItem().transformToMulti(user -> orders.getOrderForUser(user));
}
```

This code retrieves the user, and when it receives the user, the code then retrieves the orders. The `getOrderForUser` method returns `Multi<Order>`, so the result is `Multi<Order>`.

If you look carefully at the preceding code, you will say, "Hey! You're forgetting something! How does that work when we chain from a `Multi` and not a `Uni`?" You are right; we need to discuss the `Multi` case. How would you transform each item of a `Multi` into another `Uni` or `Multi`?

Let's illustrate the problem with an example. Imagine you need to retrieve the orders for all the users. So, instead of having the username as in Example 7-13, we need to retrieve all the users, and for each retrieve the orders. Example 7-14 shows the resulting code.

Example 7-14. Retrieve the orders for each user using concatenate *(chapter-7/order-example/src/main/java/org/acme/ShopResource.java)*

```
@GET
@Path("/orders")
public Multi<Order> getOrdersPerUser() {
    return users.getAllUsers()
            .onItem().transformToMultiAndConcatenate(
                user -> orders.getOrderForUser(user));

}
```

You can immediately spot a difference. Instead of `transformToMulti`, we have `transformToMultiAndConcatenate`. But why *AndConcatenate*? It relates to the order of the item sent downstream. It gets the `Multi` for the first user, emits the items downstream, and then handles the one for the next user, and so on. In other words, it takes the `Multi` instances one by one and concatenates them. This approach preserves the order, but also limits the concurrency as we retrieve the orders, one user at a time.

If you don't need to preserve the order, you can use the `transformToMultiAndMerge` method.[4] In this case, it invokes `getOrderForUser` concurrently. It merges the items from the resulting `Multi` as they come, and so may interleave the orders from different users (Example 7-15).

Example 7-15. Retrieve the orders for each user by using merge

```
@GET
@Path("/orders")
public Multi<Order> getOrdersPerUser() {
    return users.getAllUsers()
        .onItem().transformToMultiAndMerge(user -> orders.getOrderForUser(user));
}
```

 chapter-7/mutiny-examples/src/main/java/org/acme/MultiTransformAsync.java lets you execute these examples. They highlight the ordering difference.

Recovering from Failure

As we said, failures are inevitable. We must handle them.

What can be done in such an unfortunate case? In the Mutiny world, failures are events. So, you can observe and process them. You can use `invoke` or `transform` as for any other events. But you can also handle the failure and recover gracefully.

One of the most common approaches consists of recovering with a specific fallback item. Let's imagine we want to create a new user, but the insertion fails because the name needs to be unique. We can return a message indicating the failure, as shown in Example 7-16.

Example 7-16. Recover from failure with a fallback item (chapter-7/order-example/src/main/java/org/acme/ShopResource.java)

```
public Uni<String> addUser(String name) {
    return users.createUser(name)
        .onItem().transform(id -> "New User " + name + " inserted")
        .onFailure().recoverWithItem(
            failure -> "User not inserted: " + failure.getMessage());
}
```

---

4 `transformToMultiAndConcatenate` is called `concatMap` in traditional reactive programming libraries. `transformToMultiAndMerge` is generally named `flatMap`.

While a failure is an event, it's a terminal one. That's not a problem if you are dealing with Uni; you won't get the item, just the failure. So, the Uni would replace the failure with the fallback item. With Multi, you won't get any more items after the failure. The recovery emits the fallback item followed by the completion event.

Another common possibility is to retry. Remember, retry only if your system can endure it. In this case (and only in this case), you can retry. Retry resubscribing to the upstream source, as shown in Example 7-17.

Example 7-17. Retry on failure

```
public Uni<String> addUser(String name) {
    return users.createUser(name)
            .onItem().transform(id -> "New User " + name + " inserted")
            .onFailure().retry().atMost(3);
}
```

You can limit the number of retries or introduce a delay between them by using atMost and configuring the backoff; see Example 7-18.

Example 7-18. Retry on failure at most n times with delay between attempts (chapter-7/ mutiny-examples/src/main/java/org/acme/UniFailure.java)

```
Uni<String> retryAtMost = uni
        .onFailure().retry()
            .withBackOff(Duration.ofSeconds(3))
            .atMost(5);
```

> *chapter-7/mutiny-examples/src/main/java/org/acme/UniFailure.java* lets you execute these examples to help you understand the various possibilities.

The onFailure group contains a lot more possibilities.

Combining and Joining Items

The next common pattern consists of combining the items from multiple upstream sources. For example, imagine we want to generate recommendations. We would pick a random user and a recommended product. We could sequentially execute both, but they are independent, so we can execute them concurrently, and when we have both results, generate the recommendation (Example 7-19).

Example 7-19. Combine `Uni` instances (chapter-7/order-example/src/main/java/org/ acme/ShopResource.java)

```
@GET
@Path("/random-recommendation")
public Uni<String> getRecommendation() {
    Uni<UserProfile> uni1 = users.getRandomUser();
    Uni<Product> uni2 = products.getRecommendedProduct();
    return Uni.combine().all().unis(uni1, uni2).asTuple()
            .onItem().transform(tuple -> "Hello " + tuple.getItem1().name +
                    ", we recommend you "
                    + tuple.getItem2().name);
}
```

This snippet gets two `Uni`s. The first one retrieves a random user, and the second one gets a recommended product. Then we combine both and aggregate their results into a tuple. When both operations complete, Mutiny collects the items into a tuple and emits this tuple downstream. We can transform it and generate the recommendation. If the `Uni` fails, it propagates the failure downstream.

Combining `Uni` operations is common when we want to execute operations concurrently and join their results. But we can do the same with `Multi` too. In this case, we associate the items from several `Multi` operations. For example, we can generate a stream of recommendations, associating random users and recommended products, as shown in Example 7-20.

Example 7-20. Join `Multis` (chapter-7/order-example/src/main/java/org/acme/ ShopResource.java)

```
@GET
@Path("/random-recommendations")
public Multi<String> getRandomRecommendations() {
    Multi<UserProfile> u = Multi.createFrom().
        ticks().every(Duration.ofSeconds(1)).onOverflow().drop()
        .onItem().transformToUniAndConcatenate(
            x -> users.getRandomUser());
    Multi<Product> p = Multi.createFrom().ticks().every(
        Duration.ofSeconds(1)).onOverflow().drop()
        .onItem().transformToUniAndConcatenate(
            x -> products.getRecommendedProduct());

    return Multi.createBy().combining().streams(u, p).asTuple()
            .onItem().transform(tuple -> "Hello "
                    + tuple.getItem1().name
                        + ", we recommend you "
                    + tuple.getItem2().name);
}
```

When joining `Multi`s, the resulting stream completes as soon as one of the joined `Multi` sends the completion event. Indeed, it won't be possible to combine the items anymore.

Selecting Items

When dealing with `Multi`, you may want to select the items to propagate downstream and discard the others. For example, we can retrieve all the orders and then select only the orders containing more than three products (see Example 7-21).

Example 7-21. Select items (chapter-7/order-example/src/main/java/org/acme/OrderService.java)

```java
public Multi<Order> getLargeOrders() {
    return getAllOrders()
            .select().where(order -> order.products.size() > 3);
}
```

The `select.where` operation lets you select the item. For each item, the operation calls the predicates and decides whether the item should be propagated downstream. It drops the items not passing the predicate.

An asynchronous variant of the `select.when` operator is also available. It lets you select the items to keep, using an asynchronous predicate. Example 7-22 shows how to select the orders for a specific username. For each order, the code retrieves the associated user and selects only when the username matches.

Example 7-22. Select items with an asynchronous predicate (chapter-7/order-example/src/main/java/org/acme/OrderService.java)

```java
public Multi<Order> getOrdersForUsername(String username) {
    return getAllOrders()
            .select().when(order ->
                    users.getUserByName(username)
                        .onItem().transform(u -> u.name.equalsIgnoreCase(username))
            );
}
```

Selection can also drop any duplicate items. In Example 7-23, we list the ordered products.

Example 7-23. Select distinct items (chapter-7/order-example/src/main/java/org/acme/ProductService.java)

```java
public Multi<Product> getAllOrderedProducts() {
    return orders.getAllOrders()
            .onItem().transformToIterable(order -> order.products)
            .select().distinct();
}
```

For each order, we retrieve the products and generate `Multi<Product>`. Then, we select only distinct items, dropping duplicates. Note that we can't use `distinct` on unbounded streams, as it needs to keep in memory all the already seen items.

In addition to selection, Mutiny provides a `skip` group. It provides the opposite functionality, and so allows skipping items matching predicates and repetitions.

Collecting Items

Finally, when dealing with bounded `Multi`, you may want to accumulate the items into a list or a collection. The resulting structure is emitted when the `Multi` completes.

Let's reuse the previous example. We know that the set of ordered products is bounded, so, we can collect the product into a list, as shown in Example 7-24.

Example 7-24. Collect items into a list (chapter-7/order-example/src/main/java/org/acme/ProductService.java)

```java
public Uni<List<Product>> getAllOrderedProductsAsList() {
    return getAllOrderedProducts()
            .collect().asList();
}
```

Note that the method returns `Uni<List<Product>>`. The method emits the list (containing the products) when the `Multi` returned by `getAllOrderedProducts` completes.

The `collect` group provides other methods to aggregate items into maps, collections, or events, using your own collector (Example 7-25).

Example 7-25. Other collection methods

```java
Uni<List<String>> itemsAsList = multi.collect().asList();
Uni<Map<String, String>> itemsAsMap = multi.collect().asMap(item ->
    getKeyForItem(item));
Uni<Long> count = multi.collect().with(Collectors.counting());
```

Summary

This chapter was a brief introduction to the Mutiny API. It did not provide a complete overview of the possibilities but presented key patterns we will use later in this book. Remember:

- Mutiny is an event-driven reactive programming API.
- You observe and transform events.
- Mutiny provides two main classes: `Uni` and `Multi`.
- The Mutiny API is navigable and offers you guidance to pick the right operator.

With this in mind, we can now start using the reactive services and facilities offered by Quarkus.

## CHAPTER 8

HTTP with Reactive in Mind

Even when building a reactive system, HTTP is unavoidable. HTTP is a prevalent protocol, and REST, for instance, is a well-known approach to designing services and APIs. The problem with HTTP, as mentioned in Chapter 4, is the request/response interaction scheme that leads to undesirable time coupling. Also, to implement space decoupling, you often need proxies that would route the requests or advanced service discovery and load-balancing mechanism.

But let's face it: we need to be pragmatic, and HTTP has plenty of great features. We recommend using HTTP at the edge of your system (the places interacting with external entities), as shown in Figure 8-1 For example, HTTP is often used on the front tier to expose an API easily consumable by other external services. Besides, we often use HTTP at the various integration points with other external services, such as consuming services exposed using a REST API.

Integrating HTTP should not prevent or limit the responsiveness of the reactive system you are building. As a consequence, we need to implement this integration carefully. It's not rare to see a system using a so-called asynchronous HTTP client, which can do more harm than provide benefits as it may rely on a hidden thread pool.

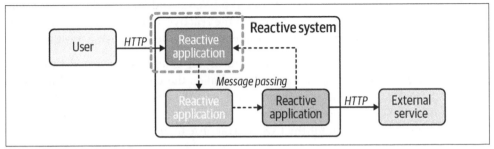

Figure 8-1. Using HTTP at the edge of a reactive system

This chapter explores the features Quarkus offers to expose HTTP endpoints and the ways we can implement these endpoints. In Figure 8-1, this part is circled with a dotted line; the right side, HTTP service consumption, is covered in Chapter 12.

The Journey of an HTTP Request

To understand the benefits of using Quarkus to handle HTTP in a reactive way, we need to look under the hood. As shown in Chapter 6, Quarkus is based on a reactive engine, so every facet of Quarkus benefits from this engine to provide asynchronous and nonblocking features. Naturally, that also includes HTTP. However, while we implemented HTTP endpoints in the previous Quarkus applications, the code was not benefiting from all the features that engine provides. Let's see how Quarkus handles HTTP requests and where we can unleash the power of the reactive engine.

To handle HTTP requests, you need an HTTP server. This server listens on a specific port (8080, in the case of Quarkus) and waits for incoming connections. When the server receives a new connection, it reads the frame and assembles the HTTP request. Typically, the server parses the HTTP method (for example, GET or POST), the invoked path, the body, and so on. Several frames can compose an HTTP request, and large bodies are split among multiple frames.

Once the HTTP request is assembled, Quarkus determines how to handle it. It checks for *interceptors* (to handle security or logging concerns) and looks for the endpoint that can process the request. This lookup is based on the path, but can also include content type negotiation. Once the endpoint method is found, Quarkus invokes the method, and it's up to the method to process the request.

Let's imagine that we call a synchronous method and that the result of the method is the payload of the HTTP response. Quarkus captures that result and builds an HTTP response. It then writes the response into the appropriate HTTP connection, encoding content accordingly.

So far, so good—but not very reactive, right? One of the essential pieces in this exchange is the HTTP service. The HTTP server used by Quarkus is nonblocking, highly efficient, and concurrent. It's powered by Vert.x and handles the HTTP interaction by using the I/O thread. So, it follows the reactive approach we explained previously in Figure 4-1 and can handle multiple HTTP connections using few threads.

Once this HTTP server receives a request, the server delegates that request to Quarkus to handle the lookup. This *routing* layer builds the chain of responsibility that handles the request (typically the interceptors and the endpoint) and invokes it. In the case of a JAX-RS endpoint, the routing layer would delegate the lookup to the JAX-RS framework and wait for the JAX-RS response to be computed.

But, wait—are we still on the I/O thread? If so, how can we prevent the user endpoint from blocking the I/O thread inadvertently? Fortunately, Quarkus has a routing layer that decides how the request must be handled (Figure 8-2).

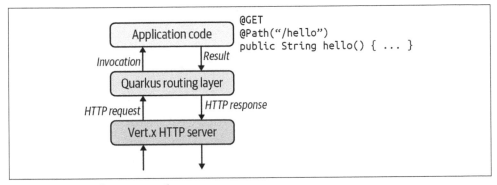

Figure 8-2. Quarkus routing layer

In the previous Quarkus application we used in Chapter 2, the requests were always dispatched on a worker thread, avoiding any risk of blocking. It was not ideal in terms of reactive principles. Let's see what Quarkus can do to improve this situation.

Say Hello to RESTEasy Reactive!

In the previous application we used in Chapter 2, we relied on *classic* RESTEasy, which follows the old-school model of associating a thread to each request. However, as we have seen before, that model does not scale and lacks responsiveness. Fortunately, Quarkus offers an alternative: *RESTEasy Reactive*. It's the same development model, except that this variant is aware of the reactive engine and relies on it.

Let's have a look and experiment with the features offered by RESTEasy Reactive. Go to *https://code.quarkus.io* and select the following extensions:

- RESTEasy Reactive
- RESTEasy Reactive Jackson

Then, click "Generate your application" and unzip it.

The reactive version is quite similar to the classic RESTEasy version. Example 8-1 shows the generated HTTP endpoint. You may notice the introduction of the `@Non Blocking` annotation. This is one of the essential differences with classic RESTEasy; RESTEasy Reactive can dispatch the requests on the I/O thread.

Example 8-1. An HTTP endpoint using RESTEasy Reactive

```
package org.acme;

import io.smallrye.common.annotation.NonBlocking;

import javax.ws.rs.GET;
import javax.ws.rs.Path;
import javax.ws.rs.Produces;
import javax.ws.rs.core.MediaType;

@Path("/hello-resteasy-reactive")
public class ReactiveGreetingResource {

    @GET
    @Produces(MediaType.TEXT_PLAIN)
    @NonBlocking
    public String hello() {
        return "Hello RESTEasy Reactive";
    }
}
```

Let's run this application using mvn quarkus:dev, and point your browser to *http://localhost:8080/hello-resteasy-reactive*. You should see this:

```
Hello RESTEasy Reactive
```

OK, well, that's nothing fancy, and not very attractive so far.

First, let's enhance our endpoint and, in addition to Hello RESTEasy Reactive, add the name of the thread handling the request (Example 8-2).

Example 8-2. Requests are processed on the I/O thread

```
@GET
@Produces(MediaType.TEXT_PLAIN)
@NonBlocking
public String hello() {
    return "Hello RESTEasy Reactive from " + Thread.currentThread().getName();
}
```

Because Quarkus runs in dev mode, there is no need to restart the application, as it will auto-update itself. Refresh your browser and you should see something like Example 8-3.

Example 8-3. Output of the application indicating the thread used for the processing

```
Hello RESTEasy Reactive vert.x-eventloop-thread-5
```

The endpoint method is invoked from the I/O thread![1] Much more reactive, but… wait…how do we handle blocking logic now? With RESTEasy Reactive, you can use the @NonBlocking and @Blocking annotations to indicate on which thread you want the request to be handled.[2] Let's illustrate this. Create another endpoint method with the same code as the hello method, but target a different path and without the @NonBlocking annotation, as illustrated in Example 8-4.

Example 8-4. Requests are processed on a worker thread when @Blocking is used

```
@GET
@Produces(MediaType.TEXT_PLAIN)
@Path("/blocking")
public String helloBlocking() {
    return "Hello RESTEasy Reactive from " + Thread.currentThread().getName();
}
```

Refresh your browser again, and voilà:

```
Hello RESTEasy Reactive executor-thread-198
```

What Happens If I Block the I/O Thread Inadvertently?

Quarkus will warn you if you attempt to block an I/O thread for too long or if you try to execute a blocking operation from an I/O thread.

RESTEasy Reactive proposes a set of defaults to avoid having to use the @NonBlocking annotation:

- Method returning an object, such as String in the previous example, is executed on a worker thread, except if the @NonBlocking annotation is used. In this case, the method uses an I/O thread.

- Method returning Uni is executed on an I/O thread, except if the method is annotated with @Blocking. In this case, the method uses a worker thread.

- Method returning Multi is executed on an I/O thread, except if the method is annotated with @Blocking. In this case, the method uses a worker thread.

---

1 Vert.x event loop threads are I/O threads.

2 Methods returning instances of Multi or Uni are automatically considered nonblocking if not specified otherwise.

What's the Benefit?

By dispatching the request on the I/O thread, you are allowing the application to handle the request in a reactive manner. You are not only embracing the reactive principles, but also increasing the throughput of your application.

Let's have a deeper look at the throughput difference. We will compare *classic* and *reactive* RESTEasy by using wrk (*https://oreil.ly/kkvBU*). This benchmark is far from being irreproachable (we run everything on the same machine); it's there just to illustrate the benefits. Also note that the result may differ from machine to machine. The benchmark is just about calling a *hello* endpoint concurrently and measuring the response time. In *chapter-8/simple-benchmark/classic*, you get the version using RESTEasy *classic*. In *chapter-8/simple-benchmark/reactive*, you get the RESTEasy *reactive* variant.

First, go into *chapter-8/simple-benchmark/classic*, build the application using mvn package, and run it using *java -jar target/quarkus-app/quarkus-run.jar*. Once the application is started in another terminal, run Example 8-5.

Example 8-5. Use wrk to stress the application endpoint

```
> wrk -t 10 -c50 -d40s http://localhost:8080/hello
Running 40s test @ http://localhost:8080/hello
```

This command hammers the *hello* endpoint for 40 seconds, using 10 threads and 50 connections. This is a simple test, but it will give us an idea of the benefits. You should get a report with the result in the terminal. For us, we got the result in Example 8-6.

Example 8-6. Benchmark result

```
  Thread Stats   Avg      Stdev     Max    +/- Stdev
    Latency    49.35ms   83.26ms 643.82ms   84.52%
    Req/Sec     2.97k     1.81k   10.66k    64.59%
  1167359 requests in 40.07s, 92.40MB read
Requests/sec:  29132.34
Transfer/sec:     2.31MB
```

Close the application, and build and run the version using RESTEasy Reactive, as shown in Example 8-7.

Example 8-7. Build and run a reactive application

```
> cd chapter-8/simple-benchmark/reactive
> mvn package
> java -jar target/quarkus-app/quarkus-run.jar
```

Run the same `wrk` command in another terminal (Example 8-8).

Example 8-8. Use wrk to stress the application endpoint

```
> wrk -t 10 -c50 -d40s http://localhost:8080/hello
Running 40s test @ http://localhost:8080/hello
  10 threads and 50 connections
  Thread Stats   Avg      Stdev     Max   +/- Stdev
    Latency   600.42us  357.14us  26.17ms   98.24%
    Req/Sec     8.44k    606.47    15.90k    93.71%
  3364365 requests in 40.10s, 221.39MB read
Requests/sec:  83895.54
Transfer/sec:      5.52MB
```

Now, let's compare the number of requests per second: 29,000 for classic RESTEasy versus 84,000 for RESTEasy Reactive. RESTEasy Reactive provides almost three times more throughput.

So far, we compared a reactive framework against a blocking one. But what about the @Blocking annotation, which instructs Quarkus to call the endpoint with a worker thread? Would @Blocking reduce the performance gain? Well, let's test it. In *chapter-8/simple-benchmark/reactive-blocking*, a variant of the application uses RESTEasy Reactive but without the @NonBlocking annotation. So, it invokes the method on a worker thread. Let's run our benchmark against that version, as shown in Example 8-9.

Example 8-9. Build and run reactive blocking applications

```
> cd chapter-8/simple-benchmark/reactive-blocking
> mvn package
> java -jar target/quarkus-app/quarkus-run.jar
```

In another terminal, run the `wrk` command (Example 8-10).

Example 8-10. Stress the application endpoint by using wrk

```
> wrk -t 10 -c50 -d40s http://localhost:8080/hello
Running 40s test @ http://localhost:8080/hello
  10 threads and 50 connections
  Thread Stats   Avg      Stdev     Max   +/- Stdev
    Latency    35.99ms   66.23ms 783.62ms   85.87%
    Req/Sec     5.22k     3.53k   22.22k    71.81%
  2016035 requests in 40.05s, 132.66MB read
Requests/sec:  50339.41
Transfer/sec:      3.31MB
```

Even when using a worker thread, the application serves 50,000 requests per second. That's more than 1.5 times the throughput of RESTEasy classic.

RESTEasy Reactive offers a solid and highly concurrent alternative to the traditional one-thread-per-request approach. And, thanks to the @Blocking and @NonBlocking annotations, you can even use it when dealing with asynchronous and synchronous logic. At the end of this chapter, you will see how RESTEasy Reactive produces a reactive score of your endpoint. Next, we will look at this integration because returning Hello is nice, but it's rarely enough.

Asynchronous Endpoints Returning Uni

One way to avoid the temptation to write blocking code is to design your HTTP endpoint method to return a Uni instance. Uni represents an asynchronous computation that may not have produced a result yet. When an endpoint returns a Uni instance, Quarkus subscribes to it, and when the Uni emits the result, it writes this result into the HTTP response. If, unfortunately, the Uni emits a failure, the HTTP response conveys that failure as an HTTP internal server error, bad request, or not found error, depending on the failure. While *waiting* for the outcome of the Uni, the thread can be used to handle other requests.

There's no need to use @NonBlocking when returning a Uni. RESTEasy Reactive recognizes it and automatically considers it nonblocking. Let's see how this works in practice. In this example, we will use the Vert.x filesystem asynchronous API. Of course, Quarkus offers other more convenient ways to serve files, but this is just to illustrate the purpose.

> You can find the related code in the *chapter-8/mutiny-integration-examples* directory.

As we said in Chapter 6, Quarkus is based on Vert.x. If you add the quarkus-vertx extension, you get access to the *managed* Vert.x instance, as shown in Example 8-11.

Example 8-11. Inject the Vert.x instance

```
@Inject Vertx vertx;
```

Be sure to import io.vertx.mutiny.core.Vertx. Note that we inject the Mutiny variant of Vert.x. This variant exposes all the Vert.x API using Mutiny, which is convenient in Quarkus. So, reading a file can be done as in Example 8-12.

Example 8-12. Read a file with the Vert.x filesystem API

```
Uni<String> uni = vertx.fileSystem().readFile(path)
        .onItem().transform(buffer -> buffer.toString("UTF-8"));
```

Accessing the filesystem is, in most cases, a blocking operation. However, thanks to the Vert.x API, we get a nonblocking variant, already providing a Uni instance! But it's a Uni<Buffer>, and to get String, we need to transform the emitted result.[3] In other words, Example 8-12 reads a file specified with a *path*. This operation returns Uni. When the content is ready to be consumed, Uni emits Buffer as an item, and we transform Buffer into a String object. All this, without blocking the thread!

But that's not all! We can return that Uni directly and let Quarkus subscribe and handle the heavy lifting for us, as illustrated in Example 8-13.

Example 8-13. Return a file read with the Vert.x filesystem API (chapter-8/mutiny-integration-examples/src/main/java/org/acme/MutinyExampleResource.java)

```
package org.acme.reactive;

import io.smallrye.mutiny.Uni;
import io.vertx.core.file.FileSystemException;
import io.vertx.mutiny.core.Vertx;
import org.jboss.resteasy.reactive.server.ServerExceptionMapper;

import javax.inject.Inject;
import javax.ws.rs.GET;
import javax.ws.rs.Path;
import javax.ws.rs.core.Response;
import java.time.Duration;

@Path("/")
public class MutinyExampleResource {

    @Inject
    Vertx vertx;

    @GET
    @Path("/lorem")
    public Uni<String> getLoremIpsum() {
        return vertx.fileSystem().readFile("lorem.txt")
                .onItem().transform(buffer -> buffer.toString("UTF-8"));
    }

}
```

---

3 Buffer is a convenient way to represent a bag of bytes in Vert.x.

Quarkus subscribes to the returned Uni and sends the emitted item to the HTTP response. If the Uni emits a failure, it sends an HTTP error.

Let's see this in action. Start the application, located in *chapter-8/mutiny-integration-examples*, with `mvn quarkus:dev` and invoke the endpoint by using Example 8-14.

Example 8-14. Retrieve the lorem file

```
> curl http://localhost:8080/lorem
Lorem ipsum dolor sit amet, consectetur adipiscing elit, sed do eiusmod tempor
incididunt ut labore et dolore magna aliqua. Ut enim ad minim veniam, quis
nostrud exercitation ullamco laboris nisi ut aliquip ex ea commodo consequat.
Duis aute irure dolor in reprehenderit in voluptate velit esse cillum dolore
eu fugiat nulla pariatur. Excepteur sint occaecat cupidatat non proident,
sunt in culpa qui officia deserunt mollit anim id est laborum.
```

Most Quarkus APIs have reactive variants using Mutiny, such as the mailer service, database access (we will look at Hibernate Reactive in Chapter 9), messaging, templating, gRPC, and so on. Besides, the Mutiny variant of Vert.x gives you access to a vast reactive ecosystem ranging from network protocols (DNS, TCP, UDP, HTTP), to messaging (Apache Kafka, AMQP, RabbitMQ, MQTT) via data accesses and web utilities.

Dealing with Failure and Customizing the Response

Just because a method is asynchronous doesn't mean it cannot fail. For example, the file we are trying to serve may not be available, so we need to handle such a failure. But, first, let's see what Quarkus does by default.

Let's add an example with a failing operation with the following endpoint (as shown in Example 8-15).

Example 8-15. Read a missing file with the Vert.x filesystem API (chapter-8/mutiny-integration-examples/src/main/java/org/acme/MutinyExampleResource.java)

```
@GET
@Path("/missing")
public Uni<String> getMissingFile() {
    return vertx.fileSystem().readFile("Oops.txt")
            .onItem().transform(buffer -> buffer.toString("UTF-8"));
}
```

Invoke the endpoint by using Example 8-16.

Example 8-16. Propagation of failures

```
> curl -f -v http://localhost:8080/missing
*   Trying ::1...
* TCP_NODELAY set
* Connection failed
* connect to ::1 port 8080 failed: Connection refused
*   Trying 127.0.0.1...
* TCP_NODELAY set
* Connected to localhost (127.0.0.1) port 8080 (#0)
> GET /missing HTTP/1.1
> Host: localhost:8080
> User-Agent: curl/7.64.1
> Accept: */*
>
* The requested URL returned error: 500 Internal Server Error
* Closing connection 0
curl: (22) The requested URL returned error: 500 Internal Server Error
```

Quarkus returns 500 Internal Server Error. This makes sense; there's clearly a bug in our code.

Let's see what we can do. As you have seen in Chapter 7, Uni provides failure-handling capabilities that we can use here. Example 8-17 shows how we can recover with a simple message.

Example 8-17. Recover on failure (chapter-8/mutiny-integration-examples/src/main/java/org/acme/MutinyExampleResource.java)

```
@GET
@Path("/recover")
public Uni<String> getMissingFileAndRecover() {
    return vertx.fileSystem().readFile("Oops.txt")
            .onItem().transform(buffer -> buffer.toString("UTF-8"))
            .onFailure().recoverWithItem("Oops!");
}
```

This returns oops, as you can see in Example 8-18.

Example 8-18. Failure recovery

```
> curl http://localhost:8080/recover
oops!
```

We can also customize the HTTP response and return a proper 404 Not Found error (Example 8-19).

Example 8-19. Response customization (chapter-8/mutiny-integration-examples/src/main/java/org/acme/MutinyExampleResource.java)

```
@GET
@Path("/404")
public Uni<Response> get404() {
    return vertx.fileSystem().readFile("Oops.txt")
            .onItem().transform(buffer -> buffer.toString("UTF-8"))
            .onItem().transform(content -> Response.ok(content).build())
            .onFailure().recoverWithItem(
                    Response.status(Response.Status.NOT_FOUND).build());
}
```

The signature of the endpoint is a bit different. Instead of returning Uni<String>, we return Uni<Response>. The emitted item (Response) represents the HTTP response we want to send back. In Example 8-20, we set that on any failure we return a 404 Not Found.

Example 8-20. Customize the HTTP response

```
 curl -v http://localhost:8080/404
*   Trying ::1...
* TCP_NODELAY set
* Connection failed
* connect to ::1 port 8080 failed: Connection refused
*   Trying 127.0.0.1...
* TCP_NODELAY set
* Connected to localhost (127.0.0.1) port 8080 (#0)
> GET /404 HTTP/1.1
> Host: localhost:8080
> User-Agent: curl/7.64.1
> Accept: */*
>
< HTTP/1.1 404 Not Found
< content-length: 0
<
* Connection #0 to host localhost left intact
* Closing connection 0
```

 You can use Response to customize the response—for example, by adding headers.

An alternative is to register an exception mapper for the FileSystemException, as illustrated in Example 8-21.

Example 8-21. Declare an exception mapper (chapter-8/mutiny-integration-examples/src/main/java/org/acme/MutinyExampleResource.java)

```
@ServerExceptionMapper
public Response mapFileSystemException(FileSystemException ex) {
    return Response.status(Response.Status.NOT_FOUND)
            .entity(ex.getMessage())
            .build();
}
```

With such a mapper defined, Quarkus captures the failure emitted by `Uni` and invokes the mapper to produce the appropriate `Response`.

And what about time-out? While the chances of having a time-out when reading from the filesystem are relatively low, it becomes much more critical when dealing with a remote service. Handle time-out as shown in Example 8-22.

Example 8-22. Handling timeout

```
return vertx.fileSystem().readFile("slow.txt")
        .onItem().transform(buffer -> buffer.toString("UTF-8"))
        .ifNoItem().after(Duration.ofSeconds(1)).fail();
```

You can specify the exception to emit in this case, and if you need, register an exception mapper.

When implementing an HTTP endpoint with RESTEasy Reactive, ask yourself if you can use the Mutiny integration to compose asynchronous actions and fully benefit from the performance and efficiency of the reactive engine of Quarkus. Of course, you can use `@Blocking`, but there is a cost to consider.

Streaming Data

Returning `Uni` is perfect when we have a single piece of data to send into the response. But what about *streams*?

In addition to `Uni`, Quarkus lets you return a `Multi` instance. Quarkus subscribes to the returned `Multi` and writes the items emitted by this `Multi`, one by one, into the HTTP response. It's an efficient way to deal with streams and limit the application's memory consumption, as you don't have to buffer the entire content in memory. Indeed, Quarkus uses HTTP *chunked* responses by setting the `Transfer-Encoding` header (*https://oreil.ly/QcHFs*) when dealing with `Multi`. That feature from HTTP allows writing into the response chunk after chunk.

As with `Uni`, a method retuning a `Multi` is considered nonblocking by default. There's no need to use `@NonBlocking`.

But when returning `Multi`, we need to ask ourselves: What envelope do we want? Do we want to stream bytes? Do we want to send a JSON array instead? Or maybe individual events using Server-Sent Events? Quarkus supports all these, and that's what we are going to see in this section.

Raw Streaming

Let's start with *raw* streaming, basically no envelope. This model is great for writing large payloads in response, as we can write them chunk by chunk, in order.

Raw streaming is straightforward with Quarkus and RESTEasy Reactive: just return `Multi`. Let's look at an example. You have probably heard about the book *War and Peace*. It's what we would call a brick, more than 1,200 pages! Let's say that we want to accumulate the full content of *War and Peace* and return it in an HTTP response as a single batch. It's doable, but let's make the book easy to digest by streaming the content (Example 8-23).

Example 8-23. Stream responses (chapter-8/mutiny-integration-examples/src/main/java/org/acme/StreamResource.java)

```
@GET
@Path("/book")
@Produces(MediaType.TEXT_PLAIN)
public Multi<String> book() {
    return vertx.fileSystem().open("war-and-peace.txt",
                new OpenOptions().setRead(true))
            .onItem().transformToMulti(AsyncFile::toMulti)
            .onItem().transform(b -> b.toString("UTF-8"));
}
```

This code opens the book text from the filesystem, using the Vert.x filesystem API, and reads it chunk by chunk. `AsyncFile::toMulti` is responsible for reading the file (and `AsyncFile`) and emitting the content chunk by chunk. As we did previously in Example 8-13, we transform the content into UTF-8 strings.

You can find this code in *chapter-8/mutiny-integration-examples*. Run the application by using `mvn quarkus:dev` and then test it with Example 8-24.

Example 8-24. Consume chunked responses

```
> curl http://localhost:8080/book -N ❶
```

❶   -N instructs `curl` to read the response chunk by chunk (it disables the buffering).

We get the content, but it's hard to see that it was sent as a set of chunks. Let's update the endpoint to send a chunk every second (Example 8-25).

Example 8-25. Pace streamed responses (chapter-8/mutiny-integration-examples/src/main/java/org/acme/StreamResource.java)

```java
@GET
@Path("/book")
@Produces(MediaType.TEXT_PLAIN)
public Multi<String> bookWithTicks() {
    Multi<Long> ticks = Multi.createFrom().ticks().every(Duration.ofSeconds(1));
    Multi<String> book = vertx.fileSystem().open("war-and-peace.txt",
        new OpenOptions().setRead(true))
            .onItem().transformToMulti(AsyncFile::toMulti)
            .onItem().transform(b -> b.toString("UTF-8"));
    return
            Multi.createBy().combining().streams(ticks, book).asTuple()
                    .onItem().transform(Tuple2::getItem2);
}
```

Example 8-25 combines two streams. First, it creates a periodic stream, emitting a tick every second (`ticks`). Then it retrieves the stream reading the book (`book`). The combination creates a stream of tuples that will be emitted every second. Each tuple contains a tick (`getItem1`) and the chunk (`getItem2`). We just need to forward the chunk, dropping the tick.

Now, rerun the `curl` command, and you will see the content appearing chunk by chunk every second. Don't wait until the end because there are many chunks; just hit Ctrl-C to interrupt.

Streaming JSON Array

The *War and Peace* example is interesting for binary content or simple text, but you may want to send a more structured response, such as a JSON array. Imagine you are building a response that is a JSON array, but a potentially large one. Each item is a JSON object. You could build that structure in memory and flush everything in a single batch, but it may be more efficient to push the JSON objects one by one. First, that approach would save some memory on our part, and the client receiving the data may be able to start processing the items immediately. To stream a JSON array, you need to adapt the produced content type. In the previous example, we just used `text/plain`. To create a JSON array, we need to set it to `application/json`.

We recommend using the `MediaType` class that provides constants for the most common content types. A typo can quickly become a debugging nightmare.

Let's imagine we have a bunch of books. Each `Book` has an ID, a title, and a list of authors (Example 8-26).

*Example 8-26. The **Book** structure (chapter-8/mutiny-integration-examples/src/main/java/org/acme/StreamResource.java)*

```java
public static class Book {
    public final long id;
    public final String title;
    public final List<String> authors;

    public Book(long id, String title, List<String> authors) {
        this.id = id;
        this.title = title;
        this.authors = authors;
    }
}
```

Let's imagine we have a *service* that lets us retrieve our collection of books as a `Multi`. In other words, we have a service offering the API in Example 8-27.

Example 8-27. Stream books API

```java
Multi<Book> getBooks();
```

To build a JSON array from this method, we can return an instance of `Multi` produced by the `getBooks` method (Example 8-28).

Example 8-28. Stream books (chapter-8/mutiny-integration-examples/src/main/java/org/acme/StreamResource.java)

```java
@Inject BookService service;

@GET
@Path("/books")
@Produces(MediaType.APPLICATION_JSON)
public Multi<Book> books() {
    return service.getBooks();
}
```

If you call this endpoint by using the command in Example 8-29, you will get all the books.

Example 8-29. Consume the stream of books

```
> curl -N http://localhost:8080/books
[{"id":0,"title":"Fundamentals of Software Architecture","authors":["Mark
Richards","Neal Ford"]},{"id":1,"title":"Domain-Driven Design","authors":
["Eric Evans"]},{"id":2,"title":"Designing Distributed Systems",
"authors":["Brendan Burns"]},{"id":3,"title":"Building Evolutionary
Architectures","authors":["Neal Ford","Rebecca Parsons","Patrick Kua"]},
```

```
{"id":4,"title":"Principles of Concurrent and Distributed Programming",
"authors":["M. Ben-Ari"]},{"id":5,"title":"Distributed Systems Observability",
"authors":["Cindy Sridharan"]},{"id":6,"title":"Event Streams in Action",
"authors":["Alexander Dean","Valentin Crettaz"]},{"id":7,"title":"Designing
Data-Intensive Applications","authors":["Martin Kleppman"]},{"id":8,
"title":"Building Microservices","authors":["Sam Newman"]},{"id":9,
"title":"Kubernetes in Action","authors":["Marko Luksa"]},{"id":10,
"title":"Kafka - the definitive guide","authors":["Gwenn Shapira","Todd Palino",
"Rajini Sivaram","Krit Petty"]},{"id":11,"title":"Effective Java",
"authors":["Joshua Bloch"]},{"id":12,"title":"Building Event-Driven
Microservices","authors":["Adam Bellemare"]}]
```

The result is a well-formed JSON array containing our books, serialized as JSON objects. But, again, it's hard to see that it was streamed. We can use the same approach as we did before to limit the emission to one per second, as in Example 8-30.

Example 8-30. Produce a book every second (chapter-8/mutiny-integration-examples/src/main/java/org/acme/StreamResource.java)

```
@GET
@Path("/books")
@Produces(MediaType.APPLICATION_JSON)
public Multi<Book> booksWithTicks() {
    Multi<Long> ticks = Multi.createFrom().ticks().every(Duration.ofSeconds(1));
    Multi<Book> books = service.getBooks();

    return
            Multi.createBy().combining().streams(ticks, books).asTuple()
                    .onItem().transform(Tuple2::getItem2);
}
```

With this code, if you rerun the `curl` command, you will see the items appearing one by one.

Using Server-Sent-Events

Raw streams and JSON arrays are helpful for bounded streams. But, sometimes, we have to deal with unbounded ones.

Server-Sent Events (*https://oreil.ly/NjQNL*) (SSE) was designed with this use case in mind. It provides a way to stream potentially unbounded structured data using HTTP.

To produce an SSE response, you set the produced content type to `text/event-stream`. Let's try this. Imagine we want to stream events from a financial market. Each event is a `Quote` containing the name of a company and the new stock value (Example 8-31).

Example 8-31. The `Quote` structure (chapter-8/mutiny-integration-examples/src/main/java/org/acme/StreamResource.java)

```java
public static class Quote {
    public final String company;
    public final double value;

    public Quote(String company, double value) {
        this.company = company;
        this.value = value;
    }
}
```

Now, let's imagine a service emitting a `Quote` every second to represent the fluctuation of the market. We can produce an SSE response by returning that stream directly (Example 8-32).

Example 8-32. Stream quotes (chapter-8/mutiny-integration-examples/src/main/java/org/acme/StreamResource.java)

```java
@Inject Market market;

@GET
@Path("/market")
@Produces(MediaType.SERVER_SENT_EVENTS)
public Multi<Quote> market() {
    return market.getEventStream();
}
```

By setting the produced content to SSE, Quarkus writes the response accordingly. Each individual `Quote` is encoded to JSON automatically (Example 8-33).

Example 8-33. Consume the SSE response

```
> curl -N http://localhost:8080/market
data:{"company":"MacroHard","value":0.9920107877590033}

data:{"company":"Divinator","value":16.086577691515345}

data:{"company":"Divinator","value":6.739227006693276}

data:{"company":"MacroHard","value":1.9383421237456742}

data:{"company":"MacroHard","value":38.723702725212156}

data:{"company":"Divinator","value":44.23789420202483}

data:{"company":"Black Coat","value":171.42142746079418}
```

```
data:{"company":"MacroHard","value":44.37699080288775}

data:{"company":"Black Coat","value":37.33849006264873}
...
```

A client reading SSE, such as a JavaScript `EventSource` (*https://oreil.ly/scARA*), can process the quotes one by one as they come.

Reactive Score

So far, we have looked at various features of RESTEasy Reactive and Quarkus. But what about tooling around Reactive?

We already experienced dev mode, which made us highly productive, but there is more. RESTEasy Reactive produces a *reactive score* for your endpoints, indicating how *responsive* the endpoints are.

To compute this score, RESTEasy Reactive looks at the execution model (typically, an endpoint using worker threads will get a lower score), instantiation scheme (favoring singleton over request-based instantiation), the usage of marshaller and reflection-based mechanisms (such as object mapper), and so on.

Let's look at the score in an example. In *chapter-8/reactive-scores*, an application contains a bunch of endpoints using various features. Launch the application in dev mode by using `mvn quarkus:dev`, and then open a browser.

 This reactive score page is part of the Quarkus dev console. Each extension can contribute to the dev console. In dev mode, access the dev console using *http://localhost:8080/q/dev*. In our example, you can navigate to *http://localhost:8080/q/swagger-ui/* to try all the defined endpoints.

You can see scores going from 50/100 (rather bad) to 100/100 (excellent!) in our application (Figure 8-3). You can click each method to understand the given score. This feature is handy when trying to improve the concurrency and the efficiency of your application. If you realize that you have a bottleneck, check the score and try to improve it. The effect on your application will be immediate.

```
POST /scores/json                                          100/100

GET /scores/json                                            83/100

GET /scores/json-blocking                                   50/100

GET /scores/json-uni                                        83/100

GET /scores/simple                                         100/100

GET /scores/simple-blocking                                 66/100

GET /scores/stream                                         100/100

GET /scores/stream-json                                     83/100

GET /scores/stream-sse                                     100/100

GET /scores/uni                                            100/100
```

Figure 8-3. Endpoint scores

Summary

HTTP is unavoidable. Although it does not enforce reactive principles, Quarkus offers a way to expose HTTP APIs without renouncing to those reactive principles.

Thanks to RESTEasy Reactive, you get a familiar declarative development model that is a lot more efficient and performant. We only scratched the surface. RESTEasy Reactive also supports Bean Validation to automatically validate the incoming payloads or OpenAPI to describe your API.

You may wonder how to consume HTTP endpoints. This is covered in Chapter 12. But, there is one aspect we didn't discuss yet: data and how to reactively access data stores. This is the topic of the next chapter.

## CHAPTER 9

Accessing Data Reactively

In Chapter 5, we explained the scalability and robustness problems in the use of blocking I/O for applications. This chapter focuses on interacting with databases and how Quarkus ensures that the data layers of an application stack can be asynchronous and utilize nonblocking I/O too.

The Problem with Data Access

Accessing relational data previously involved blocking I/O while communicating with a database. As already discussed in Chapter 5, we want to avoid blocking I/O in our applications, at any level of the stack. Interacting with a database often takes a nontrivial amount of time to complete, depending on the number of records involved, creating an even larger impact on our application with blocking I/O to access a database! What do we mean by this? Let's say we've developed a small database application; we've all developed many of those over the years. We often refer to them as *CRUD* applications because they provide create, read, update, and delete operations for records in a database.

Every exposed endpoint in our API needs to interact with the database. We will ignore caches and how they reduce the number of requests made to a database in certain situations. With each endpoint method calling the database, every execution performs blocking I/O, reducing concurrency.

Why are we forced to use blocking I/O when interacting with databases? APIs for interacting with databases, such as Open Database Connectivity (ODBC) and Java Database Connectivity (JDBC), were designed with a synchronous and blocking approach. The Java Persistence API (JPA), which came many years later, though coalescing the object-relational mapping (ORM) landscape around a common API, was still designed on the existing synchronous and blocking behavior of JDBC.

Without a reactive programming approach to data access, the entirety of an application stack can never be truly reactive. An application could be reactive only up to a point. Though still beneficial, concurrency and throughput are still prevented from reaching their full potential concurrency.

That's a lot of words explaining how database access with JDBC and JPA is not reactive, and therefore blocking, but what does that access look like? As you saw in "The Imperative Model" on page 112 with application logic, it's a similar problem for the database interaction, as illustrated in Figure 9-1.

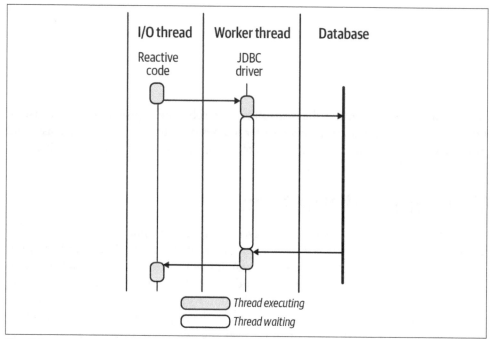

Figure 9-1. Blocking database client

When we're communicating with a database over JDBC, or the higher abstraction JPA, the JDBC driver uses a request-and-response interaction. However, as shown in Figure 9-1, the JDBC driver blocks the thread until any response is received. This blocking approach occupies an entire thread for each database interaction. Depending on how you've configured database connection pooling, it's possible to run out of threads for an application before reaching the maximum number of database connections.

When dealing with a large number of database records to search or retrieve, and network latency between our application and the database, a problem with thread starvation or resource utilization will likely occur.

Nonblocking Interactions with Relational Databases

With recent work by various projects, such as Vert.x client APIs (*https://oreil.ly/ GSE6G*) for PostgreSQL, MySQL, IBM Db2, Oracle, and Microsoft SQL Server, Java applications are now able to interact with databases in an asynchronous manner with nonblocking I/O.

How are things different with these new clients compared to JDBC? When using nonblocking database clients, we're able to avoid a blocked thread, as shown in Figure 9-2.

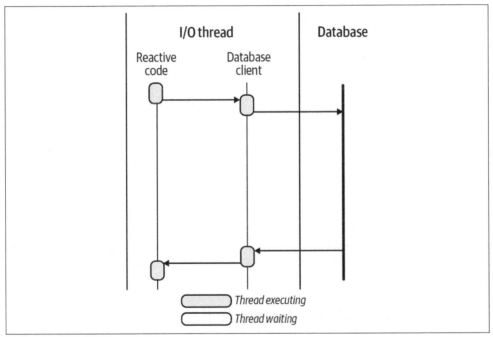

Figure 9-2. Nonblocking database client

In addition, it's now possible for the database client, instead of a worker, to execute on the I/O thread. Now we have a compounded benefit of using these new nonblocking clients: reducing the number of worker threads an application might need, as database communication with these new clients can occur on the same thread as any reactive application code!

In Figure 9-2, we see a single database connection being used for the database client to communicate. However, when a client API and database supports it, we can utilize pipelining to share a single database connection for several requests. Figure 9-3 shows how pipelining in the database client works.

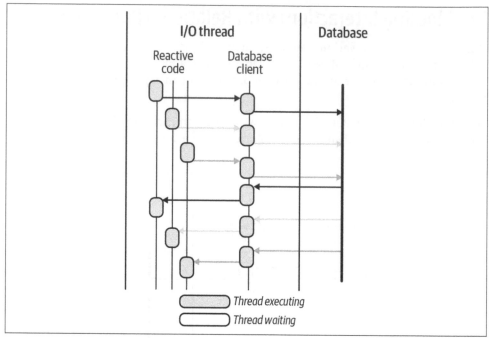

Figure 9-3. Nonblocking database client with pipelining

Each color in Figure 9-3 is a separate database request. Though we have different reactive handlers calling the database, the database client is able to utilize a single connection to the database instead of, in this case, three. We want to take advantage of nonblocking advancements such as this whenever we can, to squeeze more and more out of the same amount of resources for an application.

Using a Reactive ORM: Hibernate Reactive

Hibernate ORM enables developers to more easily write applications whose data outlives the application process. As an ORM framework, Hibernate is concerned with data persistence as it applies to relational databases. Hibernate provides both imperative and reactive APIs.

These APIs support two facets: nonblocking database clients, covered in the previous section, and reactive programming as a means of interacting with relational databases. Most of the existing Hibernate internals are still utilized, but Hibernate Reactive introduces a new layer for utilizing reactive and nonblocking APIs to communicate with database clients. The reactive APIs work in concert with JPA annotations, Hibernate annotations, and Bean Validation as well.

It's time to dive in and use Hibernate with reactive APIs! With Quarkus, Hibernate Reactive is even better, because we have the option to use Hibernate Reactive with

Panache. This thin layer simplifies the use of the Hibernate ORM. It provides two models. Your entities can be managed as active records, as the entity class provides methods to retrieve, update, and query instances of that entity class. You can also use a repository model, in which a repository class provides these functions, keeping the entity structure *pure.* See the *chapter-9/hibernate-reactive* directory for all Hibernate Reactive project code. First we need the dependency for Hibernate Reactive (Example 9-1).

Example 9-1. Hibernate Reactive dependency (chapter-9/hibernate-reactive/pom.xml)

```
<dependency>
    <groupId>io.quarkus</groupId>
    <artifactId>quarkus-hibernate-reactive-panache</artifactId>
</dependency>
```

Notice we used the Panache version of Hibernate Reactive. If we didn't want to use Panache, we could have used the `quarkus-hibernate-reactive` dependency instead. As mentioned previously, we need a reactive database client too. For this example, we will use the PostgreSQL client (Example 9-2).

Example 9-2. PostgreSQL database client dependency (chapter-9/hibernate-reactive/ pom.xml)

```
<dependency>
    <groupId>io.quarkus</groupId>
    <artifactId>quarkus-reactive-pg-client</artifactId>
</dependency>
```

With Dev Services (*https://oreil.ly/eKY8W*), a Quarkus feature starting the required pieces of infrastructure automatically, we don't need the Docker Maven plug-in to start a database for running tests. Quarkus will automatically start the database for us! To take advantage of Dev Services, we need a database driver, which we just added in Example 9-2, and to set `db.kind` for informing Quarkus of the database type being used. Let's set that up now in `application.properties` (Example 9-3).

Example 9-3. PostgreSQL database client config (chapter-9/hibernate-reactive/src/main/ resources/application.properties)

```
quarkus.datasource.db-kind=postgresql
%prod.quarkus.datasource.username=quarkus_test
%prod.quarkus.datasource.password=quarkus_test
%prod.quarkus.datasource.reactive.url=vertx-reactive:postgresql://
    localhost/quarkus_test
```

With Dev Services, all the properties except db.kind are specified with the prod configuration profile. We could also remove the properties from the prod profile completely, preferring to set them with environment variables, or a ConfigMap in Kubernetes.

We have a `Customer` entity that extends `PanacheEntity`. We won't cover `Customer` in detail here, as it utilizes the usual annotations from JPA, Bean Validation, and Hibernate Validator. The full source can be viewed at *chapter-9/hibernate-reactive/src/main/java/org/acme/data/Customer*.

Let's take a look at the implementation of a CRUD application using Hibernate Reactive and RESTEasy Reactive to expose a REST API. First up is a method to retrieve all customers from the database (Example 9-4).

Example 9-4. Retrieve all customers (chapter-9/hibernate-reactive/src/main/java/org/acme/data/CustomerResource.java)

```
public Multi<Customer> findAll() {
  return Customer.streamAll(Sort.by("name"));
}
```

We use `streamAll` on `Customer`, from Panache, to retrieve all instances into `Multi`. Each customer can have orders associated with them, and when we retrieve a single customer, we also want to retrieve their orders. Though we have a single application, we will consider the orders to be coming from an external service.

First we define `Uni` to retrieve `Customer` and throw an exception if one was not found, as shown in Example 9-5.

Example 9-5. Find a customer (chapter-9/hibernate-reactive/src/main/java/org/acme/data/CustomerResource.java)

```
Uni<Customer> customerUni = Customer.<Customer>findById(id)
    .onItem().ifNull().failWith(
        new WebApplicationException("Failed to find customer",
        Response.Status.NOT_FOUND)
    );
```

Next the orders of a customer are retrieved as a `List` into a separate `Uni` (see Example 9-6).

Example 9-6. Retrieve customer orders (chapter-9/hibernate-reactive/src/main/java/org/acme/data/CustomerResource.java)

```
Uni<List<Order>> customerOrdersUni = orderService.getOrdersForCustomer(id);
```

Lastly, the two are combined by a mapper, taking the results of each Uni to set the orders on the customer. The resulting Uni is transformed into a JAX-RS Response to complete the endpoint execution (Example 9-7).

Example 9-7. Combine `customer` and `orders` (chapter-9/hibernate-reactive/src/main/java/org/acme/data/CustomerResource.java)

```
return Uni.combine()
    .all().unis(customerUni, customerOrdersUni)
    .combinedWith(((customer, orders) -> {
      customer.orders = orders;
      return customer;
    })
    .onItem().transform(customer -> Response.ok(customer).build());
```

So far, everything we've done hasn't required a transaction, as we've only been reading database records. Example 9-8 shows how we can use transactions to store a new customer.

Example 9-8. Create a customer (chapter-9/hibernate-reactive/src/main/java/org/acme/data/CustomerResource.java)

```
return Panache
    .withTransaction(customer::persist)
    .replaceWith(Response.ok(customer).status(Response.Status.CREATED).build());
```

We use `Panache.withTransaction` to inform Panache that we want a transaction to wrap the Uni Supplier we pass into it. In this instance, we use `customer.persist` as the code to be wrapped with a transaction. Though Uni<Void> is returned on success, we can use `replaceWith` to create the necessary Uni<Response>.

Next we use `withTransaction` to update the customer name. First we retrieve a customer by ID. Then, when we receive an item that is not null, we invoke a runnable to update the name on the retrieved entity (Example 9-9).

Example 9-9. Update a customer (chapter-9/hibernate-reactive/src/main/java/org/acme/data/CustomerResource.java)

```
return Panache
    .withTransaction(
        () -> Customer.<Customer>findById(id)
            .onItem().ifNotNull().invoke(entity -> entity.name = customer.name)
    )
```

We then utilize `onItem` to generate an outcome of a successful response or return a not found response if the item is null.

The last method we need for a CRUD application with Hibernate Reactive provides the ability to delete a customer. Again we use `withTransaction`, passing it the Panache method to delete a customer by its ID. Deleting an entity returns `Uni<Boolean>`. We need to use `map` to convert it to a JAX-RS response based on its success (Example 9-10).

Example 9-10. Delete a customer (chapter-9/hibernate-reactive/src/main/java/org/acme/data/CustomerResource.java)

```
return Panache
    .withTransaction(() -> Customer.deleteById(id))
    .map(deleted -> deleted
        ? Response.ok().status(Response.Status.NO_CONTENT).build()
        : Response.ok().status(Response.Status.NOT_FOUND).build());
```

You've now seen how to create, retrieve, update, and delete entities with Panache and Hibernate Reactive! To see how the endpoints can be tested, take a look at */chapter-9/hibernate-reactive/src/test/java/org/acme/data/CustomerEndpointTest* in the book's code examples.

What About NoSQL?

We've shown how we can have reactive APIs with a traditional ORM such as Hibernate, but what about NoSQL? Are we able to take advantage of reactive APIs when an application needs a NoSQL database instead of a relational one? Yes, we can!

Quarkus has several extensions for communicating with NoSQL databases, including MongoDB, Redis, and Apache Cassandra. Do all these extensions support reactive APIs? Currently, the MongoDB, Redis, and Cassandra clients have support for reactive APIs.

In the next section, we will develop a CRUD application with the same functionality as the Hibernate Reactive example in the previous section.

Interacting with Redis

Let's develop a customer CRUD application with Redis! For this example, we will extract interactions into a separate service we can inject into a REST resource. Check out */chapter-9/redis/src/main/java/org/acme/data/CustomerResource* in the code examples to see how the service is used.

First we need the Redis client dependency for the project; see Example 9-11.

Example 9-11. Redis client dependency (chapter-9/redis/pom.xml)

```
<dependency>
    <groupId>io.quarkus</groupId>
    <artifactId>quarkus-redis-client</artifactId>
</dependency>
```

As we did with the Hibernate Reactive example, we will utilize `docker-maven-plugin` to run a Redis container for test execution. Check out *chapter-9/redis/pom.xml* in the book source for the details.

Next we configure the Redis client as to where the host of the server is located. Include the config in Example 9-12 in `application.properties`.

Example 9-12. Redis client config (chapter-9/redis/src/main/resources/ application.properties)

```
quarkus.redis.hosts=redis://localhost:6379
```

To be able to use the Redis client, we need to `@Inject` it, as shown in Example 9-13.

Example 9-13. Inject Redis client (chapter-9/redis/src/main/java/org/acme/data/ CustomerService.java)

```
@Inject
ReactiveRedisClient reactiveRedisClient;
```

So we don't create an unintentional key clash in Redis, we will prefix a customer ID, as shown in Example 9-14.

Example 9-14. Key prefix (chapter-9/redis/src/main/java/org/acme/data/ CustomerService.java)

```
private static final String CUSTOMER_HASH_PREFIX = "cust:";
```

Let's start out with retrieving a list of all the customers from Redis (Example 9-15).

Example 9-15. Retrieve all customers (chapter-9/redis/src/main/java/org/acme/data/ CustomerService.java)

```
public Multi<Customer> allCustomers() {
  return reactiveRedisClient.keys("*")
      .onItem().transformToMulti(response -> {
        return Multi.createFrom().iterable(response).map(Response::toString);
      })
      .onItem().transformToUniAndMerge(key ->
          reactiveRedisClient.hgetall(key)
```

```
            .map(resp ->
                constructCustomer(
                    Long.parseLong(
                        key.substring(CUSTOMER_HASH_PREFIX.length())),
                    resp)
        )
    );
}
```

ReactiveRedisClient provides an API aligned with the commands available with Redis, making it easier to use in Java if you are already familiar with using Redis commands. In Example 9-15, we use keys with a wildcard to retrieve all keys, which returns Uni<Response>. This particular Response class represents the response from Redis.

On receiving the response (the item) from Redis, we use transformToMulti to separate the single response into individual keys. In the lambda, we create a Multi of string keys from the response directly, as it's an Iterable, and map the value to the string of the key. The result of the execution is Multi<String>.

We're not done just yet; we need to convert the stream of keys into a stream of customers. Reading the code provides a good idea of what happens. Starting with Multi<String>, on each item produced we call transformToUniAndMerge. We use their key, or item, with the Redis client to retrieve all the fields and values matching the key, or hash. The response from hgetall is mapped to a Customer instance using constructCustomer. Finally, the customer Unis instances are merged into a Multi for returning.

To retrieve a single customer, we call hgetall and, depending on the size of the response, either return null or use constructCustomer to create a customer (Example 9-16). We need to check the size of the response to find out whether any fields and values were returned. If the size is zero, the response was empty because the key could not be found.

Example 9-16. Retrieve customer (chapter-9/redis/src/main/java/org/acme/data/CustomerService.java)

```
public Uni<Customer> getCustomer(Long id) {
  return reactiveRedisClient.hgetall(CUSTOMER_HASH_PREFIX + id)
      .map(resp -> resp.size() > 0
          ? constructCustomer(id, resp)
          : null
      );
}
```

To store a customer record into Redis, we use hmset to store multiple fields and values for a single key. From a Redis perspective, it doesn't matter whether we're storing a new customer or updating an existing one; we use hmset for both. We should split the behavior into a separate method to reuse it in both places, as shown in Example 9-17.

Example 9-17. Store customer (chapter-9/redis/src/main/java/org/acme/data/CustomerService.java)

```
return reactiveRedisClient.hmset(
    Arrays.asList(CUSTOMER_HASH_PREFIX + customer.id, "name", customer.name)
)
    .onItem().transform(resp -> {
      if (resp.toString().equals("OK")) {
        return customer;
      } else {
        throw new NoSuchElementException();
      }
    });
```

Using hmset, we need to ensure that an odd number of arguments are passed to it. The first argument is the hash for the record, followed by matching pairs of field and value for as many fields to be set. We get a simple reply of OK if it succeeds, using transform to return the customer on success or throw an exception.

With storeCustomer in place, let's look at createCustomer; see Example 9-18.

Example 9-18. Create customer (chapter-9/redis/src/main/java/org/acme/data/CustomerService.java)

```
public Uni<Customer> createCustomer(Customer customer) {
  return storeCustomer(customer);
}
```

We have a nice clean method for createCustomer for responding with Uni<Customer>! There wasn't much to that one, so let's look at updateCustomer in Example 9-19.

Example 9-19. Update customer (chapter-9/redis/src/main/java/org/acme/data/CustomerService.java)

```
public Uni<Customer> updateCustomer(Customer customer) {
  return getCustomer(customer.id)
      .onItem().transformToUni((cust) -> {
        if (cust == null) {
          return Uni.createFrom().failure(new NotFoundException());
        }
        cust.name = customer.name;
        return storeCustomer(cust);
```

```
        });
}
```

First we reuse `getCustomer` from the service to retrieve the existing customer from Redis. When an item is returned from `getCustomer`, we transform it into another `Uni` with a mapper. The mapper first checks whether the item we received, the customer, is null, returning a `Uni` failure containing an exception if it is. Then we set the new name onto the customer before calling `storeCustomer`, creating the `Uni` the mapper returns.

Lastly, we need a way to delete a customer. For this, we use `hdel` on the Redis client, which returns the number of removed fields or 0 if the key could not be found (Example 9-20). We map `Uni<Response>` to `Uni<Boolean>`, checking whether one field was removed (in this case, the customer name) to return `true`, or `null` if there were no responses. On the produced item, we fail with `NotFoundException` if the item is `null`, or succeed and transform the item into a null item.

Example 9-20. Delete a customer (chapter-9/redis/src/main/java/org/acme/data/CustomerService.java)

```java
public Uni<Void> deleteCustomer(Long id) {
  return reactiveRedisClient.hdel(Arrays.asList(CUSTOMER_HASH_PREFIX + id, "name"))
      .map(resp -> resp.toInteger() == 1 ? true : null)
      .onItem().ifNull().failWith(new NotFoundException())
      .onItem().ifNotNull().transformToUni(r -> Uni.createFrom().nullItem());
}
```

This section gave a brief look into utilizing some methods of the reactive client for Redis. There are many more methods we didn't cover, but this section provided guidance on how they can be generally used.

Data-Related Events and Change Data Capture

Change data capture, or *CDC*, is an integration pattern for extracting events from sources that don't typically operate with events and messaging, such as databases. CDC has many benefits, including being able to produce change events from a legacy application without modifying the application.

Another benefit is that CDC doesn't care about the languages an application is developed in, as it interacts with the database. This approach can greatly simplify the effort to produce a consistent-looking change event from a database that has polyglot applications writing to it. Having to update possibly dozens of applications written in different languages to produce a consistent-looking change event from them all can be challenging and time-consuming.

Writing to a database involves transactions, or usually should, and poses an additional complexity when also writing an event to a messaging system. In Figure 9-4, we need to make sure that if either the database update fails or producing a message fails, everything rolls back and undoes any changes.

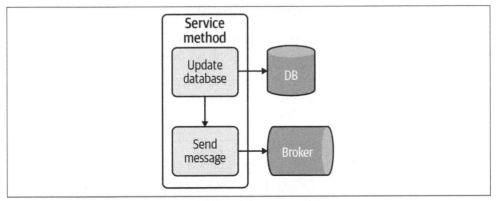

Figure 9-4. Writing to a database and message broker

Such a situation can be particularly complex when transaction rollback can occur outside our application code because of a failure to return an HTTP response, for instance. With CDC, this concern goes away because we worry only about writing to the database itself.

Any change events can flow from the updated database with CDC, ensuring that we're never sending an event we shouldn't because the transaction has been committed before CDC sees the change, as shown in Figure 9-5.

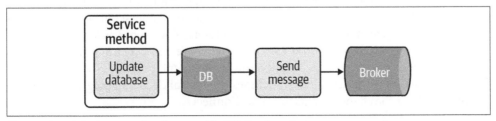

Figure 9-5. Writing to a database, with CDC triggering message creation

One impact for developers to be aware of is that CDC does not provide strong consistency. *Strong consistency* means that any data viewed immediately after an update is consistent for all observers of the data, regardless of whether the viewers are in parallel or distributed processes. For relational databases, this is guaranteed as it's part of the design of the database. With CDC, there is a period of time between the update happening in the database, and when the message of the update is received and processed by the furthest downstream system consuming the messages.

The lack of strong consistency, or *eventual consistency*, is not a deterrent for the use of CDC. We want developers to be aware of the consistency guarantees of the CDC pattern, to bear it in mind during application design.

Using Debezium to Capture Change

Debezium (*https://debezium.io/*) is a distributed platform for CDC. Debezium is durable and fast, enabling applications to respond promptly and never miss an event!

Figure 9-6 shows where Debezium fits in an application architecture using CDC. Debezium provides Kafka Connect source connectors for several databases, including MySQL, MongoDB, PostgreSQL, Oracle, Db2, and SQL Server.

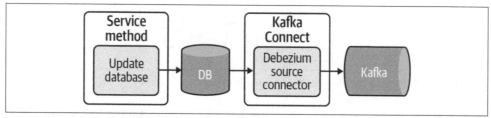

Figure 9-6. CDC with Debezium

We will briefly show how we can enhance the Hibernate Reactive example from the previous section with Debezium. Full details can be found in the source code (*https://oreil.ly/XTQQp*) for the book.

Though this example includes a copy of the code from Hibernate Reactive, it would also work by using the example directly, as the application code is not impacted by the introduction of Debezium. The main piece to understand is the *docker-compose.yml* file. This file starts the Kafka containers, ZooKeeper as a dependency of Kafka, a PostgreSQL database, and Kafka Connect. We will use the container images from the Debezium project to simplify the deployment process. For example, the PostgreSQL container image already includes the logical decoding plug-ins necessary to communicate the change events to Kafka Connect.

Start all the containers with `docker compose up`, and then build and start the application with `java -jar target/quarkus-app/quarkus-run.jar`. Once all containers have started, we install the Debezium source connector for PostgreSQL into Kafka Connect (Example 9-21).

Example 9-21. Install the Debezium source connector

```
curl -i -X POST -H "Accept:application/json" -H "Content-Type:application/json" \
    http://localhost:8083/connectors/ -d @register.json
```

Here, *register.json* is the data we're passing to the Kafka Connect endpoint. The file provides the details of the database to connect to and the Debezium connector to use, as shown in Example 9-22.

Example 9-22. Debezium source connector definition

```
{
  "name": "customer-connector",
  "config": {
    "connector.class": "io.debezium.connector.postgresql.PostgresConnector",
    "tasks.max": "1",
    "database.hostname": "postgres",
    "database.port": "5432",
    "database.user": "quarkus_test",
    "database.password": "quarkus_test",
    "database.dbname": "quarkus_test",
    "database.server.name": "quarkus-db-server"
  }
}
```

The installation of the source connector will trigger the creation of Kafka topics for the tables discovered by the connector. We can verify what topics were created by running docker exec -ti kafka bin/kafka-topics.sh --list --zookeeper zoo keeper:2181.

Next we run an *exec* shell in the Kafka container to consume messages from the topic for the customer database, quarkus-db-server.public.customer (Example 9-23).

Example 9-23. Consume messages from Kafka

```
docker-compose exec kafka /kafka/bin/kafka-console-consumer.sh \
    --bootstrap-server kafka:9092 \
    --from-beginning \                       ❶
    --property print.key=true \
    --topic quarkus-db-server.public.customer
```

❶ Remove this setting to skip the initial four messages created when the application started.

When Example 9-23 is done, create a new customer in a separate terminal window, as shown in Example 9-24.

Example 9-24. Create a customer

```
curl  X POST  II "Content-Type:application/json" http://localhost:8080/customer \
    -d '{"name" : "Harry Houdini"}'
```

In the terminal running Example 9-23, we see the JSON message created by the connector (Example 9-25).

Example 9-25. CDC message from creating a customer

```
{
  "schema": {
    "type":"struct",
    "fields": [{
      "type":"int64",
      "optional":false,
      "field":"id"
    }],
    "optional":false,
    "name":"quarkus_db_server.public.customer.Key"
  },
  "payload": {
    "id":9                          ❶
  }
}
{
  "schema": {
    // JSON defining the schema of the payload removed for brevity

    "optional": false,
    "name": "quarkus_db_server.public.customer.Envelope"
  },
  "payload": {
    "before": null,
    "after": {
      "id": 9,                      ❶
      "name": "Harry Houdini"       ❷
    },
    "source": {
      "version": "1.5.0.Final",
      "connector": "postgresql",
      "name": "quarkus-db-server",
      "ts_ms": 1627865571265,
      "snapshot": "false",
      "db": "quarkus_test",
      "sequence": "[null,\"23870800\"]",
      "schema": "public",
      "table": "customer",
      "txId": 499,
      "lsn": 23871232,
      "xmin": null
    },
    "op": "c",
    "ts_ms": 1627865571454,
    "transaction": null
```

```
    }
}
```

❶ The ID of the record created with the POST

❷ Name of the created customer

Experiment with other HTTP commands, such as updating a customer name, to compare the JSON received in the Kafka topic.

Summary

Data with reactive applications has been limited until recently, as there weren't reactive database clients available. With the introduction of Vert.x client APIs for databases such as PostgreSQL, we can now create a reactive application that is reactive for the entirety of the stack.

We don't always want to utilize database client APIs directly. We like simplified APIs such as that provided by Hibernate ORM. Hibernate Reactive gives us such an ability, building on the maturity of Hibernate ORM to add reactive-specific APIs.

Relational databases aren't the only option either. We also have reactive clients for Redis and MongoDB. With event-driven architecture, we want to have the ability to create events from database interactions. This is where CDC shines, with its ability to extract changes from database tables and create change events to feed into Kafka.

We've now reached the end of Part III! We dove deeper into Quarkus and saw that it unifies the imperative and reactive programming models, offering greater flexibility for developers in choosing their application stack. We then journeyed through Uni and Multi to learn about the preferred reactive programming library in Quarkus, Mutiny. Continuing with newer innovations in Quarkus, we explored RESTEasy Reactive to develop JAX-RS resources in a completely nonblocking manner while still providing the ability to block when needed, before finishing up with reactive database clients with Hibernate Reactive and Redis.

In Part IV, we focus on typical patterns we need when developing reactive applications, such as messaging with Kafka and AMQP. Then we delve into aspects of the system's underlying messaging to better appreciate the trade-offs and their abilities. We take a look at communicating with external services with HTTP clients, while still utilizing nonblocking I/O. Lastly, though not necessarily an application pattern per se, we will look at observability, as it is critical to understand and implement it for distributed systems.

## PART IV

Connecting the Dots

## CHAPTER 10

Reactive Messaging: The Connective Tissue

In Part III, you saw many features to develop reactive applications with Quarkus. But, as you remember from Part II, we don't want to limit ourselves to reactive applications; we want to build reactive systems. That's what we are going to do now.

Reactive systems use asynchronous message passing among their components. However, while middleware and frameworks can sometimes hide this message-passing aspect, we believe it's far more efficient to make it apparent. It not only helps you write event-driven code (*on event x, do y*), but also helps decompose your application into a set of components receiving and producing messages. Thus, Quarkus offers a message-driven development model that is simple but powerful to consume, process, and create messages. This chapter focuses on this model, how it relates to Reactive Streams, and how it makes building message-driven and event-driven applications straightforward.

From Reactive Applications to Reactive Systems

When you talk to a Java developer about messaging, you can feel the frustration. For years, JMS has been the de facto standard for messaging. However, that API didn't age well, and new messaging technologies such as Kafka and Pulsar use concepts that do not work well with JMS. In addition, JMS is a blocking API, which prevents us from implementing reactive principles.

While Quarkus can use JMS, we are going to look at another approach called *Reactive Messaging*. This MicroProfile specification builds reactive and event-driven applications. Quarkus implements version 2.*x* of the specification but also provides many extensions.

Applications using Reactive Messaging can send, consume, and process messages in a protocol-agnostic way. For example, as you will see in Chapter 11, you will be able to use Apache Kafka or AMQP or even combine both. Reactive Messaging also provides a natural development model for developers used to Contexts and Dependency Injection (CDI), a standard dependency injection framework. Typically, you can summarize Reactive Messaging to a couple of annotations. But before seeing it in action, let's describe a few concepts that it relies on.

Channels and Messages

When using Reactive Messaging, your applications and components forming them interact using *messages*, represented with the `org.eclipse.microprofile.reactive.messaging.Message<T>` class. A *message* is an envelope that has a payload of type `T`. In addition, a message can have metadata and provides acknowledgment methods to notify the framework of the successful or failed processing of a message.

Messages transit on *channels*. You can picture channels as pipes. A channel can be internal to an application or mapped, by a connector, to an external message queue or topic (Figure 10-1).

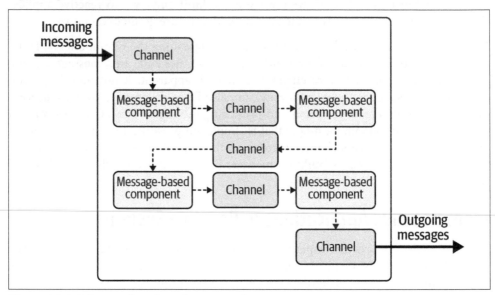

Figure 10-1. Message-based application architecture

Your application reads from channels and writes to channels. You can split your application into a set of components, with all of them reading and writing to different channels. That's it. Reactive Messaging binds everything all together, and so constructs streams in which messages flow.

Producing Messages

Reactive Messaging provides multiple ways to produce messages, but let's start with the simplest and probably more natural one for developers familiar with imperative programming: emitters. `Emitter` is an object that is attached to a channel and emits messages to that channel.[1] Example 10-1 illustrates the use of `MutinyEmitter`.

Example 10-1. Use an emitter to send messages

```
@Channel("my-channel")
MutinyEmitter<Person> personEmitter;

public Uni<Void> send(Person p) {
    return personEmitter.send(p);
}
```

To access an emitter, you just inject it in your CDI bean. The target channel is indicated using the `@Channel` annotation.

 There's no need to use the `@Inject` annotation, as Quarkus detects the injection for you.

In Example 10-1, we don't produce a `Message` instance; we just send a payload (`Person`), automatically wrapped into a message. Note that the send method returns `Uni<Void>`. This `Uni` produces a `null` item when the message processing completes successfully. Otherwise, it produces a failure indicating why the processing failed.

An emitter can also send an instance of `Message` directly, as shown in Example 10-2.

Example 10-2. Injection and use of an emitter

```
@Channel("my-second-channel")
MutinyEmitter<Person> messageEmitter;

public void sendMessage(Person p) {
    messageEmitter.send(
            Message.of(p,
                    () -> {
                        // Acknowledgment callback
                        return CompletableFuture.completedFuture(null);
                    },
```

---

1 In this book, we use `MutinyEmitter`, but you can use plain `Emitter` instead, providing a slightly different API.

```
                    failure -> {
                        // Negative-acknowledgment callback
                        return CompletableFuture.completedFuture(null);
                    })
        );
}
```

When sending a `Message`, you can directly pass the acknowledgment callbacks. We cover acknowledgment in "Acknowledgments" on page 187.

Emitters are convenient when you want to decide when to send a message. They allow imperative code to emit messages that will be handled in a reactive manner. For example, you can use an emitter in an HTTP endpoint and send a message when you receive a request.

Another way to produce messages is with the `@Outgoing` annotation. It instructs Reactive Messaging to send the output of the method to the specified channel. Note that methods annotated with `@Outgoing` can't be called from your code; Reactive Messaging calls them for you. You may wonder about the benefits. It looks a bit less flexible than emitters. But there is a trick: `@Outgoing` allows producing streams (`Multi`) directly (Example 10-3).

Example 10-3. Usage of `@Outgoing`

```
@Outgoing("my-channel")
Multi<Person> produceAStreamOfPersons() {
    return Multi.createFrom().items(
            new Person("Luke"),
            new Person("Leia"),
            new Person("Obiwan")
    );
}
```

You can produce infinite streams every second, as demonstrated in Example 10-4.

Example 10-4. Generate infinite streams by using `@Outgoing`

```
@Outgoing("ticks")
Multi<Long> ticks() {
    return Multi.createFrom().ticks()
            .every(Duration.ofSeconds(1))
            .onOverflow().drop();
}
```

When the application starts, Reactive Messaging connects all the elements to the channels. Under the hood, it creates reactive streams (covered in Chapter 5). So, your application is a set of reactive streams, enforcing the backpressure protocol. The consumption rate is controlled by the downstream subscribers. This is the reason we need onOverflow.drop in the preceding example. Otherwise, if the downstream subscriber does not consume fast enough, it would fail (you can't apply backpressure in time).

As for Emitter, you can produce a stream of messages (Example 10-5).

Example 10-5. Produce a stream of messages by using @Outgoing

```
@Outgoing("my-channel")
Multi<Message<Person>> produceAStreamOfMessagesOfPersons() {
    return Multi.createFrom().items(
            Message.of(new Person("Luke")),
            Message.of(new Person("Leia")),
            Message.of(new Person("Obiwan"))
    );
}
```

Here, our messages are just wrapping the payload. As we have seen in the example, you can pass the acknowledgment callbacks.

Attentive readers may have observed a significant difference between the emitter and the @Outgoing approaches. Reactive Messaging handles the @Outgoing method completely (invoking it), so enforcing the backpressure protocol is no problem. But with the emitter, Reactive Messaging can't. If your code uses an emitter to send messages faster than the consumption rate, you may be in trouble!

Fortunately, to avoid this, you can configure an overflow strategy when using an emitter. This strategy describes what happens when the downstream does not consume fast enough. @OnOverflow offers six strategies. The most common, demonstrated in Example 10-6, consists of using a buffer.

Example 10-6. Usage of the @OnOverflow annotation

```
@Channel("channel")
@OnOverflow(value = OnOverflow.Strategy.BUFFER, bufferSize = 100)
MutinyEmitter<Person> emitterUsingABufferOnOverflow;

@Channel("channel")
@OnOverflow(value = OnOverflow.Strategy.UNBOUNDED_BUFFER)
MutinyEmitter<Person> emitterUsingAnUnboundedOnOverflow;

@Channel("channel")
@OnOverflow(value = OnOverflow.Strategy.DROP)
MutinyEmitter<Person> emitterDroppingMessageOnOverflow;

@Channel("channel")
@OnOverflow(value = OnOverflow.Strategy.LATEST)
```

```
MutinyEmitter<Person> emitterDroppingOlderMessagesOnOverflow;

@Channel("channel")
@OnOverflow(value = OnOverflow.Strategy.FAIL)
MutinyEmitter<Person> emitterSendingAFailureDownstreamOnOverflow;

@Channel("channel")
@OnOverflow(value = OnOverflow.Strategy.THROW_EXCEPTION)
MutinyEmitter<Person> emitterThrowingExceptionUpstreamOnOverflow;
```

The OnOverflow strategies are similar to those in Mutiny:

- BUFFER, the default, uses a buffer to store the messages. The size can be config-ured; the default is 256.

- UNBOUNDED_BUFFER is like BUFFER but uses an unbounded buffer. Be cautious when using this strategy as it can lead to memory issues.

- DROP and LATEST drop the newest and oldest message, respectively.

- FAIL sends a failure downstream. Remember, failures are terminal for Reactive Streams. So, you can use the emitter after this.

- THROW_EXCEPTION throws an exception upstream to the caller of the send method. The caller can then react; for example, it can't wait until the downstream subscriber catches up.

Consuming Messages

Let's have a look at the other side of the message pipe. To consume messages, you can inject the stream by using the @Channel annotation, as shown in Example 10-7.

Example 10-7. Inject a channel

```
@Channel("my-channel")
Multi<Person> streamOfPersons;

// ...

void init() {
    streamOfPersons
            .subscribe().with(
                    person -> { /* ... */ },
                    failure -> { /* ... */ }
    );
}
```

As you can see, you must subscribe to the injected stream. Remember, if you don't subscribe, nothing will happen, and you won't receive any messages. Note that your code can inject multiple streams and consume them.

You can also inject a stream of messages. In this case, you must acknowledge the messages manually (Example 10-8).

Example 10-8. Inject a stream of messages

```
@Channel("my-channel")
Multi<Message<Person>> streamOfPersons;

// ...

void init() {
    streamOfPersons
            .subscribe().with(
                message -> {
                    Person person = message.getPayload();
                    try {
                        // do something
                        // acknowledge
                        message.ack();
                    } catch (Exception e) {
                        message.nack(e);
                    }
                },
                failure -> { /* ... */ }
    );
}
```

Acknowledgment is automatically done for you when injecting a stream of payloads. Messages give you more control on the acknowledgment, as well as the possibility to reject a message by using nack. In addition, you can access the message metadata. But, remember, with more power comes greater responsibility.

The @Channel injection is convenient when you want to access the stream directly or when you want to control the subscription.

Reactive Messaging also offers a more declarative way to consume messages: the @Incoming annotation. This annotation is the opposite of @Outgoing. Reactive Messaging invokes the annotated method for each message transiting on the specified channel (Example 10-9).

Example 10-9. An example of a method using @Incoming

```
@Incoming("my-channel")
void consume(Person person) {
```

```
    // ...
}
```

Example 10-9 provides a convenient way to process every incoming `Person`. You don't need to worry about acknowledgment; it's done for you. You can also receive `Message`, as demonstrated in Example 10-10.

Example 10-10. An example of a method using @Incoming and receiving messages

```
@Incoming("my-channel")
CompletionStage<Void> consume(Message<Person> person) {
    // ...
    return person.ack();
}
```

In this case, as for `@Channel` injecting a stream of messages, you need to handle the acknowledgment yourself. Remember: more control, but more responsibility.

Processing Messages

Now that you have seen the two ends, let's look at the middle of the pipeline: processing. To process messages, you combine `@Incoming` and `@Outgoing`, as shown in Example 10-11.

Example 10-11. Method using @Incoming and @Outgoing

```
@Incoming("from")
@Outgoing("to")
Person process(String name) {
    return new Person(name);
}
```

In this snippet, we read strings from the `from` channel. For each received string, we create a `Person` instance that is sent to the `to` channel. This method is synchronous and accepts an individual payload and returns an individual payload. That's not the only supported signature. Reactive Messaging supports more than 30 signatures, allowing asynchronous processing (such as returning `Uni`), or even stream processing (where you receive and return `Multis`),[2] see Example 10-12.

Example 10-12. Example of stream manipulation

```
@Incoming("from")
@Outgoing("to")
```

---

2 You can find the list of supported signatures on GitHub (*https://oreil.ly/hewBO*).

```
Multi<Person> processStream(Multi<String> inputStream) {
    return inputStream
            .onItem().transform(Person::new);
}
```

In addition to payloads, you can process messages. But as for the consumption of messages, you need to be more attentive. Indeed, you often need to *chain* messages, or link the incoming message with the one you produce, as shown in Example 10-13.

Example 10-13. Process messages

```
@Incoming("from")
@Outgoing("to")
Message<Person> processMessage(Message<String> msg) {
    return msg.withPayload(new Person(msg.getPayload()));
}
```

In this snippet, look at the `withPayload` method. The `Message` interface provides various `with` methods that link messages together. You may wonder why it's so important to link them. It's all about acknowledgment. You have seen this word a couple of times already, so it's time to explain what it means.

Acknowledgments

Acknowledgment is an essential aspect of any messaging system. When you use a message broker, the consumers, receiving and processing messages, must indicate to the broker when the message processing completes (successfully or not). Then the broker can decide to dispatch the next message, or to redeliver the same one if the processing failed. While the broker strategy is dependent on the broker itself, acknowledgment is a well-known concept that most messaging protocols use one way or another.

In Reactive Messaging, each message must be *acked* (acknowledged successfully) or *nacked* (acknowledged negatively, or not acked). The `Message` interface offers the `ack` and `nack` methods to indicate the successful or failed processing of the message, respectively. Both methods are asynchronous and return `CompletionStage<Void>`. Indeed, when using a remote broker, acknowledging a message means telling the broker whether the message has been processed successfully. You will see in Chapter 11 how these acknowledgments are integrated with Apache Kafka and AMQP 1.0.

When using individual payloads, Reactive Messaging handles the acknowledgment (positive or negative) for you. However, when you receive messages, you need to call these methods or produce a message that is *linked* to the incoming one. This link is essential. When the downstream consumer receives your message and acknowledges it, that consumer also acknowledges the linked message. These links form a chain of messages, and acknowledgments go up the chain until they reach the top (generally, a message produced by an emitter or from an external destination).

As depicted on Figure 10-2, the chain allows indicating the outcome of the processing, even when the processing is composed of several steps, potentially asynchronous ones.

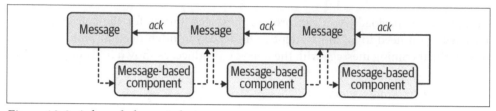

Figure 10-2. Acknowledgment chain

Let's consider an example to illustrate the behavior. Imagine receiving a message from a broker, transforming the content, and then sending this message to a remote service. For each message from the broker, this process creates a chain:

```
[(a) message from broker] -> [(b) message with the transformed content]
```

When everything is fine, the framework acknowledges the message (b), which acknowledges the message (a). The successful acknowledgment logic of the message is executed. However, if interacting with the remote service fails, it calls the nack method on the message (b), which also calls nack on the message (a). And so, it executes the negative acknowledgment logic attached to the message (a).

In more advanced scenarios, this chain can be too rigid, and you'll want more control. Typically, you may want to decide when to acknowledge a specific message, or decide to acknowledge before the processing instead of after. When using Message, you have full control and can decide to deliberately not chain messages or wait for a certain condition to acknowledge. For example, when producing multiple messages from a single one, you would acknowledge the message when all the produced messages have been acknowledged. Regardless of the use case, when using Message, don't forget to call ack or nack. Alternatively, you can use the @Acknowledgment annotation to decide where to split the chain in a more declarative manner.

Acknowledgment is essential, and with Reactive Messaging, all messages must be either *acked* or *nacked*. It's vital to implement the elasticity and resilience patterns from reactive systems. But how do we connect the applications and message brokers? That's what you are going to see in the next section.

Connectors

Connectors are specific components that map a channel to something managed externally, such as a queue or a topic. They are specific to a particular protocol or technology. There are two kinds of connectors:

Inbound connectors
> These receive messages and feed the channels. They must enforce the Reactive Streams backpressure protocol and create messages with the appropriate ack and nack logic.

Outbound connectors
> These receive messages from within the application and send them to external destinations. So they map internal messages to the external format and track the outcome to call the ack or nack method on the incoming messages.

Quarkus offers multiple connectors. Chapter 11 covers the Kafka and AMQP connectors in detail. The HTTP connector allows binding HTTP and WebSockets with your message processing. The Camel connector allows integrating legacy systems. In your application configuration, you need to specify a connector used for each channel mapped to an external destination.

Building Message-Based Applications

Enough talking; it's time to see Reactive Messaging in action. This example is located in the *chapter-10/hello-messaging* directory. To use Reactive Messaging, you need to have a dependency on quarkus-smallrye-reactive-messaging in your *pom.xml* file; see Example 10-14.

Example 10-14. Dependency for the Reactive Messaging extension (chapter-10/hello-messaging/pom.xml)

```
<dependency>
    <groupId>io.quarkus</groupId>
    <artifactId>quarkus-smallrye-reactive-messaging</artifactId>
</dependency>
```

As you will see in the next chapter, you will also need to add dependencies for the connectors. However, in this chapter, we won't use connectors.

A Reactive Messaging application includes beans containing methods annotated with @Incoming and @Outgoing. Example 10-15 contains a single bean with three methods.

*Example 10-15. Hello messaging application (chapter-10/hello-messaging/src/main/
java/org/acme/HelloMessaging.java)*

```java
package org.acme;

import io.smallrye.mutiny.Multi;
import org.eclipse.microprofile.reactive.messaging.Incoming;
import org.eclipse.microprofile.reactive.messaging.Outgoing;

import javax.enterprise.context.ApplicationScoped;
import java.time.Duration;

@ApplicationScoped
public class HelloMessaging {

    @Outgoing("ticks")
    public Multi<Long> ticks() {
        return Multi.createFrom().ticks()
                .every(Duration.ofSeconds(1))
                .onOverflow().drop();
    }

    @Incoming("ticks")
    @Outgoing("hello")
    public String hello(long tick) {
        return "Hello - " + tick;
    }

    @Incoming("hello")
    public void print(String msg) {
        System.out.println(msg);
    }

}
```

The methods form a processing pipeline. The first method, `ticks`, generates messages on the `ticks` channel. The method returns a `Multi` emitting a number every second. This number is wrapped into a simple message automatically. Then, the method `hello` consumes these ticks and produces a `String`, sent to the `hello` channel. Finally, the `print` method receives these messages and displays them on the console. We get the pipeline in Example 10-16.

Example 10-16. The processing pipeline

```
ticks() ---> [ticks] ---> hello() ----> [hello] ----> print()
```

If you go into the *chapter-10/hello-messaging* directory and run `mvn quarkus:dev`, you will see Example 10-17.

Example 10-17. Hello messages

```
Hello - 1
Hello - 2
Hello - 3
```

As you can see, building a message-processing pipeline is pretty straightforward. Beneath the hood, Reactive Messaging creates a reactive stream and creates the acknowledgment chain. That's what we are going to illustrate in the next section.

Message and Acknowledgment

To better understand the message chain, let's look at the chapter-10/messages-example directory. In this module, we create a specific implementation of `Message` (`MyMessage`), which displays on the console when a message is *acked* or *nacked* (Example 10-18).

Example 10-18. An implementation of Message (chapter-10/messages-example/src/main/java/org/acme/MyMessage.java)

```java
public class MyMessage implements Message<String> {

    private final String payload;

    public MyMessage(String payload) {
        this.payload = payload;
    }

    public MyMessage(long l) {
        this(Long.toString(l));
    }

    @Override
    public String getPayload() {
        return payload;
    }

    @Override
    public Supplier<CompletionStage<Void>> getAck() {
        return () -> {
            System.out.println("Acknowledgment for " + payload);
            return CompletableFuture.completedFuture(null);
        };
    }

    @Override
    public Function<Throwable, CompletionStage<Void>> getNack() {
        return reason -> {
            System.out.println("Negative acknowledgment for "
```

```
                    + payload + ", the reason is " + reason);
            return CompletableFuture.completedFuture(null);
        };
    }
}
```

The application itself, shown in Example 10-19, is similar to the one from the previous section. We generate a message every second, but this time, it's an instance of MyMessage instead of a payload automatically wrapped into a message. The hello method receives these messages and creates a new one with a different payload. The print method is unchanged.

Example 10-19. Usage of messages (chapter-10/messages-example/src/main/java/org/ acme/MessageExample.java)

```
@Outgoing("ticks")
public Multi<MyMessage> ticks() {
    return Multi.createFrom().ticks().every(Duration.ofSeconds(1))
            .onOverflow().drop()
            .onItem().transform(MyMessage::new);
}

@Incoming("ticks")
@Outgoing("hello")
public Message<String> hello(Message<String> tick) {
    return tick.withPayload("Hello " + tick.getPayload());
}

@Incoming("hello")
public void print(String msg) {
    System.out.println(msg);
}
```

Look at the hello method. It returns a new message built from the receiving one. The with methods link the two messages to form the chain. When the returned message is acknowledged, the received message is also acknowledged.

If you run mvn quarkus:dev from the *chapter-10/messages-example* directory, you should see this:

```
Hello 1
Acknowledgment for 1
Hello 2
Acknowledgment for 2
Hello 3
Acknowledgment for 3
```

When the print method invocation completes for a specific message, it acknowledges this message (created in the hello method), which also acknowledges the one

---

emitted by the `tick` method. That's why you can see "Acknowledgment for …" on the console.

Failures and Negative Acknowledgment

Message processing may fail, and in this case, we expect the failing message to be *nacked*. To illustrate this, let's update the code to throw an exception when it processes the third message, as shown in Example 10-20.

Example 10-20. Throwing an exception acknowledges the message negatively

```
@Incoming("hello")
public void print(String msg) {
    if (msg.contains("3")) {
        throw new IllegalArgumentException("boom");
    }
    System.out.println(msg);
}
```

Restart the application. Now the third message is nacked:

```
Hello 0
Acknowledgment for 0
Hello 1
Acknowledgment for 1
Hello 2
Acknowledgment for 2
2021-05-14 14:49:54,052 ERROR [io.sma.rea.mes.provider]
(executor-thread-1) SRMSG00200:
The method HelloMessaging#print has thrown an exception:
java.lang.IllegalArgumentException: boom
        at HelloMessaging.print(HelloMessaging.java:28)
        // ....
Negative acknowledgment for 3,
the reason is java.lang.IllegalArgumentException: boom
Hello 4
Acknowledgment for 4
```

Throwing an exception calls the `nack` method on the message and goes up the chain to call nack on the `MyMessage` instance.

In this example, our `ack` and `nack` implementations are simplistic. But they demonstrate how `ack` and `nack` can notify a message broker about the processing outcome.

Stream Manipulation

Manipulating messages one by one is straightforward, but sometimes we need to do more complicated processing. To achieve this, Reactive Messaging allows manipulating the stream of messages directly. Instead of an individual message or payload, the method receives a Multi and produces another Multi (Example 10-21).

Example 10-21. Stream manipulation with Reactive Messaging (chapter-10/stream-example/src/main/java/org/acme/StreamingExample.java)

```java
@ApplicationScoped
public class StreamingExample {

    @Outgoing("ticks")
    public Multi<Long> ticks() {
        return Multi.createFrom().ticks().every(Duration.ofSeconds(1))
                .onOverflow().drop();
    }

    @Incoming("ticks")
    @Outgoing("groups")
    public Multi<List<String>> group(Multi<Long> stream) {
        // Group the incoming messages into groups of 5.
        return stream
                .onItem().transform(l -> Long.toString(l))
                .group().intoLists().of(5);
    }


    @Incoming("groups")
    @Outgoing("hello")
    public String processGroup(List<String> list) {
        return "Hello " + String.join(",", list);
    }


    @Incoming("hello")
    public void print(String msg) {
        System.out.println(msg);
    }

}
```

You can find the complete code in the *chapter-10/stream-example* directory. The method group takes the stream of ticks as input and groups the items into lists of five elements. The processGroup method takes each group and processes them:

```
Hello 0,1,2,3,4
Hello 5,6,7,8,9
Hello 10,11,12,13,14
...
```

Although this example uses just the group operator, you can use the whole Mutiny API to orchestrate asynchronous calls, skip messages, handle failure recovery, or apply complex manipulations.

Blocking Processing

Reactive Messaging implements the reactive principles. It avoids blocking the caller thread, but sometimes it's not possible to do otherwise. Imagine lengthy processing or using a blocking API.

When facing such a situation, you can use the `@Blocking` annotation, which automatically switches the processing to a worker thread and then switches back to the I/O thread (see Example 10-22).

Example 10-22. Annotate methods with `@Blocking` (chapter-10/blocking-example/src/main/java/org/acme/BlockingExample.java)

```
@Incoming("ticks")
@Outgoing("hello")
@Blocking
public String hello(long tick) {
    // Simulate a long operation
    try {
        Thread.sleep(1000);
    } catch (InterruptedException e) {
        Thread.currentThread().interrupt();
    }
    return "Hello - " + tick;
}
```

In the *blocking-example* directory, you can find a modified version of our simple pipeline simulating a long operation in the `hello` method. Using `Thread.sleep` is blocking, so it cannot be executed on the I/O thread. Fortunately, thanks to the `@Blocking` annotation, that method is invoked on a worker thread. The `@Blocking` annotation is particularly interesting when integrating with blocking APIs. However, please don't abuse it, as it reduces the concurrency of your application.

Retrying Processing

Intermittent failures happen. Network disruptions or temporary unavailability are part of the life of any distributed system.

To handle this case, you can use the Mutiny API and use `onFailure.retry`, but you can also use the SmallRye Fault-Tolerance and its `@Retry` annotation. First, you need to declare a dependency on Fault-Tolerance, as shown in Example 10-23.

Example 10-23. Dependency for the fault-tolerance support (chapter-10/fault-tolerance-example/pom.xml)

```
<dependency>
    <groupId>io.quarkus</groupId>
    <artifactId>quarkus-smallrye-fault-tolerance</artifactId>
</dependency>
```

Then, you can use the `@Retry` annotation that automatically catches exceptions and retries the invocation. In *chapter-10/fault-tolerance-example*, you can see the code in Example 10-24.

Example 10-24. Retry the processing of messages (chapter-10/fault-tolerance-example/src/main/java/org/acme/FaultToleranceExample.java)

```
@Incoming("ticks")
@Outgoing("hello")
@Retry(maxRetries = 10, delay = 1, delayUnit = ChronoUnit.SECONDS)
public String hello(long tick) {
    maybeFaulty(); // Randomly throws an exception
    return "Hello - " + tick;
}
```

The `maybeFaulty` method throws exceptions randomly. So the `@Retry` annotation is used to retry the processing of the message, hoping for a better outcome. Remember, don't retry if your processing is not idempotent! It can have terrible consequences. It might be better to store the faulty messages on a dead-letter queue (this is covered in the next chapter).

Putting Everything Together

The last few sections have demonstrated some features offered by Reactive Messaging. These examples are simplistic on purpose. Let's now work on a more realistic pipeline where we receive HTTP requests, manipulate the body, and write it into a database. We will use RESTEasy Reactive and Hibernate Reactive, which we have seen in Chapters 8 and 9. While the application could be perfectly implemented without Reactive Messaging, we use it to illustrate how to build more complex pipelines.

The code of this application is in the *chapter-10/database-example* directory. Four classes compose the application. First, the `Person` class is a Hibernate Reactive Panache entity. This entity contains two fields: the name (unique) and the age. In this application, the user posts `Person` instances (sent as JSON), which are sent to the Reactive Messaging pipeline (as illustrated in Example 10-25).

Example 10-25. The `Person` structure (chapter-10/database-example/src/main/java/org/ acme/Person.java)

```
package org.acme;

import io.quarkus.hibernate.reactive.panache.PanacheEntity;

import javax.persistence.Column;
import javax.persistence.Entity;

@Entity
public class Person extends PanacheEntity {

    @Column(unique = true)
    public String name;

    public int age;

}
```

The `HTTPEndpoint` class uses an emitter to send the received `Person` instances to the upload channel. In addition, this class has two methods. The `upload` method receives the `Person` sent by the user and emits it. The `getAll` method returns the list of the stored `Person` instances from the database. In Example 10-26, we use this method to verify that everything works as expected. The `upload` method returns `Uni<Response>`. It creates the HTTP response asynchronously when the emitted message is acknowledged positively (then it returns a `202 - Accepted` response), or negatively (then it returns a `400 - Bad Request` response with the error message). So, when the processing is successful, the user receives its response after the insertion in the database completes.

Example 10-26. The HTTP endpoint (chapter-10/database-example/src/main/java/org/ acme/HttpEndpoint.java)

```
package org.acme;

import io.smallrye.mutiny.Uni;
import io.smallrye.reactive.messaging.MutinyEmitter;
import org.eclipse.microprofile.reactive.messaging.Channel;

import javax.ws.rs.GET;
import javax.ws.rs.POST;
import javax.ws.rs.Path;
import javax.ws.rs.core.Response;
import java.util.List;

@Path("/")
public class HttpEndpoint {
```

```
@Channel("upload")
MutinyEmitter<Person> emitter;

@POST
public Uni<Response> upload(Person person) {
    return emitter.send(person)
            .replaceWith(Response.accepted().build())
            .onFailure()
            .recoverWithItem(t ->
                    Response.status(Response.Status.BAD_REQUEST)
                            .entity(t.getMessage()).build());
}

@GET
public Uni<List<Person>> getAll() {
    return Person.listAll();
}

}
```

The `Processing` bean receives the uploaded `Person` instances and validates and for-mats the input (Example 10-27).

Example 10-27. Process `Person` instances (chapter-10/database-example/src/main/java/org/acme/Processing.java)

```
package org.acme;

import org.eclipse.microprofile.reactive.messaging.Incoming;
import org.eclipse.microprofile.reactive.messaging.Outgoing;

import javax.enterprise.context.ApplicationScoped;

@ApplicationScoped
public class Processing {

    @Incoming("upload")
    @Outgoing("database")
    public Person validate(Person person) {
        if (person.age <= 0) {
            throw new IllegalArgumentException("Invalid age");
        }

        person.name = capitalize(person.name);

        return person;
    }

    public static String capitalize(String name) {
        char[] chars = name.toLowerCase().toCharArray();
```

```
        boolean found = false;
        for (int i = 0; i < chars.length; i++) {
            if (!found && Character.isLetter(chars[i])) {
                chars[i] = Character.toUpperCase(chars[i]);
                found = true;
            } else if (Character.isWhitespace(chars[i])) {
                found = false;
            }
        }
        return String.valueOf(chars);
    }

}
```

It forwards the result to the `database` channel. The `Database` class reads this channel and writes the received `Person` to the database. To achieve this, we use the `withTran saction` and `persist` methods offered by Panache, as shown in Example 10-28.

Example 10-28. Persist the entities in the database (chapter-10/database-example/src/main/java/org/acme/Database.java)

```
package org.acme;

import io.quarkus.hibernate.reactive.panache.Panache;
import io.smallrye.mutiny.Uni;
import org.eclipse.microprofile.reactive.messaging.Incoming;

import javax.enterprise.context.ApplicationScoped;

@ApplicationScoped
public class Database {

    @Incoming("database")
    public Uni<Void> write(Person person) {
        return Panache.withTransaction(person::persist)
                .replaceWithVoid();
    }

}
```

This pipeline only passes payloads. So, when the last step completes, it acknowledges the message, which, going through the chain of messages, notifies the emitter.

Run the application with `mvn quarkus:dev` from the *chapter-10/database-example* directory. No need to provision a database; Quarkus starts a test database for you. Then, in a terminal, send a `Person` instance by using Example 10-29.

Example 10-29. Upload a new person

```
>  curl -v --header "Content-Type: application/json"  \
   POST --data '{"name":"Luke", "age":19}' \
   http://localhost:8080
```

You should get a `202 - Accepted` response. If you try to send an invalid payload, as shown in Example 10-30, you will get a `400` response.

Example 10-30. Upload an invalid person

```
>  curl -v --header "Content-Type: application/json" \
   POST --data '{"name":"Leia"}' \
   http://localhost:8080
```

You can use `curl` to check the stored instances.

Summary

In addition to having a reactive engine and providing asynchronous and nonblocking ways to deal with HTTP and databases, Quarkus comes with a message-based model called Reactive Messaging.

Remember:

- Reactive Messaging allows receiving, processing, and consuming messages transiting on channels.

- The channel can be internal to the application, as you have seen in this chapter, or mapped to external destinations, as you will see in the next chapter.

- Reactive Messaging supports positive and negative acknowledgment. You can decide the amount of control you need.

- Reactive Messaging allows handling messages individually or supports the Mutiny API to implement more complex transformations.

In the next chapter, we will look at two connectors that will allow interacting with Apache Kafka and AMQP to build reactive systems.

## CHAPTER 11

The Event Bus: The Backbone

In Chapter 10, we discussed Reactive Messaging and utilizing its annotations to produce, consume, and process messages, as well as to bridge imperative and reactive programming. This chapter dives deeper into the backbone of a reactive system built with Reactive Messaging, focusing on Apache Kafka and Advanced Message Queuing Protocol (AMQP).[1]

Kafka or AMQP: Picking the Right Tool

Plenty of messaging solutions let you implement event-driven architecture, event streaming, and reactive systems in general. Recently, Apache Kafka became a prominent player in this space. AMQP is another approach for messaging that should not be immediately ruled out. Both have pros and cons. Your choice depends entirely on your use cases, and to a lesser extent the existing skills and experience of a team.

Rather than favoring one event bus over another, this section details the characteristics and behaviors of each, along with their relative strengths and weaknesses. We want to provide you sufficient information about each system, enabling you to determine how they may fit into the use cases for a particular system.

At a high level, Kafka can be described as smart consumers with a dumb broker, while AMQP has a smart broker but dumb consumers. Sometimes the choice comes down to the amount of flexibility needed when implementing a solution.

Sure it's cliché, but there really is no one-size-fits-all event bus. Each situation has specific requirements and use cases to be fulfilled, requiring careful evaluation of the pros and cons of each. Note that other messaging solutions might be better for your

---

1 Throughout this chapter, we will be talking about AMQP 1.0.

use case, such as the Solace PubSub+ Platform (*https://solace.com*), Microsoft Azure Event Hubs (*https://oreil.ly/eXz0E*), RabbitMQ (*https://rabbitmq.com*), or NATS (*https://nats.io*).

Building Reactive Systems with Kafka

Since 2011, when Apache Kafka was open sourced by LinkedIn, it has skyrocketed to becoming one of the most prominent actors in the event-driven space. Fueled by the rise of microservices, serverless architecture, and distributed systems in general, Kafka is a popular choice for developers needing a messaging backbone.

While Chapter 10 already gave examples of using Kafka, we didn't explain the important details of how it works underneath, which are necessary to understand it well. This chapter dives a bit deeper and explains how to use Kafka as the connective tissue in a reactive system. We don't intend to cover Kafka in full detail, but enough to appreciate how Kafka operates to effectively develop a reactive system. First off, we need to cover the basics of Kafka.

Apache Kafka

Kafka is a powerful distributed commit log, and if you're a developer, you're probably familiar with another distributed commit log, Git! When communicating with Kafka, we use a *record*, or event, as the piece of information we want written to the log, and which we then read from the log later. The log contains a *topic* for each record grouping we want to track (Figure 11-1).

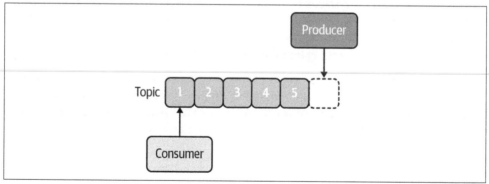

Figure 11-1. Kafka topic

A record can hold only four pieces of information:

Key

  Assigned by Kafka when writing a record into the log, but can also be used in partitioning, which we cover later

Value

The actual value, or payload, we want to be stored in the log for retrieval by consumers

Timestamp

Optionally set when we create the record, or set by Kafka when the record is written to the log

Headers

Optional metadata about the record to provide extra information to Kafka, or for downstream consumers to utilize

Figure 11-2 outlines the process of interacting with the log.

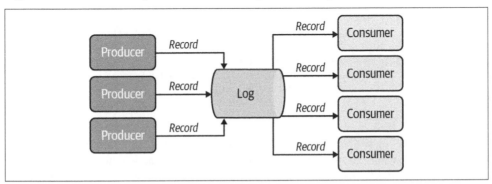

Figure 11-2. Producing and consuming records

With a record created, we write it to the log in Kafka with a producer. We can have one or many producer instances writing the same type of record to the log, because the way we write records to the log is decoupled from the way they're consumed. Once a record is written to the log, we use a consumer to read the record from the log and perform whatever processing is needed with it.

When writing records to the log, a producer always appends. A producer cannot insert or delete records. An append-only approach means Kafka can offer high scalability for writes. Because there is no contention or locking for existing records, every write is a new record.

Separation of producers and consumers is a key concept with Kafka. This decoupling of time between when records are written to the log and consumed from it is key for reactive systems. Granted, this is 100% achievable only when the log retention policies are sufficiently long enough to prevent any produced records from being removed before they're consumed! We don't want to log all the records and have them deleted by Kafka before we consume them years later.

In Chapter 10, you saw how to produce messages with @Outgoing. Let's modify that example slightly to also set a key for the record, as shown in Example 11-1.

Example 11-1. Configure the Kafka outgoing metadata

```
@Outgoing("my-channel")
Multi<Message<Person>> produceAStreamOfMessagesOfPersons() {
    return Multi.createFrom().items(
            Message.of(new Person("Luke"))
                .addMetadata(OutgoingKafkaRecordMetadata.builder()
                    .withKey("light").build()),
            Message.of(new Person("Leia"))
                .addMetadata(OutgoingKafkaRecordMetadata.builder()
                    .withKey("light").build()),
            Message.of(new Person("Obiwan"))
                .addMetadata(OutgoingKafkaRecordMetadata.builder()
                    .withKey("light").build()),
            Message.of(new Person("Palpatine"))
                .addMetadata(OutgoingKafkaRecordMetadata.builder()
                    .withKey("dark").build())
    );
}
```

Here we have a key to indicate whether the person is part of the *light* or *dark* side of the force. To switch to producing the message to Kafka, we need to make two changes. First, modify *pom.xml* to include the SmallRye Reactive Messaging for Kafka dependency (Example 11-2).

Example 11-2. Kafka connector dependency (/Users/clement/Documents/book/code-repository/chapter-11/processor/pom.xml)

```
<dependency>
    <groupId>io.quarkus</groupId>
    <artifactId>quarkus-smallrye-reactive-messaging-kafka</artifactId>
</dependency>
```

Lastly, configure the dependency, as shown in Example 11-3.

Example 11-3. Configure the Kafka connector to write records (chapter-11/processor/src/main/resources/application.properties)

```
mp.messaging.outgoing.my-channel.connector=smallrye-kafka
mp.messaging.outgoing.my-channel.topic=starwars
mp.messaging.outgoing.my-channel.value.serializer=\
    org.apache.kafka.common.serialization.StringSerializer
```

The configuration indicates the connector we're using, smallrye-kafka, the name of the topic the channel should be writing to, and the serializer for converting the payload content. If the topic being written to matches the name of the channel, we would not need the topic configuration, as the channel name is the default.

On the consuming side, we can read the key with Example 11-4.

Example 11-4. Extract the incoming Kafka metadata

```
@Incoming("my-channel")
CompletionStage<Void> consume(Message<Person> person) {
    String msgKey = (String) person
            .getMetadata(IncomingKafkaRecordMetadata.class).get()
            .getKey();
    // ...
    return person.ack();
}
```

We also need similar configuration as outgoing for us to use Kafka; see Example 11-5.

Example 11-5. Configure the Kafka connector to poll records (chapter-11/processor/src/ main/resources/application.properties)

```
mp.messaging.incoming.my-channel.connector=smallrye-kafka
mp.messaging.incoming.my-channel.topic=starwars
mp.messaging.incoming.my-channel.value.deserializer=\
    org.apache.kafka.common.serialization.StringDeserializer
```

So far, we've been generically referring to write records to and consume records from a log. As you have seen in Figure 11-1, a *topic* is a log, a means of organizing and durably storing records. This log is for a specific type of record, or group of records, enabling us to customize the behavior specifically to the needs of those records. For instance, if the records are of extremely high volume and not meaningful to the application for longer than a week, we could change the retention policy for one topic to retain records for only that period of time, even if they haven't been consumed. We could also have another topic that has records retained for six months or even indefinitely.

Also in Figure 11-1 you can see each record as a box with a number; this represents the *offset*, or index, of where a record is written in a topic. In this instance, six records have already been written, and a producer is about to write the seventh, which is offset 6. We also see a consumer reading the record at offset 0, the first record in the topic. Though the default is for a new consumer to begin reading records from the first offset, we could decide to start at any offset we wanted.

Another way to consider a topic is as a virtual address representing an external destination. When a producer writes a record to a topic, it has no knowledge of when, if, or even where the record will be read by a consumer. Use of a virtual address, or topic, provides the means of decoupling our reactive system components from one another in space and time.

A consumer can be combined with others to form a *consumer group*. Any consumer created with the same consumer group name, or identifier, will be placed in the same consumer group. When creating a consumer without setting a consumer group identifier, we end up with a consumer group containing a single consumer by default.

So far, what we've described implies a topic with a single log of records. A *partition* is how we improve the problems associated with a single-log approach. Partitions are useful for improving the read and write performance of a topic, as we split a single topic into multiple partitions.

Instead of a single partition with a single consumer, we could have three partitions with a separate consumer reading records from each of them. Looking at this situation unscientifically, we could expect there to be three times the amount of throughput with three partitions and three consumers, as opposed to a single partition and consumer.

Though we mentioned three consumers for three partitions, in Figure 11-3 we have two consumers within a single consumer group. One consumer is assigned to read records from two partitions, to ensure that all partitions have consumers. We've now improved our throughput by partitioning the topic, enabling multiple consumers to consume records.

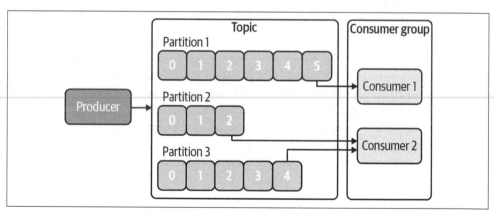

Figure 11-3. Topic partitions

In the situation shown in Figure 11-3, a producer can write a record to the topic, leaving the broker to decide which partition the record is actually written to. Alternatively, the producer can explicitly define the partition that a record should be written to. If records have a key unique to the record's contents, such as username for a Person record, it can be efficient to determine the appropriate partition with the

Kafka key-hashing algorithm. It will ensure that all records with an identical key are written to the same partition. We need to be careful, though, to ensure that any key is reasonably distributed. Otherwise, we risk creating a *hot partition* (for example, partitioning by country may see trillions of records placed in a USA partition, but only a few thousand records in the Andorra partition).

Right now we have an issue with resiliency because all our partitions are on the same broker instance. In Figure 11-4, we've replicated the topic across three partitions.

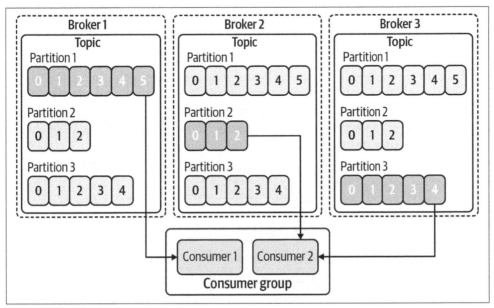

Figure 11-4. Topic partition replication

To support resiliency and ensure that consumers don't read the same record in a partition from different brokers, a *leader partition* is elected for consumers to read from. Partition 0 in the first broker, Partition 1 in the second, and Partition 2 in the third broker are the leader partitions in this example.

With the design we have in Figure 11-4, Kafka ensures that our consumers cannot read a record from a partition before it has been successfully replicated. It does this by tracking the *high watermark offset*, the offset of the last message successfully replicated across all partitions. The broker prevents consumers from reading beyond the high watermark offset, stopping unreplicated records from being read.

Point-to-Point Communication

Kafka is not a traditional messaging system. It can be confusing to implement the standard delivery patterns with it.

With *point-to-point communication*, we want the same message to be consumed once, by the same consumer or by any other consumer within the same consumer group. Note that when facing network failures, you cannot guarantee that records are consumed only once per consumer group. You need to be prepared to see duplicated messages.

We use *consumer groups* to scale a consumer in Kafka to perform identical processing with greater throughput. In Figure 11-5, only one consumer within the group is able to read records from a single topic partition, conforming to the needs of point-to-point communication. Here we see Consumer 2 unable to read records because it's part of the same consumer group as Consumer 1, effectively making Consumer 2 idle, as we have only one partition in this situation.

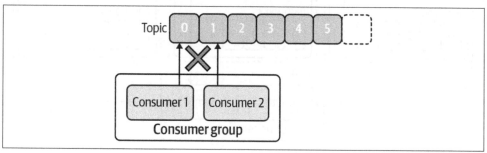

Figure 11-5. Consumer groups

Why can't we have two consumers in the same group reading from the same partition? Kafka tracks the last committed offset per partition for a given consumer group and uses the offset for restarting processing. However, consumers don't commit the offset until they've completely finished processing a record. This creates a window where multiple consumers in the same group could read the same record, thus duplicating the processing of a message.

When a new consumer subscribes to a consumer group, and Kafka does not know the last committed offset for the partition, there are two strategies. The strategies are *Earliest*, where the consumer starts reading events from the first offset of the partition, and *Latest*, which consumes only events received after the consumer subscribed.

Publish/Subscribe

Point-to-point ensures that messages are consumed once. Another popular pattern dispatches a message to multiple consumers. With a *publish/subscribe* model, we can have many subscribers, or consumers, reading the same message, usually for different purposes.

Figure 11-6 has two consumer groups consuming messages from the same topic. One consumer group has three consumers, while the other has two consumers. We see each partition being read by only a single consumer from the same consumer group, but multiple consumers across consumer groups. Though the two consumer groups are connected to the same topic and its partitions, there is no requirement for each consumer to be at the same offset. Such a requirement would remove the benefits of being able to consume records with different groups.

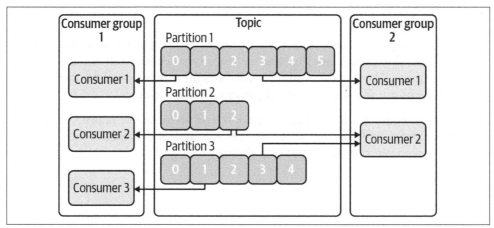

Figure 11-6. Multiple consumer groups

Elasticity Patterns

Elasticity is one of the pillars of reactive systems. The partition mechanism offered by Kafka lets us implement elasticity patterns. Figure 11-6 also highlights the elasticity patterns of consumer groups in Kafka. Consumer group 1 has three consumers, each consuming from a different partition. If a consumer fails for any reason, another consumer takes up the load of reading from the partition that is now without a consumer. Consumer elasticity ensures that all partitions are being consumed as long as at least one consumer is present. Granted, such an occurrence does reduce the throughput, but it is preferable over no records being consumed. Consumer group 2 could represent such an occurrence.

Consumer group elasticity is limited, though. As we mentioned earlier, it is not possible for multiple consumers within the same group to read from the same partition. In

Figure 11-6, with three partitions we're limited to three consumers within a single consumer group. Any additional consumers in the same group would be idle, as we cannot have multiple consumers in the same group connected to the same partition.

Elasticity is a key factor to consider when determining the number of partitions we want for a topic. With too few, we limit the throughput for processing records, while too many can lead to idle consumers if the records are not distributed across the partitions sufficiently evenly.

Dealing with Failures

Failures happen! It's the nature of distributed systems, and not one we can avoid even when developing reactive systems. However, Kafka provides us with mechanisms for appropriately dealing with failure.

Commit strategies

Each consumer periodically informs the broker of its latest *offset commit*. The number represents the last message that was successfully processed from a topic partition by the consumer. The offset commit then becomes the starting point for the new consumer of the partition when the current consumer fails or crashes.

Committing an offset is not a cheap operation. For performance reasons, we recommend not committing the offset after every record processed. Quarkus provides a few options for commit strategies to use with Kafka:

- Throttled
- Ignore
- Latest

The *Throttled* strategy, the default option, tracks the received records for a consumer and monitors their acknowledgment. When all records before a position are successfully processed, that position is committed to the broker as the new offset for that consumer group. If any record is neither acked nor nacked, it's no longer possible to commit a new offset position, and records will be continually enqueued. Without the ability to bail out, it would lead to out-of-memory errors eventually. The Throttled strategy can detect this problem by reporting a failure to the connector, enabling the application to be marked as unhealthy. Note that this situation is often an application bug causing a message to be "forgotten."

The *Ignore* strategy utilizes the default offset commit of the Kafka consumer, which occurs periodically when polling for new records. This strategy ignores message acknowledgment and relies on record processing to be synchronous. This strategy is the default when `enabled.auto.commit=true` is used. Any asynchronous processing that fails will be unknown to the process that is polling for new records to consume.

If we've set `commit-strategy` to `ignore` and `enable.auto.commit` to `false`, as shown in Example 11-6, no offset is ever committed. Every time a new consumer starts reading messages from a topic, it will always start from offset 0. In some situations, this approach is desired, but it needs to be a conscious choice.

Example 11-6. Configure the commit strategy

```
mp.messaging.incoming.my-channel.connector=smallrye-kafka
mp.messaging.incoming.my-channel.enable.auto.commit=false
mp.messaging.incoming.my-channel.commit-strategy=ignore
```

Latest will commit the offset after every message is acknowledged, which as we described earlier will impact performance of the consumer. In lower-throughput scenarios, this strategy may be preferable to have a higher confidence that the offset is accurate.

Acknowledgment strategies

In "Acknowledgments" on page 187, you learned how Reactive Messaging utilizes `ack` and `nack` to inform the upstream reactive streams of the record-processing status. These acknowledgment methods are part of the failure-handling strategies we have available for Kafka. The application configures the Kafka connector with one of these strategies.

The simplest, and default, strategy is *Fail Fast*. When an application rejects a message, the connector is notified of the failure, and the application is stopped. If the failure is transient in origin, such as network issues, restarting the application should allow processing to continue without an issue. However, if a particular record causes a consumer failure, the application will be in a perpetual loop of failure → stop → restart, as it will be continually trying to process the record causing a failure.

Another simple strategy is *Ignore*. Any nacked message is logged and then ignored as the consumer continues processing new records. The Ignore strategy is beneficial when our application handles any failure internally, and we thus don't need to inform the message producer of a failure, or when an ignored message occasionally is acceptable because of the type of messages being processed. If, on the other hand, large numbers of messages are being ignored, it is worth investigating the root cause as it's likely not an intended consequence.

The last strategy for failure handling is *Dead-Letter Queue*. It sends the failing records to a specific topic to be handled later either automatically or manually.

Dead-letter queue

This strategy has been a part of messaging systems for as long as messaging systems have existed! Instead of failing straight away, or ignoring any failures, this strategy stores the messages that fail to a separate destination, or topic. Storing the failed messages enables an administration process, human or automated, to determine the correct cause of action to resolve the failed handling.

It's important to note that the use of the Dead-Letter Queue strategy will work only when ordering of all messages is unnecessary, as we don't stop processing new messages waiting for a message failure to be resolved off the dead-letter queue (DLQ).

When choosing this strategy, the default topic is named dead-letter-topic-*[topic-name]*. For our previous examples, it would be dead-letter-topic-my-channel. It is possible to configure the topic name as shown in Example 11-7.

Example 11-7. Configure the failure strategy to use a DLQ

```
mp.messaging.incoming.my-channel.failure-strategy=dead-letter-queue
mp.messaging.incoming.my-channel.dead-letter-queue.topic=my-dlq
```

We can even retrieve the failure reason associated with the message from the dead-letter-reason header (Example 11-8).

Example 11-8. Retrieve the failure reason

```
@Incoming("my-dlq")
public CompletionStage<Void> dlq(Message<String> rejected) {
  IncomingKafkaRecordMetadata<String, String> metadata =
      rejected.getMetadata(IncomingKafkaRecordMetadata.class);
  String reason = new String(metadata.getHeaders()
    .lastHeader("dead-letter-reason").value());
}
```

Don't forget that using a DLQ requires having another application or a human operator to process the records sent to the DLQ. The records may be reintroduced in the initial topic (but the order is lost) or dropped, or a mitigation logic would need to happen.

Backpressure and Performance Considerations

There is no way to have a truly reactive system without appropriate backpressure to avoid overloading components. So how do we handle backpressure for Kafka?

The outbound connector for Kafka, used with @Outgoing or Emitter, uses the number of in-flight messages waiting for acknowledgment from the broker. *In-flight messages* are those the connector has sent to a Kafka broker for writing to a topic, but for which the connector has not received acknowledgment that the record was successfully stored.

We tweak the number of in-flight messages to adjust the backpressure of the outbound Kafka connector. The default number of in-flight messages is 1,024. Too high a number can lead to higher memory use, potentially out-of-memory errors depending on the payload size, while too few causes a reduction in throughput. We can customize the number of in-flight messages in the connector with the property `max-inflight-messages`.

On the side of the consumer, Kafka will pause the consumer and then resume it, according to the Reactive Streams requests. We've talked a lot about Kafka, so in the next section we explore it in Kubernetes!

Kafka on Kubernetes

To use Kafka on Kubernetes, we need Kafka installed. We will use the Strimzi (*https://strimzi.io*) project for installing Kafka. This project has an operator for managing Kafka deployments in Kubernetes.

Before setting up Kafka in Kubernetes, we need a Kubernetes environment. If you already have one, great! If you don't, we recommend you use minikube, as covered in "The New Kids on the Block: Cloud Native and Kubernetes Native Applications" on page 46.

> Running Kafka in minikube can require more memory than usual deployments, so we recommend starting it with at least 4 GB of RAM:
>
> ```
> minikube start --memory=4096
> ```

With a Kubernetes environment running, we need to install Strimzi, as shown in Example 11-9. Be sure to have Helm (*https://helm.sh*) installed, as we will use it to install Strimzi.

Example 11-9. Install Strimzi

```
kubectl create ns strimzi                      ❶
kubectl create ns kafka                        ❷

helm repo add strimzi https://strimzi.io/charts              ❸
helm install strimzi strimzi/strimzi-kafka-operator -n strimzi \
    --set watchNamespaces={kafka} --wait --timeout 300s      ❹
```

❶ Create a `strimzi` namespace for the Kubernetes operator.

❷ Namespace for the Kafka cluster.

❸ Add the Strimzi chart repository to Helm.

❹ Install the Strimzi operator into the `strimzi` namespace.

Once the installation has succeeded, verify that the operator is running (as illustrated in Example 11-10).

Example 11-10. Strimzi operator status

```
kubectl get pods -n strimzi
NAME                                     READY   STATUS    RESTARTS   AGE
strimzi-cluster-operator-58fcdbfc8f-mjdxg   1/1     Running   0          46s
```

Now it's time to create the Kafka cluster! First we need to define the cluster we want to create, as shown in Example 11-11.

Example 11-11. Kafka cluster definition

```
apiVersion: kafka.strimzi.io/v1beta2
kind: Kafka
metadata:
  name: my-cluster                    ❶
spec:
  kafka:
    replicas: 1                       ❷
    listeners:
      - name: plain
        port: 9092
        type: internal
        tls: false
      - name: tls
        port: 9093
        type: internal
        tls: true
    config:
      offsets.topic.replication.factor: 1
      transaction.state.log.replication.factor: 1
      transaction.state.log.min.isr: 1
    storage:
      type: ephemeral                 ❸
  zookeeper:
    replicas: 1
    storage:
      type: ephemeral
  entityOperator:
    topicOperator: {}
    userOperator: {}
```

❶ Name of the cluster.

❷ Number of Kafka replicas to create in the cluster. In production, we would want more than one, but for testing this reduces the memory requirements.

❸ We choose ephemeral storage, again to reduce the requirements from a testing perspective.

Now we use Example 11-11 to create a Kafka cluster matching the requested definition, as shown in Example 11-12.

Example 11-12. Create a Kafka cluster

```
kubectl apply -f deploy/kafka/kafka-cluster.yaml -n kafka
```

Verify that the cluster we wanted was created (Example 11-13).

Example 11-13. Kafka cluster status

```
kubectl get pods -n kafka
NAME                                           READY   STATUS    RESTARTS   AGE
my-cluster-entity-operator-765f64f4fd-2t8mk    3/3     Running   0          90s
my-cluster-kafka-0                             1/1     Running   0          113s
my-cluster-zookeeper-0                         1/1     Running   0          2m12s
```

With the cluster running, we create the Kafka topics we need (Example 11-14).

Example 11-14. Create Kafka topics

```
kubectl apply -f deploy/kafka/ticks.yaml
kubectl apply -f deploy/kafka/processed.yaml
```

To show you how Kafka works with Kubernetes, we will use an example that consists of three services: produce a *tick* every two seconds, receive the message and add details of the consumer processing it, and expose all messages via SSE. These three services will be used to showcase consumer handling with Kafka. Follow the instructions in */chapter-11/README.md* under *Application deployment* for building the required Docker images and installing the services with Helm.

Once the services are running, it's time to test it! Open the SSE endpoint in a browser, and you will see data similar to Example 11-15.

Example 11-15. SSE output: all the messages are consumed by the same pod

```
data:1 consumed in pod (processor-d44564db5-48n97)
data:2 consumed in pod (processor-d44564db5-48n97)
data:3 consumed in pod (processor-d44564db5-48n97)
```

```
data:4 consumed in pod (processor-d44564db5-48n97)
data:5 consumed in pod (processor-d44564db5-48n97)
```

We can see all the ticks consumed by a single consumer, even though we have three partitions for our topic. Let's scale up `processor` to add more consumers to the same group (Example 11-16).

Example 11-16. Increase the number of application instances

```
kubectl scale deployment/processor -n event-bus --replicas=3
```

In the browser, we now see the messages processed by three consumers of the same group, increasing throughput and concurrency (Example 11-17).

Example 11-17. SSE output: the messages are consumed by the three pods

```
data:11 consumed in pod (processor-d44564db5-2cklg)
data:12 consumed in pod (processor-d44564db5-48n97)
data:13 consumed in pod (processor-d44564db5-s6rx9)
data:14 consumed in pod (processor-d44564db5-2cklg)
data:15 consumed in pod (processor-d44564db5-s6rx9)
data:16 consumed in pod (processor-d44564db5-48n97)
data:17 consumed in pod (processor-d44564db5-2cklg)
```

If we started another `processor` instance but without `mp.messaging.incom` `ing.ticks.group.` `id=tick-consumer` set, we would see the duplication of message numbers from the new consumer, as they have their own consumer group and offset position.

Building Reactive Systems with AMQP

Advanced Message Queuing Protocol, or *AMQP*, is an application layer protocol for message-oriented middleware that has been around since 2002. The AMQP Broker is a highly advanced message broker with a tremendous amount of flexibility and customization dependent on application requirements.

We don't cover all the possible uses of the AMQP Broker here. With a huge array of possible broker topologies to support many varied use cases, there is simply too much information to even attempt to squeeze it all into this section! Robert Godfrey on InfoQ (*https://oreil.ly/xC0ar*) presents the AMQP 1.0 core features and introduces some possibilities.

Unlike Kafka, all the *smarts* are inside the AMQP Broker, which knows about topologies, clients, message statuses, what is delivered, and what is yet to be delivered.

AMQP 1.0

AMQP 1.0 is an open standard for passing business messages among applications or organizations. It consists of several layers, the lowest of which is a binary wire-level protocol for transferring a message between two processes. On top of the wire-level protocol is the messaging layer, which defines an abstract message format and encoding. The wire-level protocol is what enables many clients of different types to be able to send and receive messages with the AMQP Broker, as long as they support the same 1.0 version of the AMQP specification.

Utilizing the AMQP 1.0 connector in Quarkus requires the dependency in Example 11-18.

Example 11-18. Dependency for the AMQP connector

```
<dependency>
    <groupId>io.quarkus</groupId>
    <artifactId>quarkus-smallrye-reactive-messaging-amqp</artifactId>
</dependency>
```

Point-to-Point Communication

With AMQP, point-to-point communication is achieved with a *queue* and not a *topic*. In AMQP-speak a queue is referred to as *anycast*, meaning any consumer can read the message, but only one of them (Figure 11-7). Messages we add to a queue can be durable, as with Kafka, but they can also be nondurable. When a message is nondurable, it will be lost if the broker restarts before the message is consumed.

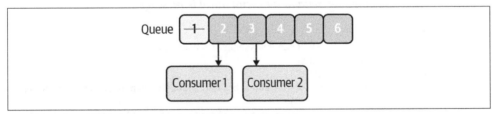

Figure 11-7. AMQP queue consumers

A key difference between Kafka and AMQP for point-to-point is that once a message is read by a consumer in AMQP, the message is removed from the queue and not retained in any way. AMQP temporarily stores messages until they've been consumed, whereas Kafka retains all messages in the log, at least until the log-retention policy begins removing older ones. This makes AMQP unsuitable for use cases that could require a replay of messages within the reactive system at some point.

We can also have many consumers reading messages from the same queue, but the broker ensures that only one of them ever reads a single message. AMQP does not have the same throughput restrictions as Kafka with respect to scaling consumers. We can have dozens of consumers reading from a single queue with AMQP, provided order is not important.

Let's send a message to AMQP! After adding the dependency we mentioned earlier (Example 11-18), we need to configure the broker properties as shown in Example 11-19, so the connector knows the location of the AMQP Broker.

Example 11-19. Configure the AMQP Broker location and credentials

```
amqp-host=amqp
amqp-port=5672
amqp-username=username
amqp-password=password

mp.messaging.outgoing.data.connector=smallrye-amqp
```

We've set the AMQP Broker configuration for host, port, username, and password globally, meaning any channel we define will use the identical AMQP Broker configuration. If desired, the configuration can be set on a per-channel basis. We've also indicated to use the `smallrye-amqp` connector for the `data` outgoing channel.

By default, the channel uses durable messages for the queue, or we make them nondurable with `mp.messaging.outgoing.data.durable=false`. We can also override the message durability directly when sending the message, as shown in Example 11-20.

Example 11-20. Use outgoing metadata to send durable messages

```
@Outgoing("data")
Multi<Message<Person>> produceAStreamOfMessagesOfPersons() {
    return Multi.createFrom().items(
        Message.of(new Person("Luke"))
            .addMetadata(OutgoingAmqpMetadata.builder().withDurable(false).build()),
        Message.of(new Person("Leia"))
            .addMetadata(OutgoingAmqpMetadata.builder().withDurable(false).build()),
        Message.of(new Person("Obiwan"))
            .addMetadata(OutgoingAmqpMetadata.builder().withDurable(false).build()),
        Message.of(new Person("Palpatine"))
            .addMetadata(OutgoingAmqpMetadata.builder().withDurable(false).build())
    );
}
```

We can then consume the message similarly to Kafka, but using the AMQP metadata object to retrieve more detailed information about the message (Example 11-21).

Example 11-21. Extract AMQP metadata from incoming messages

```
@Incoming("data")
CompletionStage<Void> consume(Message<Person> person) {
    Optional<IncomingAmqpMetadata> metadata = person
            .getMetadata(IncomingAmqpMetadata.class);
    metadata.ifPresent(meta -> {
        String address = meta.getAddress();
        String subject = meta.getSubject();
        });
    // ...
    return person.ack();
}
```

Successful receipt and processing of a message results in the connector notifying the broker with an `accepted` acknowledgment. On receiving this acknowledgment, the broker will delete the message from the queue.

Publish/Subscribe

AMQP also supports a publish/subscribe model, similarly to Kafka, allowing many subscribers for a single queue to read messages. In AMQP, a queue can be of type *multicast* (the opposite of *unicast*) to indicate that many consumers can receive the same message.

Figure 11-8 has three consumers of a multicast queue reading messages, and we see how far through the messages each of the consumers has gotten. As with unicast queues, the messages are durable by default but can also be made nondurable if desired.

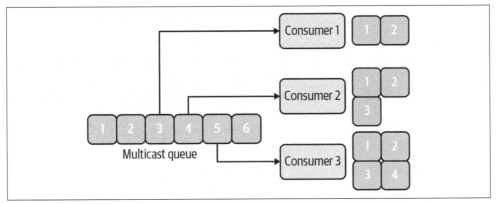

Figure 11-8. AMQP multicast queue consumers

The code for sending and receiving messages from a multicast queue is identical to the code we used for point-to-point in "Point-to-Point Communication" on page 217.

The *address* defaults to the channel name; it can be customized in configuration of the channel or set directly on the metadata of the message.

Elasticity Patterns

The elasticity patterns for AMQP with point-to-point communication are a little different. With Kafka, we can have only one consumer reading from a single partition. With AMQP, we can have as many consumers as we want reading from the same queue, given the order in which the messages are processed is not important.

Granted, we may not want a lot of consumers reading the queue from the same broker node, but we are able to cluster the brokers to spread the load across them. With a cluster of brokers, the broker is smart enough to shift messages from one broker to another if it notices the consumers of a queue on that broker are underutilized compared to other brokers.

Acknowledgment and Redelivery

When we send a message to an AMQP Broker, it is acknowledged if the broker successfully committed the message. However, this will not be the case when routers are utilized between the producer and a broker. In this situation, it is recommended to set `auto-acknowledgement` to `true` to ensure that the producer receives acknowledgment when the message is sent to the router. Any response from the broker of `rejected`, `released`, or `modified` results in the message being nacked.

The consumption side has a few more possibilities for acknowledgment. We can `fail` the message, causing the application to enter a failed state and process no further messages. The message being processed resulting in the failure is marked as `rejected` with the broker. This is the default behavior for the AMQP connector.

The Accept, Release, and Reject strategies all result in the failure being logged, and the application to continue processing additional messages. The only difference between them is in the way the AMQP messages are designated on the broker. The Accept strategy marks the message as `accepted`, the Release one marks it as `released`, and, finally, the Reject one marks it as `rejected`. When we want to continue processing messages on failure, which of the three options you set depends on how you want the AMQP Broker to handle the message.

What about redelivery? If we mark the AMQP message as `released`, the broker can redeliver the message, to the same or different consumer, at a later time. When setting a message as `modified`, we have two available strategies. Using the `modified-failed` strategy sets a `delivery-failed` attribute on the message, enabling the broker to attempt redelivery of the message while processing continues with the next message. However, using the `modified-failed-undeliverable-here` strategy also sets the `delivery-failed` attribute, and while the broker can attempt redelivery of the message, it won't do so with this consumer.

If at any point the consumer loses the session with a broker, any in-progress work will be rolled back. This allows for other consumers, or restarting of the current consumer, to accept redelivery of any messages that were in-flight at the time the session with the broker was severed.

Credit-Flow Backpressure Protocol

AMQP enables backpressure in producers with a credit system. Producers are able to send messages to a broker only as long as they have credits available, preventing producers from overloading the broker with too many messages in a small amount of time. The credits represent the number of bytes a producer can send. For example, if we had 1,000 credits, representing 1,000 bytes, a producer would be able to send 1 message of 1,000 bytes or 10 messages of 100 bytes before the credits expired.

When a producer has spent all its credits, it waits in a nonblocking manner until additional credits are granted from the broker. The default is to request additional credits every 2,000 ms, but this setting can be configured with the `credit-retrieval-period` configuration property.

When running out of credit, the connector marks the application as `not ready`. This information is then reported to the application health check. If you deploy the application to Kubernetes, the readiness health check will fail, and Kubernetes will stop sending traffic to the pod until it becomes ready again.

AMQP on Kubernetes

Setting up a production-ready AMQP Broker on Kubernetes is not a straightforward task, so we're opting to use a single Docker image to keep it simple. With a Kubernetes environment running, run an AMQP Broker container, as shown in Example 11-22.

Example 11-22. Start AMQP Broker container

```
kubectl run amqp --image=quay.io/artemiscloud/activemq-artemis-broker \
    --port=5672 --env="AMQ_USER=admin" --env="AMQ_PASSWORD=admin" \
    -n event-bus
```

Here, we start an AMQP Broker in a Kubernetes pod, but we need to expose the broker as a service to make it accessible to the services, as shown in Example 11-23.

Example 11-23. Expose AMQP Broker service port

```
kubectl expose pod amqp --port=5672 -n event-bus
```

To be able to use AMQP, we need to switch our code to utilize a different dependency and configuration, but the bulk of the services remain unchanged. For each service, comment out the `quarkus-smallrye-reactive-messaging-kafka` dependency and uncomment the `quarkus-smallrye-reactive-messaging-amqp` dependency in each *pom.xml*. In the *application.properties* file for each service, comment out the `smallrye-kafka` connector configuration and uncomment the `smallrye-amqp` connector. Don't forget to change both connectors in the `processor` service! Be sure to run `mvn clean package` on all the services after making these changes.

All the AMQP Broker configuration is present in the Helm charts, with the actual values in *values.yaml*. Follow the instructions in */chapter-11/README.md* under *Application deployment* for building the required Docker images and installing the services. They are the same steps we used for Kafka earlier in the chapter. Once the services are running, it's time to test it! Open the SSE endpoint in a browser to see data as we did with Kafka (Example 11-24).

Example 11-24. SSE output: all the messages are consumed by a single pod

```
data:2 consumed in pod (processor-7558d76994-mq624)
data:3 consumed in pod (processor-7558d76994-mq624)
data:4 consumed in pod (processor-7558d76994-mq624)
```

Let's scale up `processor` to add more consumers, as shown in Example 11-25.

Example 11-25. Increase the number of application instances (pods)

```
kubectl scale deployment/processor -n event-bus --replicas=3
```

Scaling with AMQP has a different outcome from that of scaling with Kafka; see Example 11-26.

Example 11-26. SSE output: the messages are consumed by the three pods

```
data:187 consumed in pod (processor-7558d76994-mq624)
data:187 consumed in pod (processor-7558d76994-hbp6j)
data:187 consumed in pod (processor-7558d76994-q2vcc)
data:188 consumed in pod (processor-7558d76994-q2vcc)
data:188 consumed in pod (processor-7558d76994-hbp6j)
data:188 consumed in pod (processor-7558d76994-mq624)
data:189 consumed in pod (processor-7558d76994-mq624)
data:189 consumed in pod (processor-7558d76994-hbp6j)
data:189 consumed in pod (processor-7558d76994-q2vcc)
```

We're now seeing the same message consumed by all three producers, instead of a message consumed once!

Summary

This chapter went deeper into understanding the event bus when we use AMQP or Kafka with Reactive Messaging. If we don't need metadata classes for specific Kafka or AMQP behavior, we can easily switch between the two with a dependency change and modifying configuration. We covered how each of the event bus options support point-to-point communication, publish/subscribe, acknowledgments, failure handling, and backpressure. These are all key concepts in understanding the totality of a reactive system and its components.

Kafka is the current popular choice for many event-driven reactive systems. Kafka can handle a massive number of messages and makes ordering an essential characteristic. AMQP does have a lot more flexibility than Kafka in the way it can be configured and customized. It also has higher elasticity in point-to-point scenarios, as the limit is not constrained by the number of partitions.

In the next chapter, we discuss using an HTTP client with Java interfaces representing an external service, as well as how to use the lower-level web client and why that's still useful.

## CHAPTER 12

Reactive REST Client: Connecting with HTTP Endpoints

The previous two chapters focused on messaging, the connective tissue of reactive systems. Modern message brokers provide the perfect feature set to implement the internal communication of reactive systems. However, at the frontier of your system, where you need to integrate remote services, there's a good chance you need to use HTTP. So let's be pragmatic and see how we can consume HTTP services without breaking the reactive principles.

In Chapter 8, you saw how to *expose* reactive HTTP endpoints. This chapter presents the other side: how to *consume* HTTP endpoints. Quarkus offers a nonblocking way to consume HTTP endpoints. In addition, it provides resilience features to protect the integration points against failures and slowness. It's important to notice that the called service does not have to be a reactive application. That's up to the implementation of that service.

Let's see what Quarkus offers to consume HTTP endpoints.

Interacting with an HTTP Endpoint

Quarkus provides multiple ways to consume HTTP endpoints:

Vert.x Web Client
   This low-level HTTP client is implemented on top of Vert.x and Netty (and so is inherently asynchronous and based on nonblocking I/O).

Reactive Messaging connector
   This connector sends HTTP requests for each processed message.

REST client

This type-safe approach eases the consumption of HTTP-based APIs.

Vert.x Web Client is convenient when you don't want to bother being exposed to low-level HTTP details, such as verbs, headers, bodies, and response status. The web client is flexible, and you have complete control over the HTTP request and the response processing.

To use Vert.x Web Client, you need to add the dependency shown in Example 12-1 in your project.

Example 12-1. Dependency for Mutiny Vert.x Web Client

```
<dependency>
    <groupId>io.smallrye.reactive</groupId>
    <artifactId>smallrye-mutiny-vertx-web-client</artifactId>
</dependency>
```

Then you can use it as shown in Example 12-2.

Example 12-2. Vert.x Web Client example

```
@ApplicationScoped
public class WebClientExample {

    private final WebClient client;

    @Inject
    public WebClientExample(Vertx vertx) {
        client = WebClient.create(vertx);
    }

    @PreDestroy
    public void close() {
        client.close();
    }

    public Uni<JsonObject> invokeService() {
        return client
            .getAbs("https://httpbin.org/json").send()
            .onItem().transform(response -> {
                if (response.statusCode() == 200) {
                    return response.bodyAsJsonObject();
                } else {
                    return new JsonObject()
                            .put("error", response.statusMessage());
                }
            });
    }
}
```

As you can see, you need to create and close `WebClient` yourself. It exposes a Mutiny API, so it integrates perfectly within your Quarkus application.

The HTTP reactive connector integrates with Reactive Messaging (see Chapter 10) and allows sending HTTP requests for each message. It's convenient when you design a message-processing pipeline where the outbound is an HTTP endpoint. It handles the backpressure and controls the amount of concurrency (number of in-flight requests) but does not allow processing the response.

To use this HTTP connector, you need the dependency shown in Example 12-3.

Example 12-3. Dependency for the HTTP connector

```
<dependency>
    <groupId>io.quarkus</groupId>
    <artifactId>quarkus-reactive-messaging-http</artifactId>
</dependency>
```

Then you can configure the connector as shown in Example 12-4.

Example 12-4. Use the HTTP connector to send messages using HTTP POST requests

```
mp.messaging.outgoing.my-http-endpoint.connector=quarkus-http          ❶
mp.messaging.outgoing.my-http-endpoint.method=POST                     ❷
mp.messaging.outgoing.my-http-endpoint.url=https://httpbin.org/anything ❸
```

❶ Instruct Quarkus to use the `quarkus-http` connector to manage the `my-http-endpoint` channel.

❷ Configure the HTTP method to use.

❸ Configure the URL of the service to invoke.

By default, the connector encodes the received messages to JSON. You can also configure a custom serializer. The connector also supports retries and time-out but, as said earlier, does not allow processing the response. Any non-2XX HTTP response is considered a failure and will nack the message.

The last approach, the REST client, offers a declarative way to invoke an HTTP service. It implements the MicroProfile REST Client specification (*https://oreil.ly/dX0Lv*). Instead of dealing with the HTTP requests and responses, you map the HTTP API in a Java interface. Thanks to a couple of annotations, you express how to send the request and process the response. The client uses the same JAX-RS annotations as the server side; see Example 12-5.

Example 12-5. Example of REST client

```
@Path("/v2")
@RegisterRestClient
public interface CountriesService {

    @GET
    @Path("/name/{name}")
    Set<Country> getByName(@PathParam String name);
}
```

The application uses the method from the interface directly. The rest of this chapter focuses on the REST client and how to integrate it in reactive applications, including how to handle failure gracefully.

The REST Client Reactive

We need to be careful. Lots of *asynchronous* HTTP and REST clients do not use non-blocking I/O and instead delegate the HTTP requests to an internal thread pool. This is not the case with the reactive REST client from Quarkus. It relies on the reactive architecture of Quarkus. Note that it's not because it's reactive that you can't use it in a blocking manner. As with most Quarkus features, you have the choice. Even if you decide to use the blocking way, Quarkus would continue using I/O threads and delegate the calls on a worker thread for your application.

To use the reactive REST client in Quarkus, add the dependency in Example 12-6 to your project.

Example 12-6. Dependency for the reactive REST client (chapter-12/rest-client-example/ pom.xml)

```
<dependency>
    <groupId>io.quarkus</groupId>
    <artifactId>quarkus-rest-client-reactive</artifactId>
</dependency>
```

If you plan to use JSON, which is often the case when using HTTP services, also add the dependency in Example 12-7.

Example 12-7. Dependency for the Jackson support for the reactive REST client (chapter-12/rest-client-example/pom.xml)

```
<dependency>
    <groupId>io.quarkus</groupId>
    <artifactId>quarkus-rest-client-reactive-jackson</artifactId>
</dependency>
```

The dependency adds the ability to serialize the request body into JSON and deserialize JSON payloads into objects.

Mapping HTTP APIs to Java Interfaces

The cornerstone of the REST client is a Java interface that represents the consumed HTTP endpoint. This interface represents the HTTP API your application consumes. It acts as a facade, enabling your application to avoid dealing with HTTP directly. On each method of the interface, you use JAX-RS annotations to describe how to handle the HTTP request and response. Let's consider an example. Imagine that you need to integrate the `httpbin` (*https://httpbin.org*) service. To call the */uuid* endpoint (which returns a UUID), you need to create a Java interface with the method representing the call; see Example 12-8.

Example 12-8. REST client for the `httpbin` service (chapter-12/rest-client-example/src/main/java/org/acme/restclient/HttpApi.java)

```
@RegisterRestClient(configKey = "httpbin")
public interface HttpBinService {

    @GET
    @Path("/uuid")
    String getUUID();
}
```

The first important fact about this interface is the `@RegisterRestClient` annotation. It indicates that the interface represents an HTTP endpoint. The `configKey` attribute defines the key we will use to configure the HTTP endpoint, such as the location.

For now, this interface has a single method: `getUUID`. When the application calls this method, it sends a `GET` request to `/uuid`, waits for the response, and reads the response body as `String`. We define this behavior by using the `@GET` and `@Path` annotations.

Let's add a method by using another HTTP method, as shown in Example 12-9.

Example 12-9. Send JSON payloads

```
class Person {
    public String name;
}

@POST
@Path("/anything")
String anything(Person someone);
```

Calling this method sends a POST request on /anything with a JSON payload as the body. The reactive REST client maps the instance of Person to JSON. You can also use the @Consume annotation to set content-type explicitly.

The REST client also lets you configure the request headers. These headers can be constant and defined by using the @ClientHeaderParam annotation or can be passed as a method parameter by using the @HeaderParam annotation; see Example 12-10.

Example 12-10. Pass headers

```
@POST
@Path("/anything")
@ClientHeaderParam(name = "X-header", value = "constant value")
String anythingWithConstantHeader(Person someone);

@POST
@Path("/anything")
String anythingWithHeader(Person someone,
                          @HeaderParam("X-header") String value);
```

To pass query parameters, use the @QueryParameter annotation (Example 12-11).

Example 12-11. Pass query parameters

```
@POST
@Path("/anything")
String anythingWithQuery(Person someone,
                         @QueryParam("param1") String p1,
                         @QueryParam("param2") String p2);
```

Let's now look at the response. So far, we used only String, but the REST client can map the response to objects. If we go back to the initial example (/uuid), it returns a JSON object with a single field: uuid. We can map this response into an object, as shown in Example 12-12.

Example 12-12. Receive JSON objects

```
class UUID {
    public String uuid;
}

@GET
@Path("/uuid")
UUID uuid();
```

By default, the REST client uses JSON to map the responses to objects. You can use the @Produces annotation to configure the Accept header.

If you want to handle the HTTP response yourself, to retrieve the status code or headers, you can return a `Response`, as shown in Example 12-13.

Example 12-13. Use responses

```
@GET
@Path("/uuid")
Response getResponse();
```

It's the same `Response` as in "Dealing with Failure and Customizing the Response" on page 148.

Mapping an HTTP API to a Java interface introduces a clear contract and avoids having HTTP code everywhere in the application code. It also improves testability as you can quickly mock the remote service. Finally, note that you don't have to map all the endpoints of the remote service, only the one you use in your application.

Invoking the Service

To use the interface we defined in the previous section in your application, we need to do the following:

1. Inject the REST client in the application code.
2. Configure the URL of the service.

The first step is straightforward; we just need to inject the client, as shown in Example 12-14.

Example 12-14. Use the HTTPBin REST client (chapter-12/rest-client-example/src/ main/java/org/acme/restclient/HttpEndpoint.java)

```
@Inject
@RestClient HttpBinService service;

public HttpBinService.UUID invoke() {
    return service.uuid();
}
```

The `@RestClient` qualifier indicates that the injected object is a REST client. Once it's injected, you can use any of the methods you have defined on the interface.

To configure the client, open the *application.properties* file and add the following property:

```
httpbin/mp-rest/url=https://httpbin.org
```

The `httpbin` part is the configuration key used in the `@RegisterRestClient` interface. Here we configure only the location, but you can configure a lot more (*https:// oreil.ly/rD1tL*).

Of course, the URL can also be passed at runtime by using the `httpbin/mp-rest/url` system property or the `HTTPBIN_MP_REST_URL` environment property.

Blocking and Nonblocking

As said previously, the reactive REST client from Quarkus supports both imperative (blocking) methods and reactive (nonblocking) methods. The distinction is made by using the return type. In "Mapping HTTP APIs to Java Interfaces" on page 229, all our returned types are synchronous. So Quarkus blocks the caller thread until the reception of the HTTP responses. This is not great in terms of Reactive. Fortunately, you can avoid this by changing the return types to `Uni`, as shown in Example 12-15.

Example 12-15. Use Mutiny in the REST client interfaces

```java
@RegisterRestClient(configKey = "reactive-httpbin")
public interface ReactiveHttpBinService {


    @GET
    @Path("/uuid")
    Uni<String> getUUID();

    class Person {
        public String name;
    }

    @POST
    @Path("/anything")
    Uni<String> anything(Person someone);

    class UUID {
        public String uuid;
    }

    @GET
    @Path("/uuid")
    Uni<UUID> uuid();

    @GET
    @Path("/uuid")
    Uni<Response> getResponse();

}
```

By returning `Uni` instead of the direct result type, you instruct the REST client not to block the caller thread. Even better, it will use the current I/O thread, embrace the asynchronous execution model, and avoid additional thread switches.

On the consumer side, you just use `Uni` and append the processing of the response to your pipeline (Example 12-16).

Example 12-16. Use the reactive API of the REST client

```
@Inject
@RestClient ReactiveHttpBinService service;

public void invoke() {
    service.uuid()
            .onItem().transform(u -> u.uuid)
            .subscribe().with(
                    s -> System.out.println("Received " + s),
                    f -> System.out.println("Failed with " + f)
    );
}
```

In this example, we handle the subscription ourselves. Don't forget that you often rely on Quarkus to take care of this. For example, returning `Uni` from a RESTEasy Reactive endpoint subscribes on the returned `Uni`.

Handling Failures

If you look at Example 12-16, you can see that calling the REST client can emit a failure, and you need to handle it. Quarkus provides multiple ways to handle failure gracefully. You can use the Mutiny API to handle the failure, execute retries, or recover gracefully, as shown in Chapter 7. Also, Quarkus provides a declarative way to express how to handle failures. This approach is particularly convenient when integrating remote systems (as with the REST client), because it combines the integration point and the failure management in a single location.

The `quarkus-smallrye-fault-tolerance` extension provides a set of annotations to configure:

- Fallback methods
- Retries
- Circuit breakers
- Bulkheads

`quarkus-smallrye-fault-tolerance` works for both imperative and reactive APIs. In this section, we focus only on the latter.

First, to use the Fault-Tolerance extension, add the dependency in Example 12-17 to your project.

Example 12-17. Dependency for fault-tolerance support (chapter-12/api-gateway-example/api-gateway/pom.xml)

```
<dependency>
    <groupId>io.quarkus</groupId>
    <artifactId>quarkus-smallrye-fault-tolerance</artifactId>
</dependency>
```

Fallback

A *fallback* is a method that provides an alternative result if the original invocation fails. Let's reuse the example we have seen before, shown again here in Example 12-18.

Example 12-18. The uuid method

```
@GET
@Path("/uuid")
Uni<UUID> uuid();
```

If the interaction with the remote service fails, we can generate a fallback (local) UUID, as shown in Example 12-19.

Example 12-19. Declare a fallback for the uuid method

```
import io.smallrye.mutiny.Uni;
import org.eclipse.microprofile.faulttolerance.Fallback;
import org.eclipse.microprofile.rest.client.inject.RegisterRestClient;

import javax.ws.rs.GET;
import javax.ws.rs.Path;


@RegisterRestClient(configKey = "reactive-httpbin")
public interface ReactiveHttpBinServiceWithFallbackMethod {

    class UUID {
        public String uuid;
    }

    @GET
    @Path("/uuid")
    @Fallback(fallbackMethod = "fallback")
    Uni<UUID> uuid();
```

```
    default Uni<UUID> fallback() {
        UUID u = new UUID();
        u.uuid = java.util.UUID.randomUUID().toString();
        return Uni.createFrom().item(u);
    }

}
```

The `@Fallback` annotation indicates the name of the method to call. This method must have the same signature as the original method. So, in our case, it must return `Uni<UUID>`. Our fallback implementation is simple, but you can imagine more complex scenarios such as calling an alternative service.

If you need more control on the fallback, you can also provide a `FallbackHandler`; see Example 12-20.

Example 12-20. Use a fallback handler

```
import io.smallrye.common.annotation.NonBlocking;
import io.smallrye.mutiny.Uni;
import org.eclipse.microprofile.faulttolerance.ExecutionContext;
import org.eclipse.microprofile.faulttolerance.Fallback;
import org.eclipse.microprofile.faulttolerance.FallbackHandler;
import org.eclipse.microprofile.rest.client.inject.RegisterRestClient;

import javax.ws.rs.GET;
import javax.ws.rs.Path;

@RegisterRestClient(configKey = "reactive-httpbin")
public interface ReactiveHttpBinServiceWithFallbackHandler {

    class UUID {
        public String uuid;
    }

    @GET
    @Path("/uuid")
    @Fallback(value = MyFallbackHandler.class)
    Uni<UUID> uuid();

    class MyFallbackHandler implements FallbackHandler<Uni<UUID>> {

        @Override
        public Uni<UUID> handle(ExecutionContext context) {
            UUID u = new UUID();
            u.uuid = java.util.UUID.randomUUID().toString();
            return Uni.createFrom().item(u);
        }
    }

}
```

The configured fallback handler is called with an `ExecutionContext` encapsulating the original method and the exception.

Retries

Fallback allows recovering gracefully with a local value. The Fault-Tolerance extension also allows retrying. Remember, retries should be used only when the called service is idempotent. So, before using this feature, be sure it won't harm your system.

The `@Retry` annotation instructs Quarkus to retry the invocation multiple times, hoping that the next call would be successful (Example 12-21).

Example 12-21. Declare a retry strategy

```
@GET
@Path("/uuid")
@Retry(maxRetries = 10, delay = 1000, jitter = 100)
Uni<UUID> uuid();
```

As you can see, you can configure the number of retries, as well as a delay and jitter to avoid retrying immediately. You could combine `@Retry` and `@Fallback` to invoke the fallback method if all the attempts failed.

Time-out

Failing fast is always better than having users waiting a long time. The `@Timeout` annotation enforces that an invocation completes in a timely fashion; see Example 12-22.

Example 12-22. Configure a time-out

```
@GET
@Path("/uuid")
@Timeout(value = 3, unit = ChronoUnit.SECONDS)
Uni<UUID> uuid();
```

If the invocation does not produce a result in the configured time-out, it fails. Combining `@Timeout` with `@Fallback` allows using a fallback result if the original call was unable to complete in the expected time.

Bulkheads and Circuit Breaker

The Quarkus fault-tolerance feature also provides circuit breakers and bulkheads. While the other patterns protect your application against remote failures and slowness, these two last patterns avoid hammering unhealthy or brittle services.

The first pattern, popularized a few years ago with libraries such as Hystrix (*https://oreil.ly/eLHn0*) or Resilience4j (*https://oreil.ly/yr4dO*), detects failing services and gives them time to recover (instead of continuously calling them). The circuit breaker allows your application to fail immediately to prevent repeated calls that are likely going to fail. The circuit breaker operates much like an electrical circuit breaker. A closed circuit represents a fully functional system, and an open circuit means an incomplete system. If a failure occurs, the circuit breaker triggers to open the circuit, removing the point of failure from the system.

The software circuit breaker has one more state: the half-open state. After the circuit is opened, it periodically changes to the half-open state. It checks whether the failed component is restored and closes the circuit after being considered safe and functional. To use a circuit breaker in Quarkus, just use the `@CircuitBreaker` annotation, as shown in Example 12-23.

Example 12-23. Use a circuit breaker

```
@GET
@Path("/uuid")
@CircuitBreaker
Uni<UUID> uuid();
```

You can also configure the circuit breaker; see Example 12-24.

Example 12-24. Configure a circuit breaker

```
@GET
@Path("/uuid")
@CircuitBreaker(
    // Delay before switching to the half-open state
    delay = 10, delayUnit = ChronoUnit.SECONDS,
    // The number of successful executions,
    // before a half-open circuit is closed again
    successThreshold = 2,
    // The ratio of failures within the rolling
    // window that will trip the circuit to open
    failureRatio = 0.75,
    // The number of consecutive requests in a
    // rolling window
    requestVolumeThreshold = 10
)
Uni<UUID> uuidWithConfiguredCircuitBreaker();
```

Protecting your integration point with a circuit breaker not only allows you to prevent slow responses and failures in your application, but also gives the failing service time to recover. Using a circuit breaker is handy when the service you interact with is under maintenance or heavy load.

The idea behind the bulkhead pattern is to limit the propagation of failure. You protect your application from failures happening in the remote service and avoid cascading them to the entire system and causing widespread issues. The `@Bulkhead` annotation limits the number of concurrent requests and saves an unresponsive remote service from wasting system resources.

Using the annotation helps you avoid having to deal with too many failures and avoids flooding a remote service with a high number of concurrent requests. The latter aspect is essential. With the reactive principles enabling high concurrency, you should never forget that the service you are calling may not be prepared for that load. So using the `@Bulkhead` annotation allows controlling the outbound concurrency. Yes, it will increase your response time and reduce your concurrency, but that's for the sake of the global system state.

You can configure the bulkhead with the max concurrency (`value`), and the maximum number of requests waiting for their turn, as demonstrated in Example 12-25. If the queue is full, it rejects any new invocations immediately, avoiding slow response time.

Example 12-25. Declare a bulkhead

```
@GET
@Path("/uuid")
@Bulkhead(value = 5, waitingTaskQueue = 1000)
Uni<UUID> uuid();
```

Building API Gateways with the RESTEasy Reactive Client

In Chapter 8, we showed how to implement HTTP endpoints relying on nonblocking I/O and how this implementation can use Mutiny (covered in Chapter 7) to orchestrate asynchronous tasks and avoid blocking. This approach enables high concurrency and efficient resource usage. This is the perfect combination for building API gateways.

An *API gateway* is a service that sits in front of a set of backend services. The gateway handles external requests and orchestrates other services. For example, it can delegate a request to a single service and implement more complex processes involving multiple backend services.

We can build highly concurrent, responsive, and resilient API gateways by combining Mutiny, RESTEasy Reactive, the reactive REST client, and the fault-tolerance annotations. In this section, we explain the basics of implementing such a gateway by exploring an example. Three applications compose our system:

Greeting service

Exposes an HTTP API returning `Hello` *{name}*, the name being a query parameter.

Quote service

Exposes another HTTP API returning a random funny quote about coffee.

API gateway

Exposes an HTTP API that delegates requests on `/quote` to the quote service. Requests made to `/` will call the greeting and quote services and build a JSON object encapsulating both.

You can find the full code of the system in the *chapter-12/api-gateway-example* directory. This section focuses on the API gateway component. We do not cover the code of the greeting and quote services here as they are simple. The source code of these components is available in the *chapter-12/api-gateway-example/greeting-service* and *chapter-12/api-gateway-example/quote-service* directories. The API gateway application that you can find in *chapter-12/api-gateway-example/api-gateway* is more interesting, and we explore it together.

First, let's build and run this system. To build this example, in a terminal, navigate into *chapter-12/api-gateway-example* and run `mvn package`. Then you will need three terminals:

1. In the first one, run `java -jar target/quarkus-app/quarkus-run.jar` from the *chapter-12/api-gateway-example/greeting-service* directory.

2. In the second one, run `java -jar target/quarkus-app/quarkus-run.jar` from the *chapter-12/api-gateway-example/quote-service* directory.

3. Finally, in the third one, run `java -jar target/quarkus-app/quarkus-run.jar` from the *chapter-12/api-gateway-example/api-gateway* directory.

 Ensure that ports 9010 (greeting service) and 9020 (quote service) are not used on your system. The API gateway uses port 8080.

Once all services are running, you can use `curl` to invoke the API gateway, which orchestrates the other backend services (Example 12-26).

Example 12-26. Invoke the greeting endpoint

```
> curl http://localhost:8080/
{"greeting":"Hello anonymous","quote":"I never drink coffee
at lunch. I find it keeps me awake for the afternoon."}
```

The cornerstone of the API gateway is the Gateway class, shown in Example 12-27.

Example 12-27. The Gateway class (chapter-12/api-gateway-example/api-gateway/src/ main/java/org/acme/gateway/Gateway.java)

```java
package org.acme.gateway;

import io.smallrye.mutiny.Uni;
import org.eclipse.microprofile.rest.client.inject.RestClient;

import javax.ws.rs.DefaultValue;
import javax.ws.rs.GET;
import javax.ws.rs.Path;
import javax.ws.rs.QueryParam;

@Path("/")
public class Gateway {

    @RestClient
    GreetingService greetingService;

    @RestClient
    QuoteService quoteService;

    @GET
    @Path("/quote")
    public Uni<String> getQuote() {
        return quoteService.getQuote();
    }

    @GET
    @Path("/")
    public Uni<Greeting> getBoth(
            @QueryParam("name")
            @DefaultValue("anonymous") String name) {
        Uni<String> greeting = greetingService.greeting(name);
        Uni<String> quote = quoteService.getQuote()
                .onFailure()
                    .recoverWithItem("No coffee - no quote");

        return Uni.combine().all().unis(greeting, quote).asTuple()
                .onItem().transform(tuple ->
                        new Greeting(tuple.getItem1(),
                                tuple.getItem2())
                );
```

```
        }

        public static class Greeting {
            public final String greeting;
            public final String quote;

            public Greeting(String greeting, String quote) {
                this.greeting = greeting;
                this.quote = quote;
            }
        }
    }
}
```

The `Gateway` class retrieves the two REST clients and handles the HTTP requests using them. As an API gateway can be under heavy load and high concurrency, we use RESTEasy Reactive and its Mutiny integration, so we don't need worker threads.

The `getQuote` method is straightforward. It delegates the calls to the `QuoteService`.

The `getBoth` method is more interesting. It needs to call both services and aggregate the response. As both services are unrelated, we can call them concurrently. As you have seen in Chapter 7, this can be easily achieved with Mutiny by using the `Uni.com` `bine` construct. Once we have both responses encapsulated in a tuple, we build the `Greeting` structure and emit it.

Let's look at the REST clients. `GreetingService` uses the fault-tolerance annotation to be sure we handle failures or slow responses appropriately; see Example 12-28.

Example 12-28. The `GreetingService` REST client (chapter-12/api-gateway-example/ api-gateway/src/main/java/org/acme/gateway/GreetingService.java)

```java
package org.acme.gateway;

import io.smallrye.mutiny.Uni;
import org.eclipse.microprofile.faulttolerance.*;
import org.eclipse.microprofile.rest.client.inject.RegisterRestClient;

import javax.ws.rs.GET;
import javax.ws.rs.Path;
import javax.ws.rs.QueryParam;

@RegisterRestClient(configKey = "greeting-service")
public interface GreetingService {

    @GET
    @Path("/")
    @CircuitBreaker
    @Timeout(2000)
    @Fallback(GreetingFallback.class)
    Uni<String> greeting(@QueryParam("name") String name);
```

```
class GreetingFallback implements FallbackHandler<Uni<String>> {
    @Override
    public Uni<String> handle(ExecutionContext context) {
        return Uni.createFrom().item("Hello fallback");
    }
}
}
```

Notice that the greeting method combines the circuit breaker, time-out, and fallback annotations. QuoteService is similar but does not use the fallback annotation, as you can see in Example 12-29.

Example 12-29. The QuoteService REST client (chapter-12/api-gateway-example/api-gateway/src/main/java/org/acme/gateway/QuoteService.java)

```
package org.acme.gateway;

import io.smallrye.mutiny.Uni;
import org.eclipse.microprofile.faulttolerance.CircuitBreaker;
import org.eclipse.microprofile.faulttolerance.Timeout;
import org.eclipse.microprofile.rest.client.inject.RegisterRestClient;

import javax.ws.rs.GET;
import javax.ws.rs.Path;

@RegisterRestClient(configKey = "quote-service")
public interface QuoteService {

    @GET
    @Path("/")
    @CircuitBreaker
    @Timeout(2000)
    Uni<String> getQuote();

}
```

Instead, as you may have noticed, we handle failure by using the Mutiny API in the Gateway class (Example 12-30).

Example 12-30. Recover from failures by using the Mutiny API (chapter-12/api-gateway-example/api-gateway/src/main/java/org/acme/gateway/Gateway.java)

```
Uni<String> quote = quoteService.getQuote()
    .onFailure().recoverWithItem("No coffee - no quote");
```

While, in general, we choose between using the fault-tolerance annotation or using the Mutiny API, we wanted to highlight that you have the choice and can combine the two easily. However, the getQuote method does not handle the failure and propagate the error. So, when using Mutiny to handle the failure, make sure you cover all entry points. Now, if you stop the quote service (by pressing Ctrl-C in the second terminal), you get the output in Example 12-31.

Example 12-31. Invoke the endpoint

```
> curl http://localhost:8080\?name\=luke
{"greeting":"Hello luke","quote":"No coffee - no quote"}
```

If you also stop the greeting service, by pressing Ctrl-C in the first terminal, you get Example 12-32.

Example 12-32. Invoke the greeting endpoint when there's no greeting service

```
> curl http://localhost:8080\?name\=luke
{"greeting":"Hello fallback","quote":"No coffee - no quote"}
```

This section explored the fundamental constructs to build a highly concurrent API gateway. Combining RESTEasy Reactive, the reactive REST client, fault tolerance, and Mutiny provides all the features you need to expose robust APIs to your users and handle failure gracefully. The following section illustrates how the REST client can also be used in messaging applications.

Using the REST Client in Messaging Applications

The REST client can also be helpful in messaging applications. For example, a message-processing pipeline can call a remote HTTP API for each message or forward the messages to a remote HTTP endpoint. We can use the REST client in a processing pipeline modeled with Reactive Messaging to achieve this. In this section, we explore an application receiving simple orders from an HTTP endpoint, process them, and persist them in a database:

1. `OrderEndpoint` receives `Order` and emits it into the `new-orders` channel.

2. An `OrderProcessing` component consumes the orders from the `new-order` channel and invokes the remote validation service. If the order gets validated successfully, it is sent to the `validated-orders` channel. Otherwise, the order is acknowledged negatively.

3. `OrderStorage` receives the order from the `validated-orders` channel and stores it in the database.

For the sake of simplicity, the validation endpoint runs in the same process, but invocations still use the REST client. You can find the complete code of the application in *chapter-12/http-messaging-example*, but let's go through it quickly.

As you can see in Example 12-33, the `Order` structure is simple. It contains just the name of a product and a quantity. Note that the `Order` class is a Panache entity. We will use that to store the validated orders in the database.

Example 12-33. The `Order` structure (chapter-12/http-messaging-example/src/main/java/org/acme/http/model/Order.java)

```java
package org.acme.http.model;

import io.quarkus.hibernate.reactive.panache.PanacheEntity;

import javax.persistence.Entity;
import javax.persistence.Table;

@Entity
@Table(name = "orders")
public class Order extends PanacheEntity {

    public String name;
    public int quantity;

}
```

`OrderEndpoint` is also straightforward, as you can see in Example 12-34.

Example 12-34. The `OrderEndpoint` class (chapter-12/http-messaging-example/src/main/java/org/acme/http/OrderEndpoint.java)

```java
package org.acme.http;

import io.smallrye.mutiny.Multi;
import io.smallrye.mutiny.Uni;
import io.smallrye.reactive.messaging.MutinyEmitter;
import org.acme.http.model.Order;
import org.eclipse.microprofile.reactive.messaging.Channel;

import javax.ws.rs.GET;
import javax.ws.rs.POST;
import javax.ws.rs.Path;
import javax.ws.rs.core.Response;

@Path("/order")
public class OrderEndpoint {

    @Channel("new-orders")
```

```
    MutinyEmitter<Order> emitter;

    @POST
    public Uni<Response> order(Order order) {
        return emitter.send(order)
                .log()
                .onItem().transform(x -> Response.accepted().build())
                .onFailure().recoverWithItem(
                        Response.status(Response.Status.BAD_REQUEST)
                                .build()
                );
    }

    @GET
    public Multi<Order> getAllValidatedOrders() {
        return Order.streamAll();
    }

}
```

The order method emits the received order to the new-orders channel. When the message gets acknowledged, it produces a 202 - ACCEPTED response. If the message is nacked, it creates a 400 - BAD REQUEST response.

The getAllValidatedOrders method lets us check what has been written in the database. The OrderProcessing component consumes the orders from the new-orders channel and invokes the validation service, as shown in Example 12-35.

Example 12-35. The OrderProcessing class (chapter-12/http-messaging-example/src/main/java/org/acme/http/OrderProcessing.java)

```
package org.acme.http;

import io.smallrye.mutiny.Uni;
import org.acme.http.model.Order;
import org.eclipse.microprofile.reactive.messaging.Incoming;
import org.eclipse.microprofile.reactive.messaging.Outgoing;
import org.eclipse.microprofile.rest.client.inject.RestClient;

import javax.enterprise.context.ApplicationScoped;

@ApplicationScoped
public class OrderProcessing {

    @RestClient
    ValidationService validation;

    @Incoming("new-orders")
    @Outgoing("validated-orders")
    Uni<Order> validate(Order order) {
```

```
    return validation.validate(order)
            .onItem().transform(x -> order);
  }

}
```

The validation service fails if the order is invalid. As a result, the message is nacked. If the order is valid, it sends the order to the validated-orders channel. The Order Storage component consumes this channel and writes each order in the database (Example 12-36).

Example 12-36. Persist orders in a database (chapter-12/http-messaging-example/src/main/java/org/acme/http/OrderStorage.java)

```
package org.acme.http;

import io.quarkus.hibernate.reactive.panache.Panache;
import io.smallrye.mutiny.Uni;
import org.acme.http.model.Order;
import org.eclipse.microprofile.reactive.messaging.Incoming;

import javax.enterprise.context.ApplicationScoped;

@ApplicationScoped
public class OrderStorage {

    @Incoming("validated-orders")
    public Uni<Void> store(Order order) {
        return Panache.withTransaction(order::persist)
                .replaceWithVoid();
    }

}
```

Run the application with mvn quarkus:dev from the *chapter-12/http-messaging-example* directory. As it uses Quarkus Dev Services, you don't need to provision a database in dev mode; Quarkus does it for you.

Once the application is running, add an order as shown in Example 12-37.

Example 12-37. Invoke the endpoint to add a new order

```
> curl -v  --header "Content-Type: application/json" \
  --request POST \
  --data '{"name":"coffee", "quantity":2}' \
  http://localhost:8080/order
```

You can verify that the order has been processed by using Example 12-38.

Example 12-38. Invoke the endpoint to retrieve the persisted orders

```
> curl http://localhost:8080/order
[{"id":1,"name":"coffee","quantity":2}]
```

Now try to insert an invalid order (using a negative quantity), as shown in Example 12-39.

Example 12-39. Invoke the endpoint to introduce an invalid order

```
> curl -v  --header "Content-Type: application/json" \
  --request POST \
  --data '{"name":"book", "quantity":-1}' \
  http://localhost:8080/order
```

The response is 400. You can verify that it was not inserted in the database by using code in Example 12-40.

Example 12-40. Invoke the endpoint to retrieve the persisted orders: the invalid order is not listed

```
> curl http://localhost:8080/order
[{"id":1,"name":"coffee","quantity":2}]
```

The validation step of the processing can use the fault-tolerance annotations to improve the reliability of the application (Example 12-41).

Example 12-41. Use fault-tolerance annotations

```
@Incoming("new-orders")
@Outgoing("validated-orders")
@Timeout(2000)
Uni<Order> validate(Order order) {
    return validation.validate(order)
            .onItem().transform(x -> order);
}
```

Using the REST client in the messaging application allows you to smoothly integrate remote services in a processing workflow.

Summary

This chapter focused on integrating a remote HTTP API into your reactive application without breaking the reactive principles. You learned how to do the following:

- Integrate a remote HTTP endpoint with your reactive application by using the reactive REST client
- Protect your integration point by using the fault-tolerance annotations
- Build API gateways by combining Mutiny, RESTEasy Reactive, and the REST client
- Integrate remote HTTP APIs in message-processing pipelines

The next chapter focuses on observability and how to keep your reactive system running under fluctuating load and when facing failures.

## CHAPTER 13

Observing Reactive and Event-Driven Architectures

So far, we've focused on how to develop reactive systems. What we haven't discussed is how to ensure that all the components of our reactive system are functioning as we expect them to. This is the focus of the chapter: how we monitor and observe our reactive and event-driven architecture.

Why Is Observability Important?

When an application is a single deployment, or *monolith*, we have a relatively easy time observing how the application is performing. Everything we need to observe is in one place. Whether it's checking logs for errors, monitoring the utilization of CPU and memory, or any other aspect, it's all accessible.

With a reactive and event driven architecture, instead of one deployment, it's often several, dozens, or even hundreds. We're no longer dealing with a single place to view the information we need to monitor and observe, but many places! Observability tooling provides a means for us to gather this information and provide a single place to view it again.

However, we need to gather the necessary information, or telemetry, from the components in the event-driven architecture to enable a singular view. *Telemetry* consists of any information we gather from processes for the purpose of observing a system. The most common types of telemetry are as follows:

Logs
> Textual messages often written to console output, logfiles, or exported to specific log-processing systems. We can also provide more structured logging in a JSON format to facilitate more accurate data extraction.

Metrics

A single metric measures a specific piece of information, such as HTTP server requests. Various types of metrics are available: counter, gauge, timer, and histogram, to name a few.

Traces

Represents a single request through a system, broken into specific operations.

When running distributed systems utilizing reactive or event-driven architecture, we need solid telemetry produced from the components to support sufficient reasoning about the system. Without being able to reason about the system based on what we can observe from the outside, our reactive system is not truly observable.

Let's clarify some terms. *Monitoring* and *observability* can be conflated to mean the same thing. Though there are overlaps, they do mean different things. Monitoring focuses on specific metrics and measuring them against specific goals, service-level objectives (SLOs), and alerting operations when those goals are not met. Monitoring is also called *known unknowns*, as we know what data, or metrics, to measure to see a problem, but we don't know what might cause a specific problem. *Unknown unknowns* refers to observability, because we don't know what will cause a problem, and when one occurs, it requires observation of a system from its outputs to determine the cause.

Kubernetes is a great place to run reactive systems, as it provides the mechanism to monitor, scale, and repair a system gracefully. However, we need to provide information for Kubernetes to do that properly, such as with health checks. Health checks can serve many purposes; for our needs, the readiness and liveness probes in Kubernetes can utilize them. *Readiness probes* let Kubernetes know a container is ready to begin accepting requests, and *liveness probes* let Kubernetes know if a container needs to be restarted because of unrecoverable failures when communicating with Kafka.

Throughout the rest of the chapter, we explain how to effectively monitor and observe reactive systems.

Health with Messaging

Kubernetes utilizes health checks to determine the state of a container. If containers don't provide health checks, Kubernetes is unable to determine the state of a container. This may result in users experiencing errors caused by deadlocked containers that cannot be stopped or by containers that are not ready to process requests.

We can implement three types of health checks for our containers:

Liveness Probe

This probe lets Kubernetes know a container should be restarted. If we can write a meaningful health check, it's a good way to catch situations of application deadlock or connection issues with external systems. We can possibly resolve intermittent issues by allowing a clean slate by restarting the container. The probe is periodically run based on the frequency we define. We want to ensure that the frequency is not too large, so we prevent containers being stuck for long periods of time, but not too small either, as that would increase resource consumption.

Readiness Probe

This probe informs Kubernetes when a container is ready to begin receiving traffic from a service. We can use this type of health check to provide enough time for HTTP servers and connections to external systems to be available before we begin accepting requests. This prevents users from experiencing errors because the container was not ready to process a request. This probe executes only once during the life of a container. The readiness probe is necessary to effectively allow scaling up without causing undue user errors.

Startup Probe

A recent health check addition, this probe has a similar purpose as the liveness probe. However, this probe allows us to set a different wait period before declaring the container unhealthy. This is especially beneficial in situations where a container could take a very long time to be alive, possibly due to connecting with legacy systems. We're able to set a shorter time-out for a *Liveness Probe*, while allowing a much longer time-out for a *Startup Probe*.

Each of these probes supports HTTP, TCP, or commands run inside the container itself. Nothing prevents other protocols from being used for probes, but they're currently not implemented in Kubernetes. Which probe we use for an application will depend on whether there are HTTP endpoints we can utilize for the probes, or whether we need custom commands within the container. Quarkus has an extension for SmallRye Health (*https://github.com/smallrye/smallrye-health*) to develop health checks available over HTTP.

How do these probes relate to a reactive application? Readiness indicates that a Reactive Messaging connector, such as Kafka, has successfully connected to the broker, or backend, there were no failures, and optionally the topic we intend to use exists in the broker. In this state, the connector is ready to begin sending or receiving messages. Verifying the presence of any topics is disabled by default because it's a lengthy operation requiring use of the admin client. Enabling topic verification is done by setting `health-readiness-topic verification: true`.

Liveness should fail when the Reactive Messaging connector has experienced an unrecoverable failure or a disconnection from the broker. These types of transient failures can disappear after a restart of the container. For example, the application may connect to another broker.

As we covered in "Apache Kafka" on page 202, Kafka has built-in resilience. The last committed offset is not updated until a consumer has successfully processed the record, ensuring that records are not forgotten if a consumer fails while processing it. Also, Kafka is able to rebalance consumers, within the same consumer group, if any of them fail. Any consumer(s) that might crash while processing records from a partition will be replaced with other consumers from the same group. When using Kubernetes health checks, the consumers will be rebalanced when containers stop, and rebalanced again when Kubernetes has started new instances of the containers.

It is now time to see how it all works with an example. We will take the example from Chapter 11 and extend it. We want to customize the consumer to highlight the behaviors of health checks. We will have a specific process service, `processor-health`. You can find the complete code in the *chapter-13* directory.

First we need to add the extension for SmallRye Health to the *pom.xml* of each service, as shown in Example 13-1.

Example 13-1. Dependency for the health support (chapter-13/processor-health/pom.xml)

```
<dependency>
  <groupId>io.quarkus</groupId>
  <artifactId>quarkus-smallrye-health</artifactId>
</dependency>
```

To generate the necessary Kubernetes deployment YAML, including the liveness and readiness probes, we need the Kubernetes extension. In this case, though, we use the minikube extension as we're deploying to it; see Example 13-2.

Example 13-2. Dependency for the minikube deployment feature (chapter-13/processor-health/pom.xml)

```
<dependency>
  <groupId>io.quarkus</groupId>
  <artifactId>quarkus-minikube</artifactId>
</dependency>
```

Run `mvn clean package` in the */chapter-13* directory to generate the deployment YAML. Take a look in the */target/kubernetes* directory of one of the modules and view the generated YAML. We see the desired liveness and readiness probes added to the deployment specification.

By default, the period between each liveness probe request is 30 seconds. Let's reduce it to 10 seconds to enable Kubernetes to restart our consumer, processor-health, sooner if there are problems by modifying application.properties (Example 13-3).

Example 13-3. Configure the liveness probe (chapter-13/processor-health/src/main/resources/application.properties)

```
quarkus.kubernetes.liveness-probe.period=10s
```

Example 13-4 shows how to modify Processor to simulate failures.

Example 13-4. Processor to nack every eighth message received (chapter-13/processor-health/src/main/java/org/acme/Processor.java)

```
@Incoming("ticks")
@Outgoing("processed")
@Acknowledgment(Acknowledgment.Strategy.MANUAL)                    ❶
Message<String> process(Message<Long> message) throws Exception {  ❷
    if (count++ % 8 == 0) {                                        ❸
      message.nack(new Throwable("Random failure to process a record."))
          .toCompletableFuture().join();
      return null;
    }
    String value = String.valueOf(message.getPayload());
    value += " consumed in pod (" + InetAddress.getLocalHost().getHostName() + ")";
    message.ack().toCompletableFuture().join();                    ❹
    return message.withPayload(value);
}
```

❶ Use manual acknowledgment, so we can nack messages explicitly.

❷ We need to change the method signature to use Message instead of Long to use manual acknowledgment.

❸ Every eighth message should be nacked, and we return a null instead.

❹ Explicitly ack a message.

As the default failure-strategy is fail, when we nack a message, the processing of messages fails. This message failure will cause the health check of the consumer to also fail, triggering a container restart once the next liveness probe runs. Refer to "Kafka on Kubernetes" on page 213, or the *README* of */chapter-13*, to start minikube and deploy Kafka. Then, run mvn verify -Dquarkus.kubernetes.deploy=true for each of the three services: ticker, viewer, processor. Verify that all three services are running with kubectl get pods.

With the services deployed, we can see the overall health check status by accessing /q/health of a service. We get the response shown in Example 13-5 for the processor-health service.

Example 13-5. Reactive application health check with no errors

```
{
    "status": "UP",
    "checks": [
        {
            "name": "SmallRye Reactive Messaging - liveness check",
            "status": "UP",
            "data": {
                "ticks": "[OK]",                    ❶
                "processed": "[OK]"
            }
        },
        {
            "name": "SmallRye Reactive Messaging - readiness check",
            "status": "UP",
            "data": {
                "ticks": "[OK]",
                "processed": "[OK]"
            }
        }
    ]
}
```

❶ The data within the check shows the channels we're connected to and their respective status.

We saw, when viewing the generated deployment YAML, that there are also /q/health/live and /q/health/ready endpoints. These represent the liveness and readiness probes, respectively. Access them in a browser, or via curl, to see the specific checks of each probe.

Open up the *VIEWER_URL*, from the terminal, in a browser. Based on the producer we've defined, we will see seven messages with the same processor pod name, before it hit the message that we nacked. There will be a pause while Kubernetes restarts the container; then we will see another seven messages, and this sequence repeats.

If we take a look at the pods in Kubernetes, we can see that the container for the processor service has been restarted, as shown in Example 13-6.

Example 13-6. Use `kubectl` to list pods

```
> kubectl get pods
NAME                                        READY   STATUS    RESTARTS   AGE
observability-processor-5cffd8c755-d5578    1/1     Running   2          84s
observability-ticker-bd8f6f5bb-hqtpj        1/1     Running   0          2m
observability-viewer-786dd8bc84-zbjp4       1/1     Running   0          3m
```

After several restarts in a short amount of time, the pod will be in the state of `CrashLoopBackoff`, which will slowly increase the delay between pod restarts. As we don't have a "happy" container for at least 10 minutes, we end up in a state where the pod will not restart for a while. That's not a problem for these examples, but is worth noting.

When viewing the health checks at `/q/health`, it can be difficult to "catch" the failed health check before the container restarts. To make it easier, we can modify the `quarkus.kubernetes.liveness-probe.period` of the processor service to a large period of time, like `100s`. With a longer period, we give ourselves a chance to view the failed health check before the container restarts, as shown in Example 13-7.

Example 13-7. Reactive application health check with errors

```
{
    "status": "DOWN",
    "checks": [
        {
            "name": "SmallRye Reactive Messaging - liveness check",
            "status": "DOWN",                                               ❶
            "data": {
                "ticks": "[KO] - Random failure to process a record.",      ❷
                "processed": "[KO] - Multiple exceptions caught:
                    [Exception 0] java.util.concurrent.CompletionException:
                        java.lang.Throwable: Random failure to process a record.
                    [Exception 1] io.smallrye.reactive.messaging.ProcessingException:
                        SRMSG00103: Exception thrown when calling the method
                        org.acme.Processor#process"
            }
        },
        {
            "name": "SmallRye Reactive Messaging - readiness check",
            "status": "UP",
            "data": {
                "ticks": "[OK] - no subscription yet,
                    so no connection to the Kafka broker yet"               ❸
                "processed": "[OK]"
            }
```

```
        }
    ]
}
```

❶ Liveness check is DOWN, causing the entire health check to be DOWN.

❷ The `ticks` channel is not OK, showing the failure from the exception sent in `nack`.

❸ There is no subscription, because the `process` method has failed and is no longer subscribing. The `ticks` channel is still OK; it's just waiting for a subscription.

We can now check the health of our applications and utilize them in the container orchestration of Kubernetes. Next, we see how our reactive applications can generate metrics for monitoring and utilize those metrics for autoscaling.

Metrics with Messaging

Metrics are a critical part of our applications, even more so with reactive applications. Metrics can feed monitoring systems for alerting operations and SREs of problems in applications. Before delving into how we can do that, let's explain some monitoring-related terms:

SLA (service-level agreement)
: A contract between a service provider and its customers as to the availability, performance, etc. of the service.

SLO (service-level objective)
: A goal for a service provider to reach. SLOs are internal goals used to help prevent a service provider from breaking an SLA with its customers. Developers define rules, or thresholds, for the SLOs of a service to alert Operations or SREs when we're at risk of breaking SLAs.

SLI (service-level indicator)
: A specific measurement used in measuring an SLO. These are the metrics we generate from a reactive application.

If an organization doesn't define SLAs, SLOs, and SLIs, that's OK. It's still beneficial to gather metrics from a reactive application to at least define the thresholds indicating when everything is OK and when it is not. A "good" metric for a particular reactive application can differ depending on the specific use case.

However, all reactive systems should be gathering and monitoring certain metrics:

Queue length

If the queue of messages waiting to be processed is too large, it impacts the speed at which messages flow through the system. If messages aren't flowing fast enough, a time-sensitive reactive application, such as stock trading, will see delays and problems as a result. High queue length is an indication we need to increase the number of consumers within a consumer group. It may also indicate that we need to increase the number of partitions for a topic if we're already at the maximum number of consumers.

Processing time

When a consumer takes too long to process a message, it will likely cause an increase in queue length. Long processing times can also indicate other issues with a reactive application, dependent on what work a consumer does. We could see network latency issues because of another service we're interacting with, database contention, or any other number of possible problems.

Messages processed in a time window

This metric provides an overall understanding of the throughput of a reactive application. Knowing the actual number of messages processed is likely less important than monitoring variations. A significant drop could indicate a problem in messages not being received, or large numbers of customers leaving the application too early.

Ack-to-nack ratio

We want this metric to be as high as possible, as it means we're not seeing many failures in the messages we process. If too many failures occur, we need to investigate whether it's due to upstream systems providing invalid data, or failures in the processor to handle different data types properly.

All of these metrics we've discussed are great for detecting possible bottlenecks in a reactive application. We may see several of these metrics go in a bad direction at the same time—definitely a sign we have a problem in processing messages! We can also define basic rules for detecting bottlenecks. When using HTTP, or request/reply, we should check the response time and success rate. High response times or low success rates would indicate a problem needing investigation. For messaging applications, the number of *in-flight*, not yet processed, messages is a key measurement to track.

We've covered a lot of theory, but what do we need to do to capture these metrics? The key change is to add the dependency for Micrometer,[1] and in this case we want the metrics available in the Prometheus format.

Micrometer is the preferred metrics solution for Quarkus because it offers key benefits for developers:

- Ability to switch the monitoring backend from Prometheus, to Datadog, to Splunk, to New Relic, and many others, without needing to modify existing code-creating metrics. All that's required is a dependency change to use a different registry!

- Provides `MeterBinder` implementations for many of the frameworks used in Quarkus. These provide metrics for frameworks such as JAX-RS, Vert.x, and Hibernate, without developers needing to specifically code metrics themselves.

To expose the metrics in the Prometheus format, add the dependency in Example 13-8 to your application.

Example 13-8. Dependency for the Micrometer Prometheus support (chapter-13/viewer/ pom.xml)

```
<dependency>
  <groupId>io.quarkus</groupId>
  <artifactId>quarkus-micrometer-registry-prometheus</artifactId>
</dependency>
```

With this dependency, we have an endpoint showing all the metrics of an application at /q/metrics. When using Prometheus in Kubernetes, we then need only a `Service Monitor` to inform Prometheus of this endpoint for it to scrape the metrics. For this example, we won't be utilizing Prometheus and Grafana, two common tools for monitoring metrics. Plenty of documentation online explains how to set them up in Kubernetes for readers to view the metrics in these tools.

If minikube is not still running from the earlier health example, follow the instructions in the *README* of */chapter-13* to start it, deploy Kafka, and build and deploy the three services. Verify that they're running with `kubectl get pods`, and then open the URL of the viewer. Once you've seen messages appear, open up the metrics endpoint for the processor. The URL can be found with `minikube service --url observability-processor` and then add /q/metrics to the end.

You will see metrics such those shown in Example 13-9.

---

1 Micrometer (*https://micrometer.io*) provides a facade over the instrumentation clients of popular monitoring systems, such as Prometheus.

Example 13-9. Sample of metrics for a reactive application

```
# HELP kafka_consumer_fetch_manager_records_consumed_total The total number of
# records consumed
kafka_consumer_fetch_manager_records_consumed_total \
   {client_id="kafka-consumer-ticks",kafka_version="2.8.0",} 726.0
# HELP kafka_consumer_response_total The total number of responses received
kafka_consumer_response_total
   {client_id="kafka-consumer-ticks",kafka_version="2.8.0",} 123.0
# HELP kafka_consumer_fetch_manager_fetch_latency_avg The average time taken for
# a fetch request.
kafka_consumer_fetch_manager_fetch_latency_avg \
   {client_id="kafka-consumer-ticks",kafka_version="2.8.0",} 485.6222222222222
# HELP kafka_consumer_fetch_manager_records_consumed_rate
# The average number of records consumed per second
kafka_consumer_fetch_manager_records_consumed_rate \
   {client_id="kafka-consumer-ticks",kafka_version="2.8.0",} 15.203870076019351
# HELP kafka_consumer_coordinator_assigned_partitions
# The number of partitions currently assigned to this consumer
kafka_consumer_coordinator_assigned_partitions \
   {client_id="kafka-consumer-ticks",kafka_version="2.8.0",} 3.0
# HELP kafka_producer_response_rate The number of responses received per second
kafka_producer_response_rate \
   {client_id="kafka-producer-processed",kafka_version="2.8.0",} 3.8208002687156233
# HELP kafka_producer_request_rate The number of requests sent per second
kafka_producer_request_rate \
   {client_id="kafka-producer-processed",kafka_version="2.8.0",} 3.820639852212612
# HELP kafka_producer_record_send_rate The average number of records sent per second.
kafka_producer_record_send_rate \
   {client_id="kafka-producer-processed",kafka_version="2.8.0",} 15.230982251500022
# HELP kafka_producer_record_send_total The total number of records sent.
kafka_producer_record_send_total \
   {client_id="kafka-producer-processed",kafka_version="2.8.0",}\
   726.0
# HELP kafka_producer_response_total The total number of responses received
kafka_producer_response_total \
   {client_id="kafka-producer-processed",kafka_version="2.8.0",} \
   182.0
# HELP kafka_producer_request_total The total number of requests sent
kafka_producer_request_total \
   {client_id="kafka-producer-processed",kafka_version="2.8.0",} \
   182.0
# HELP kafka_producer_request_latency_avg The average request latency in ms
kafka_producer_request_latency_avg \
   {client_id="kafka-producer-processed",kafka_version="2.8.0",} 10.561797752808989
```

Example 13-9 shows a condensed version of the metrics generated from the processor service, as the complete version would require much more space!

Metrics would also enable us to develop a Kubernetes operator to autoscale the consumers of a reactive system. The operator can use the Kafka admin API to measure the number of messages that have not been consumed. If there are fewer consumers than the number of partitions, the operator can scale up the number of replicas for a consumer to process more messages in the same time. When the number of unconsumed messages drops below a threshold, the operator can then scale back consumers from within the consumer group.

Distributed Tracing with Messaging

Distributed tracing is an extremely important part of observability for reactive systems. When we have a single application deployment, all the interactions usually occur within the same process. Additionally, reactive systems have the complexity of one service not knowing where, or often when, another service will consume the message they've created. With nonreactive systems, we're usually able to infer the connections by reading the code to see where outgoing HTTP calls are made. That is not possible with a reactive system built around messaging.

This is where distributed tracing shines, connecting the many dots—services—in a system across space and time to provide an overall perspective on the message flows. For the example, we will be using the OpenTelemetry extension, with an exporter to send the captured traces to Jaeger.[2]

First, though, let's cover some terminology:

Span

> A single operation within a trace (defined next). Many spans can be created within a single service, depending on the level of detail you want to collect. A span can have parent or child spans associated with it, representing a chain of execution.

Trace

> A collection of operations, or spans, representing a single request processed by an application and its components.

When using Reactive Messaging in Quarkus for Kafka or AMQP, spans are automatically created when messages are consumed and when they're produced. This is done by the extension propagating the existing trace and span into the headers of any produced message, which is extracted when consuming it. This process allows OpenTelemetry to chain together the spans across multiple services in different processes to provide a singular view of the flow with Jaeger.

---

2 OpenTelemetry (*https://opentelemetry.io*) is a CNCF project combining OpenCensus and OpenTracing into a single project for the collection of telemetry signals. Jaeger (*https://www.jaegertracing.io*) is a CNCF project for collecting and visualizing traces.

Let's update the example for distributed tracing! We add the Quarkus extension for OpenTelemetry to each service in *pom.xml*, as shown in Example 13-10.

Example 13-10. Jaeger exporter for OpenTelemetry dependency

```
<dependency>
  <groupId>io.quarkus</groupId>
  <artifactId>quarkus-opentelemetry-exporter-jaeger</artifactId>
</dependency>
```

For each service to be able to send the gathered spans to Jaeger, we also need to update `application.properties` for each service with the URL of the collector (Example 13-11).

Example 13-11. Jaeger collector endpoint

```
quarkus.opentelemetry.tracer.exporter.jaeger.endpoint=
http://simplest-collector.jaeger:14250
```

To simplify the deployment of Jaeger, we will deploy the *all-in-one* image, as shown in Example 13-12.

Example 13-12. Install Jaeger all-in-one

```
kubectl create ns jaeger
kubectl apply -f deploy/jaeger/jaeger-simplest.yaml -n jaeger
```

Details of the Kubernetes deployment and service for Jaeger can be examined by reviewing */deploy/jaeger/jaeger-simplest.yaml*. The key point to note is the service exposing port 14250 for collecting spans, which is the port we set in Example 13-11.

Retrieve the URL for the Jaeger UI, `minikube service --url jaeger-ui -n jaeger`, and open it in a browser. We see the initial page to search for traces, but without any services in the drop-down to search for, as nothing is running yet.

Follow the *README* for */chapter-13* to rebuild and redeploy the three services: ticker, processor, viewer. Once they're deployed, open up the viewer URL, `minikube service --url observability-viewer`, in a browser to begin receiving messages.

Once messages are appearing, go back to the Jaeger UI and refresh the page. There will now be four services to select from; choose `observability-ticker`, the first service in the reactive stream. Click the Find Traces button to retrieve the traces for the service. Select one of the traces from the list to open a view containing all the details of the spans (Figure 13-1).

Figure 13-1. Jaeger UI showing reactive system trace

In this example, we have four spans within a single trace. There is a span for each step in the reactive stream that first produces a message from the ticker services, then consumes and produces a message in the processor service, and finally consumes the message in the viewer service. In the Jaeger UI, explore the data captured within the spans for each step. In Figure 13-1, we see the details of the `ticks send` span, including the type of span, producer, and the details of where the message was sent.

 Though *ticks send* is grammatically incorrect for past tense, the name of the span is dictated by the semantic conventions of OpenTelemetry in *blob/main/specification/trace/semantic_conventions/messaging.md#span-name*. The span name is a combination of the destination, *ticks*, and the operation type, *send*.

So far, you've seen how to utilize traces when message flows are almost instantaneous between services. However, a benefit of reactive systems is being able to decouple components within the system according to time. In other words, a message flow can take hours, days, weeks, months, or even years to be completed, with messages waiting in a topic, for instance, for a lengthy amount of time before being consumed. It's also possible for the same message to be processed by a different consumer, such as an audit process, some time after it was originally consumed. Let's simulate a delayed scenario and see how the traces work.

To start, let's clear out the existing services with `kubectl delete all --all -n default`. To ensure that we're starting with a clean slate, we should also delete and recreate the existing Kafka topics, as shown in Example 13-13.

Example 13-13. Update the application deployments

```
kubectl delete kafkatopics -n kafka processed
kubectl delete kafkatopics -n kafka ticks
kubectl apply -f deploy/kafka/ticks.yaml
kubectl apply -f deploy/kafka/processed.yaml
```

To simulate delayed processing, let's deploy the ticker service and then remove it again after 20–30 seconds to have a reasonable number of messages produced (Example 13-14).

Example 13-14. Deploy and remove the ticker application

```
cd ticker
mvn verify -Dquarkus.kubernetes.deploy=true
# After 20-30 seconds
kubectl delete all --all -n default
```

Search again for traces of the `observability-ticker` service and you'll see traces with only a single span. The only span in every trace is the one from the ticker service. For the processor to receive messages from before it was running, we need to update `application.properties` to indicate we want the earliest messages; see Example 13-15.

Example 13-15. Configure the first offset to read for new consumer groups

```
mp.messaging.incoming.ticks.auto.offset.reset=earliest
```

With the change made, deploy the viewer and processor services, and open the viewer URL in a browser to receive the messages. Once the messages have been received by the viewer, go back to the Jaeger UI and search for the traces again. We see the traces that previously had only a single span now have all four spans! We successfully processed messages after some time, and Jaeger was able to associate the spans with the right trace.

In a real production system, whether the preceding process works would depend on the retention of tracing data. If we retain tracing data for a year but want to process messages older than that, Jaeger will consider them as traces with only the spans from today. Any spans from the same trace will no longer be present for Jaeger to properly link them for visualization.

Summary

This chapter detailed the importance of observability for reactive systems in Kubernetes. Observability is the key to ensuring the resiliency and elasticity of reactive systems. Health checks help systems to be resilient, by triggering the restart of services that are not healthy. Specific metrics of a reactive system can be used to provide elasticity by scaling up and down consumers as needed, dependent on message queue size, for instance.

We covered observability in Kubernetes with health checks, metrics, and distributed tracing. What we've covered only scratches the surface of observability for reactive systems, but provides sufficient detail for developers to delve deeper themselves. Though we can provide general guidelines for observability of reactive systems, specifics of what is desired will depend heavily on the use cases of the system.

We've reached the end of Part IV, where we covered patterns of Reactive Messaging and its support of event buses, connecting messages to/from HTTP endpoints, and observing reactive systems.

Conclusion

We have come to the end of this book. We have covered the principles behind reactive architectures and the technical practices to implement them with Quarkus.

A Brief Summary

In Part II, we explored reactive architectures. Reactive systems (Chapter 4) propose a different way to build distributed systems (Chapter 3). The use of message passing between the various components forming the system enables elasticity and resilience, two characteristics essential for modern applications deployed in the cloud or running in containers. But that's not all. Reactive applications must also handle the workload in a timely fashion and use resources efficiently. This last point pushes reactive applications to use nonblocking I/O and avoids creating too many OS threads ("The Role of Nonblocking Input/Output" on page 71). The resulting execution model provides better response time and improves memory consumption. However, it does not come for free. To write such an application, you must change the way you write code. You must never block the I/O threads and so must write your code using a continuation-passing style. In this book, we have looked at reactive programming and Mutiny (Chapter 5, Chapter 7).

We also covered Quarkus, a stack to write applications in Java tailored for the cloud and containers (Chapter 2). Quarkus runs on top of a reactive engine dealing with the network and nonblocking I/O. In addition, Quarkus offers a large set of reactive APIs. The combination of the engine and the API creates a breeding ground to build reactive applications (Chapter 6). Quarkus provides reactive APIs to serve HTTP endpoints (Chapter 8), as well as to interact with data sources (Chapter 9) and consume HTTP services (Chapter 12).

Quarkus also provides the connective tissue for building reactive systems (Chapter 10). This book covered Kafka and AMQP 1.0, but many more possibilities are available (Chapter 11).

Quarkus lets you design, build, and operate reactive systems. Observability is a key component for distributed systems and not a feature to be tacked on at the end of development (Chapter 13). Reactive systems are distributed systems, and failures are inevitable. Being able to observe, detect issues, emit alerts, and react is essential to keep the system running and serve its purpose.

Is That All?

This book did not offer a silver-bullet solution to build reactive systems. We have covered the principles and the building blocks to build them. But, as with everything in software, the ideal solutions always depend on the problem. We've showed you a toolbox, but it's up to you to select the best tool for your application, assemble your system following the reactive principles, and profit.

Throughout this book, we have shown many features to implement reactive applications and systems with Quarkus, but we've only scratched the surface. Quarkus offers a lot more reactive features.

We explained how you can deal with HTTP in a reactive fashion. But there are alternatives to HTTP. gRPC, for example, is a secure, polyglot, and performant RPC protocol that can replace most HTTP interactions. It uses a contract-first approach (written using Protobuf), and supports unidirectional and bidirectional streams. Quarkus lets you implement gRPC services and consume them. It relies on the reactive engine and therefore offers excellent performance and resource utilization. In addition, it integrates with the Mutiny API.

We have also covered the data space, explaining how you can interact with various databases from within your Quarkus application. Quarkus offers reactive access to databases such as PostgreSQL, MySQL, Db2, SQL Server, and Oracle. Quarkus also provides reactive APIs to interact with many NoSQL databases such as Neo4j, Cassandra, Redis, and MongoDB.

Finally, to build reactive systems, you often need a message broker, or a way to exchange messages asynchronously. In this book, we used Apache Kafka and Apache ActiveMQ. Quarkus offers a lot more. You can integrate with MQTT, RabbitMQ, or JMS. Quarkus can be combined with Apache Camel to interact with virtually any existing system without preventing *reactiveness*.

In other words, Quarkus offers a complete toolbox that lets you build reactive applications for many contexts and use cases. You have endless possibilities.

The Future of Reactive Systems

It's impossible to predict the future with a high degree of certainty. The best we can do is track meaningful trends and prepare for change. The following are some trends that we think are important to track.

HTTP is evolving. HTTP/3 comes with a better flow-control approach and parallel request transmission, improving overall communication across the system.

The use of message brokers is growing tremendously. New brokers are emerging, such as Apache Pulsar, NATS, and KubeMQ. The last two are built with Kubernetes in mind and integrate well in such an environment. Several revolutionizing projects are changing how to process messages and derive knowledge from event streams. Apache Pinot, to cite one, allows querying data coming from event streams such as Apache Kafka.

As in many other domains, the rise of machine learning and AI also influence the construction of reactive systems. Machine learning algorithms can help understand the system and adapt it to handle failures or peaks of demands. Already today, you can see Kubernetes operators collecting metrics about a system and adapting it to face the current workload.

At the code level, Project Loom is promising. It will drastically reduce the complexity of writing efficient reactive applications. Approaches to express structured concurrency such as Ballerina and Joli are still niched but may become more popular shortly.

There are many more trends. Keep an eye on the technologies that embrace the reactive principles we explained in this book.

The End of the Beginning

You now have all the tools to build *better* distributed systems that are more robust and more efficient. Quarkus, a Java stack tailored for the cloud, will let you embrace the reactive system paradigm smoothly, one step at a time. Go ahead!

We hope you enjoyed this journey. Now it's time for you to start a new one by using what you've learned.

Index

Symbols

@Blocking annotation, 195
@Channel annotation, 184
@Incoming annotation, 185
@Outgoing annotation, 182

A

accessing data (see data access)
ack (acknowledged successfully), 187
acknowledgment
  in message-based application, 191-193
  negative, 193
acknowledgment strategies, 211, 220
acknowledgments (messaging system element),
  187
ahead of time (AOT) compilation, 21, 34
AMQP (Advanced Message Queuing Protocol)
  acknowledgment and redelivery, 220
  AMQP 1.0, 106, 217
  building reactive systems with, 216-223
  credit-flow backpressure protocol, 221
  elasticity patterns, 220
  as event bus tool, 201
  on Kubernetes, 221
  point-to-point communication, 217-219
  publish/subscribe model, 219
anycast (queue), 217
AOT (ahead of time) compilation, 21, 34
Apache Kafka (see Kafka)
Apache Maven, xvii
API gateways, 238-243
asynchronous actions, chaining with Mutiny,
  131-133
asynchronous code, 83-107

  basics, 83-89
  futures, 89
  Project Loom, 91-93
  reactive programming and, 93-100
  Reactive Streams and need for flow control,
    100-106
asynchronous message passing
  reactive systems and, 62
  requirements for, 6
  time decoupling and, 70
asynchronousity, event-driven software and, 4

B

backpressure, 103
  credit-flow backpressure protocol, 221
  defined, 103
  distributed systems and, 106
  Mutiny and flow control, 128
  Reactive Streams, 103-105
  Reactive Streams and, 7
blocking I/Os
  data access and, 159-160
  nonblocking I/O versus, 71-74
blocking methods, reactive REST client and,
  232
buffers, 101
bulkheads, 236
Byzantine failures, 51

C

callbacks, 6
carrier threads, 91-93
CDC (change data capture), 170-175, 172
cgroups (control groups), 10

chaining asynchronous actions, 131-133
channels, defined, 180
circuit breakers, 236
cloud native applications
    distributed systems and, 46-48
    false assumptions related to cloud and
        Kubernetes, 52-54
    Reactive architectures and, 7
collections, 137
combining items, 134-136
commands
    events versus, 65-68
    in reactive systems, 63
commit strategies, 210
completion event, 96
CompletionStage, 89
connectors, 189
consumer groups (Kafka), 206, 208
container density, 18
container image, 48
container orchestration (see Kubernetes)
containers, 48-50, 48
continuations, 74
CPS (continuation-passing style), 74
credit-flow backpressure protocol, 221

D

data access, 159-175
    blocking I/O problems, 159-160
    data-related events and change data capture,
        170-175
    Hibernate ORM and, 162-166
    interacting with Redis, 166-170
    nonblocking interactions with relational
        databases, 161
    NoSQL, 166-170
Dead-Letter Queue strategy, 211
Debezium, 172
deployment (Quarkus), 31
design principles of reactive systems, 61-82
    anatomy of reactive applications, 79-82
    characteristics of reactive systems, 61-63
    commands, 63
    commands versus events, 65-68
    destinations and space decoupling, 68-70
    events, 64
    nonblocking I/O, 71-79
    time decoupling, 70
destinations, in reactive systems, 68-70

Dev Services, 163
distributed systems
    backpressure in, 106
    basics, 43-46
    cloud native applications, 46-48
    defined, 43
    failures in, 51
    false assumptions about, 52-54
    Kubernetes native applications, 48-50
    synchronous communication and time-
        coupling, 54-60
distributed tracing, 260-263
Docker, xvii, 37

E

Eclipse Vert.x, 117
"Eight Fallacies of Distributed Computing",
    52-53
elasticity
    AMQP and, 220
    defined, 62
    Kafka partition mechanism and, 209
emitters, 181
epoll, 77
event bus, 201-223
    building reactive systems with AMQP,
        216-223
    building reactive systems with Kafka,
        202-216
    Kafka versus AMQP, 201
event loop, 78, 115
event loop thread, 81
event-driven architecture, 121
event-driven software, 4
events
    commands versus, 65-68
    failures as, 133
    observing with Mutiny, 129
    reactive systems and, 64
    streams and, 95
    transforming with Mutiny, 130
eventual consistency, 172

F

Fail Fast acknowledgment strategy, 211
fail-stop failures, 51
failure (event), 95
failure handling
    acknowledgment strategies, 211

circuit breakers/bulkheads, 236
commit strategies, 210
dead-letter queue, 211
distributed systems and, 51
fallback, 234-236
Kafka and, 210-212
negative acknowledgment and, 193
operators and, 97
Quarkus and, 148-151
reactive REST client and, 233-238
recovery with Mutiny, 133
retries, 236
retrying processing, 195
time-out, 236
fallback, 234-236
flow control
backpressure, 103
buffering, 101
dropping items, 102
Mutiny and, 128
Reactive Streams, 103-105
Reactive Streams and, 100-106
frameworks
Quarkus versus traditional, 18-21
time to first request, 11
futures, 89

G

GraalVM, 34-36

H

health checks, 250-256
heap size
Quarkus, 16
Thorntail, 14
Hibernate Reactive, 162-166, 172, 196
high watermark offset, 207
hot partition (Kafka), 207
HTTP, 139-158
asynchronous endpoints returning Uni, 146-148
dealing with failure/customizing the response, 148-151
Reactive Messaging example, 196-200
reactive score, 157
request-handling basics, 140
RESTEasy Reactive and, 141-143
RESTEasy Reactive benefits, 144-146
streaming data, 151-157

HTTP endpoints
building API gateways with RESTEasy Reactive client, 238-243
connecting with, 225-248
failure handling, 233-238
interacting with, 225-228
reactive REST client and, 228-232
using the REST client in messaging applications, 243-247

I

idempotence, 59
Ignore acknowledgment strategy, 211
Ignore commit strategy, 210
imperative methods, 232
imperative model, 112-115, 116-120
in-flight messages, 212
inbound connector, 189
intermittent failures, 51
invoke method (Mutiny), 129
item (event), 95

J

Jaeger, 260
Jib, 29
JMS (Java Message Service), 179
joining items (Mutiny), 134-136
JSON array, streaming, 153-155

K

Kafka
about, 202-207
backpressure/performance considerations, 106, 212
building reactive systems with, 202-216
elasticity patterns, 209
as event bus tool, 201
failure handling, 210-212
installing, 213
on Kubernetes, 213-216
point-to-point communication model, 208
publish/subscribe model, 209
Kubernetes
AMQP on, 221
deploying a Quarkus application in, 28-34
deploying to, xvii
false assumptions related to cloud and Kubernetes, 52-54

health checks with messaging, 250-256
Kafka on, 213-216
location transparency, 68
running an application with, 48-50

L

Latest commit strategy, 211
lazy initialization, 11
leader partition (Kafka), 207
lists, collecting items for, 137
liveness probe, 251
location transparency, 68
Loom, 91-93

M

Maven, xvii
message queues, 66
message-based applications, building, 189-196
    failures and negative acknowledgment, 193
    message and acknowledgment, 191-193
messages
    consuming, 184-186
    defined, 64, 180
    idempotence, 59
    independence of system components and,
        67
    in message-based applications, 191-193
    processing, 186
    producing, 181-184
    reactive systems and, 64
messaging
    distributed tracing with, 260-263
    health checks with, 250-256
    metrics with, 256-260
    using the REST client in messaging applica-
        tions, 243-247
minikube, 29-34
monitoring (see observability)
Multi class (Mutiny), 126-128
    combining Multi operations, 135
    Reactive Streams backpressure protocol
        and, 128
    streaming data and, 151
multicast (queue), 219
multireactor pattern, 78
Mutiny, 117, 123-138
    basics, 120
    chaining asynchronous actions with,
        131-133

    collecting items with, 137
    combining/joining items, 134-136
    flow control, 128
    observing events with, 129
    programming issues addressed by, 123
    Quarkus and, 125
    recovering from failure, 133
    selecting items for propagation down-
        stream, 136
    transforming events with, 130
    Uni and Multi classes, 126-128
    unique characteristics of, 124

N

nack (acknowledged negatively), 187, 193
native executables, 34-38
Netty, 79
nonblocking I/O
    asynchronous code/patterns, 83-89
    blocking I/Os versus, 71-74
    interactions with relational databases, 161
    mechanism of operation, 74-77
    reactor pattern and event loop, 77-79
    role in reactive systems, 71-79
nonblocking methods, reactive REST client
    and, 232
NoSQL databases, 166-170

O

object-relational mapping (ORM), 162-166
observability, 249-264
    distributed tracing with messaging, 260-263
    health with messaging, 250-256
    importance of, 249
    metrics with messaging, 256-260
    observing events with Mutiny, 129
offset (Kafka), 205
offset commit, 210
operators, reactive programming and, 96-100
ORM (object-relational mapping), 162-166
outbound connector, 189

P

Panache, 162-166
parallel composition, 86
partition (Kafka), 206
permanent failures, 51
pipelines, 90, 94

pods, 30
point-to-point communication
    AMQP and, 217-219
    Kafka and, 208
poll, 76
proactor pattern, 78, 119
Project Loom, 91-93
Prometheus, 258
publish/subscribe model
    AMQP and, 219
    Kafka and, 209

Q

Quarkus
    about, xiv
    basics, 9-39
    creating your first application in, 21-28
    deploying an application in Kubernetes,
        28-34
    event-driven architecture with, 121
    failure handling, 148-151
    going native, 34-38
    HTTP request handling, 140
    Java on the cloud and, 9-18
    Mutiny usage in, 125
    reactive engine (see reactive engine)
    RESTEasy Reactive, 141-143
    sample application, 15-18
    traditional frameworks versus, 18-21

R

raw streaming, 152
Reactive
    cloud native applications and, 7
    defined, 4
    explanation of term, xiii
    foundation of ideas behind, 4
    landscape, 5-7
    limitations, 8
reactive (term), 3
reactive engine, 9, 111-122
    imperative model and, 112-115
    reactive model and, 115
    unification of reactive and imperative,
        116-120
"The Reactive Manifesto", 6, 61
Reactive Messaging, 179-200
    acknowledgments, 187
    blocking processing, 195

building message-based applications,
    189-196
channels and messages, 180
connectors, 189, 227
consuming messages, 184-186
event bus (see event bus)
HTTP example, 196-200
processing messages, 186
producing messages, 181-184
retrying processing, 195
stream manipulation, 193-195
reactive methods, 232
reactive model, 115, 116-120
reactive ORM, 162-166
reactive programming, 93-100
    basics, 93-100
    common definition, 93
    libraries, 100
    Mutiny, 120
    operators, 96-100
    Reactive Streams and need for flow control,
        100-106
    streams and, 94-96
reactive REST client
    blocking/nonblocking methods, 232
    failure handling, 233-238
    HTTP endpoints and, 228-232
    mapping HTTP APIs to Java interfaces,
        229-232
reactive score, 157
Reactive Streams
    backpressure and, 7
    basics, 103-105
    connectors and, 189
    distributed systems and, 106
    flow control and, 100-106
    protocol issues/solutions, 106
reactive systems, 61-82
    anatomy of reactive applications, 79-82
    building with AMQP, 216-223
    building with Kafka, 202-216
    characteristics of, 6-7, 61-63
    commands, 63
    commands versus events, 65-68
    design principles, 61-82
    destinations and space decoupling, 68-70
    events, 64
    nonblocking I/O, 71-79
    Reactive Messaging and, 179-200

time decoupling, 70
reactor pattern, 77
readiness probe, 251
record (Kafka), 202
redelivery, AMQP and, 220
Redis, 166-170
relational databases, nonblocking interactions
    with, 161
replay mechanism, 66
resident set size (RSS), 12
resilience, in reactive systems, 63
responsiveness, in reactive systems, 63
REST client, 227-228
    in messaging applications, 243-247
    reactive REST client and HTTP endpoints,
        228-232
RESTEasy Reactive
    basics, 141-143
    benefits of, 144-146
    building API gateways with RESTEasy
        Reactive client, 238-243
    classic RESTEasy versus, 144-146
    reactive score, 157
retries, 59, 195, 236
RSocket, 106
RSS (resident set size), 12
RX-JS, 100
RxPY, 100

S
selecting items (Mutiny), 136
Selector, 76
sequential composition, 86
Server-Sent Events API (SSE), 155-157
service, defined, 33
SLA (service-level agreement), 256
SLI (service-level indicator), 256
SLO (service-level objective), 256
SmallRye Mutiny (see Mutiny)
sockets, 71
space decoupling, 68-70
SSE (Server-Sent Events API), 155-157
startup probe, 251
stream manipulation, 193-195
streaming data
    HTTP response, 151-157
    JSON array, 153-155
    raw streaming, 152
    using Server-Sent Events, 155-157

streams
    buffering, 101
    dropping items, 102
    reactive programming and, 94-96
    Reactive Streams, 103-105
    Reactive Streams and flow control, 100-106
Strimzi project, 213
strong consistency, 171
subscription, 96
synchronous calls, distributed systems and,
    54-60

T
telemetry, 249
Thorntail, 13-15
threads
    asynchronous code and, 83-85
    blocking I/Os and, 72
    carrier, 91-93
    data access and, 160
    event handlers and, 81
    HTTP requests and, 140-146
    imperative programming and, 112-115,
        118-120
    nonblocking I/Os and, 76
    Reactive Messaging and, 195
    Reactive model and, 115
    reactive REST client and, 228, 232
    virtual, 91-93
Throttled commit strategy, 210
time decoupling, reactive systems and, 70
time to first request, 11
time-coupling, distributed systems and, 54-60
time-out, 236
topic (Kafka), 202, 205
transforming events (Mutiny), 130
transient failures, 51

U
unbounded streams, Server-Sent Events and,
    155-157
Uni class (Mutiny), 126-128
    asynchronous endpoints returning Uni
        instance, 146-148
    combining Uni operations, 135

V
Vert.x, 80, 117

managed instance, 146
Quarkus reactive engine and, 120

Vert.x Web Client, 226
virtual threads, 91-93

About the Authors

Clement Escoffier is Reactive architect at Red Hat. He has had several professional lives, from academic positions to management. Currently, he is working mainly as a Quarkus and Vert.x developer. He has been involved in projects and products touching many domains and technologies including OSGi, mobile app development, continuous delivery, and DevOps. His main area of interest is software engineering—the processes, methods, and tools that make the development of software more efficient as well as more fun. Clement is an active contributor to many open source projects such as Apache Felix, iPOJO, Wisdom Framework, and Eclipse Vert.x, SmallRye, Eclipse MicroProfile, and Quarkus.

Ken Finnigan is a senior principal software engineer for Red Hat Middleware and has been a consultant and software engineer for over 20 years with enterprises throughout the world. Ken leads the SmallRye project, which implements the Eclipse MicroProfile specifications while also looking to innovate with Kubernetes-native development. Ken is also part of the team developing Quarkus to be Supersonic Subatomic Java. As part of his work on SmallRye, Ken is heavily involved in the Eclipse MicroProfile community to develop specifications for Java microservices in the cloud. Ken previously served as the project lead for Thorntail and LiveOak, along with other JBoss projects. Ken is the author of *Enterprise Java Microservices* and two other books.

Colophon

The animal on the cover of *Reactive Systems in Java* is the African leopard (*Panthera pardus*). The leopard is known for its well-camouflaged, spotted fur as well as its predatorial prowess. Leopards are ambush predators, meaning they pounce on their prey before it has a chance to react. Their diet consists of antelope, gazelle, pigs, primates, and domestic livestock. Their tremendous strength allows them to tackle prey up to 10 times their own weight.

Leopards are vulnerable on the IUCN list, as populations are threatened by habitat loss and fragmentation. Humans are the leopard's primary predators, as they're hunted as trophy animals or killed for attacking farmers' livestock.

Many of the animals on O'Reilly covers are endangered; all of them are important to the world.

The cover illustration is by Karen Montgomery, based on a black-and-white engraving from *Braukhaus Lexicon*. The cover fonts are Gilroy Semibold and Guardian Sans. The text font is Adobe Minion Pro; the heading font is Adobe Myriad Condensed; and the code font is Dalton Maag's Ubuntu Mono.

Lightning Source UK Ltd.
Milton Keynes UK
UKHW032229081221
395333UK00008B/11

9 781492 091721